Praise for *How to Write like Tolstoy*

'Insightful...[Cohen] escorts his readers to Iris Murdoch for sage counsel on launching a novel, to Salman Rushdie for shrewd guidance on developing an unreliable narrator, to Rudyard Kipling for a cagey hint on creating memorable minor characters, and to Leo Tolstoy for a master's help in transforming personal experience into fictional art. Even readers with no intentions of writing a novel will relish the opportunity to join their favourite authors at the workbench.'

Booklist

'...interesting, charming, and engaging...Cohen reveals the possibilities that lie in wait when authors practise selection and intention, sparking the literary imagination.'

Library Journal, starred review

'Cohen's myriads of examples are lush and instructive...he is a generous tour guide through his literary world.'

Kirkus

'Elegant...Cohen [tells] amusing, often discursive stories about great literature and authors, mixed with the writers' own observations, which he hopes will further inspire readers and would-be writers.'

Publishers Weekly

HOW TO WRITE LIKE
TOLSTOY

Leo Tolstoy, by Nikolai Ge, painted in 1882,
when Tolstoy was fifty-four.

HOW TO WRITE LIKE
TOLSTOY

A Journey into the Minds of

Our Greatest Writers

Richard Cohen

ONEWORLD

A Oneworld Book

First published in Great Britain and Australia by Oneworld Publications, 2016

ISBN 978-1-78607-021-0
eISBN 978-1-78607-022-7

Permissions and acknowledgements can be found on page 321
Book design by Dana Leigh Blanchette
Chapter title background image: © iStockphoto.com

Printed and bound in Great Britain by Clays Ltd, St Ives plc

Oneworld Publications
10 Bloomsbury Street
London WC1B 3SR
England

For Toby, Mary and Guy

Contents

From the Goethe card deck, by Guido Zibordi Marchesi:
The Three of Hearts.

PREFACE

PETER CAREY: I was finally a writer.
INTERVIEWER: What was it that was clicking?
CAREY: Age, experience, a simpler form, practice, reading, influence, getting beyond influence.

THE PARIS REVIEW, 2006

There are three rules for writing a novel. Unfortunately, no one knows what they are.

W. SOMERSET MAUGHAM (ATTRIB.)

At a New Year's Eve dinner party in Los Angeles, some time in the 1980s, the magician Ricky Jay was entertaining his fellow guests with elaborate tricks using a simple deck of cards when one of his dining companions said, "Come on, Ricky, why don't you do something truly amazing?" After an awkward moment (for all the tricks *had* been amazing), Jay asked the guest to name a card. "The three of hearts," the man replied. Jay shuffled the pack, gripped it in his right hand, then sprung it, cascading all fifty-two cards so that they flew the length of the dining table and pelted an open wine bottle.

"What was your card again?"

"Three of hearts."

"Look in the bottle."

The man did as bidden and found, curled inside the neck, the three of hearts.

Any good magician's effects, his tricks of illusion or distraction, are akin, in at least the sense of amazement they induce, to what great writers do. Vladimir Nabokov once referred to "the flawless magic of Tolstoy's style." Take the scene in *Anna Karenina* where Konstantin Levin, a thirty-two-year-old landowner, proposes to Princess Ekaterina "Kitty" Alexandrovna Shcherbatskaya. Levin is a passionate yet shy aristocrat who, unlike his Moscow friends, lives in the country on his large estate. He actually proposes twice. On the first occasion, Kitty, just eighteen, clumsily turns him down, telling him that her marrying him is impossible. She believes she is in love with the handsome Count Alexei Vronsky and that he will soon propose to her. Vronsky regards his flirting with Kitty as mere sport and turns his attentions to Anna. Levin is crushed by Kitty's refusal and returns to his estate, abandoning any hope of marriage and resolving to forget Kitty.

With his earnestness and soul-searching, his concern for equality and his committed life on a country estate, Levin shares many similarities with his creator (consciously so: in Russian, "Levin" means "of Lev," and Lev is the spelling of Tolstoy's first name). In some ways he is a bumbling figure, a little easy to mock, but our hearts go out to him, and we long for Kitty to change her mind, but cannot guess how it will come about after so much misunderstanding.

Eventually, a mutual cousin manoeuvres the two of them so that they find themselves alone in a family drawing room. Kitty goes to a card-table, sits down, and taking a piece of chalk starts to draw circles on the green cloth. For a while neither of them speaks. Kitty's eyes, Tolstoy tells us, "shine with a gentle gleam." Levin leans over, takes the chalk from her and writes "w, y, s, i, i, i, w, i, i, t, o, a."

These letters were the initials of the words, "When you said, 'It is impossible,' was it impossible *then*, or *always*?"

It was highly unlikely that Kitty would be able to make out this complicated question. All the same, Levin looked at her as if his life depended on whether she could guess these words or not. She glanced back at him gravely, then resting her forehead on her hand tried to decipher it. Occasionally she would look up at him, asking him with her eyes: "Is what I think right?"

"I know what it is," she said at last, blushing.

"What is this word?" he asked, pointing to the *i* of the word *impossible*.

"That stands for *impossible*. But the word is not right."

He quickly rubbed out what he had written, gave the chalk to her, and stood up.

She wrote: *t, I, c, n, a, d. . . .*

At once his face lit up; he had understood the reply: *"Then I could not answer differently."*

He looked at Kitty timidly. "Only *then*?"

"Yes."

"*But*—but now?"

"Read this. I will tell you what I wish, what I wish very much." She quickly traced the initials, *t, y, m, f, a, f, w, t, p.* This meant: *"That you might forgive and forget what took place."*

He seized the chalk with trembling fingers, and crushing

it wrote down the initials of the words: "*I have nothing to for-give and forget. I have never ceased to love you.*"

Kitty looked at him, and her smile died away.

"I understand," she said in a low voice.

I first read this scene when I was twenty, have re-read it many times since, and still wonder at its effect on me. How could a combi-nation of words on a page—*translated* words—so take over my inner world? How had Tolstoy created an encounter that enraptured me, making me feel for these two make-believe characters so strongly (and, indeed, miss supper in college hall as a result)? Later, I discov-ered that the chalk game was a retelling of Tolstoy's real-life proposal to Sonia Behrs, just as the scene in which Levin insists on showing his future wife the diaries recounting his youthful debaucheries also came straight from the author's own experiences. How had Tolstoy taken such intimate events and spun them into fiction?

This is what the current book attempts to pin down, with a deck that spans a lifetime of reading. "Who cares for you?" cries Alice, about to step out of her Wonderland. "You're nothing but a pack of cards!" Only we do come to care, and that is where the magic comes in. Of course a novelist is not just performing a trick; he is creating a whole world that takes in themes, character, argument, cultural con-texts, and much else besides. But do not forget that sense of magic and wonder: the secret in the bottle.

I was an only child brought up in the seaside resort of Brighton and spent much of my early years with books. I devoured comics too, some half-dozen a week, identified totally with William Brown (while also taking in such creations as Jennings, Desperate Dan, and Billy Bunter along the way) before graduating to *Alice's Adventures in Wonderland* (still the only book I have read ten times), *Kidnapped,* and all of Stevenson, Jules Verne, John Buchan (Ah! *The Thirty-Nine Steps* and the man who "held up a hand which lacked three fingers"),

Edith Nesbitt, most of Dumas and Rider Haggard, then (I confess) every single Agatha Christie story, and so on and on. Becoming involved in the lives of fictional characters has not only been my main pastime, it has shaped my moral world.

Besides my own writing, I have been editing other people's prose since 1969, working on most kinds of fiction and non-fiction (a short list would include Kingsley Amis, Anthony Burgess, Sebastian Faulks, Jean Auel, Fay Weldon, John Le Carré, A. Alvarez, Victoria Glendinning, Richard Holmes, V. S. Pritchett, Hilary Spurling, Madeleine Albright, Simon Winchester, Vanessa Redgrave, Dian Fossey, Studs Terkel, John Keegan, and Jonathan Spence). I have also spent several years as a visiting professor in creative writing.

This book describes how any three of hearts ends up inside the bottle—how the authors I have read, and worked with, came to compose their books and how they made their creative choices, for good and occasionally for bad.

How to Write Like Tolstoy began as a by-product of my university teaching. However, as the book took shape my aims evolved too. Although a secondary purpose is to give practical writing advice, I became swept up in how great novelists had dealt with particular problems—how Charles Dickens and George Eliot, for instance, tackled the business of rounding off a novel; how William Faulkner experimented with different narrators and points of view; or how Elmore Leonard polished his use of dialogue.

I have written about what I hope will catch the attention of anyone who lights up when they read imaginative literature of real quality. The American writer and teacher Richard G. Stern said that he would never hesitate to bring into his classes "the work of masters." This, he explained, was "not meant to cheapen the marvellous but to evoke it. The hope is to make students fall in love with sublimity and to show them it's not out of reach." I have tried to do something similar, as far as possible using the words of the authors themselves to help explain their craft, aiming to take readers on a journey into the concerns, techniques, tricks, flaws and, occasionally, obsessions of our most luminous writers.

Can one, in fact, teach people to write? Brendan Behan (1923–64), who famously described himself as "a drinker with a writing problem," was invited by a prestigious American university to deliver an afternoon lecture about his craft. Behan's reputation as boozer and rabble-rouser meant that the lecture hall was filled to capacity, with students standing at the back and perched in the aisles, but the appointed hour came and went, with still no sign of the great man. Time laboured on; the stage remained empty. After forty-five minutes or so, a more than usually dishevelled Behan stumbled in, and the audience waited, in equal parts expectant, curious, and alarmed.

"Good afternoooon," he crooned. "Now, hands up all of you who want to be writers." Nearly everyone raised an arm. Behan viewed this forest with disgust. "Well, then," said he. "Go on back home and frickin' *write*." With that, he reeled off the stage.

The question of whether one can teach writing hardly ends there. Kurt Vonnegut, who for many years was on the faculty of the prestigious Iowa Writers' Workshop, held that one could not make writers, and likened himself to a golf pro who could, at best, take a few shots off someone's game. Ann Beattie, a staff member at the University of Virginia, asked if writing could be taught, replied: "Does anybody ever say, 'Here's X; I taught X how to be a creative writer'?" Teachers, she suggested, can't put the writing gifts into you, but if they find them there they can try to keep you from going in obviously wrong directions.

One can extend this approach. The novelist and long-time teacher John Gardner believed that "writing ability is mainly a product of good teaching supported by a deep-down love of writing," and pointed out that Hemingway, although on record (and echoing

Behan) as declaring that the only way for a writer to learn his craft was to go away and write, took hours of tutorials from Gertrude Stein. He wrote to her: "Isn't writing a hard job though? It used to be easy before I met you. I certainly was bad. Gosh, I'm awfully bad now but it's a different kind of bad."

Then take George Orwell, who began his career as an embarrass-ingly clumsy writer. When, at the age of twenty-four, he moved into cheap lodgings in London, he was befriended by the distinguished poet Ruth Pitter. She was the first person to be shown his apprentice efforts, finding them awkward and Orwell "like a cow with a mus-ket." The two would go for long walks along the Embankment dis-cussing his stories, or meet for dinner over a bottle of cheap red wine when she would be unsparing in her criticism; but however much she teased him, she also helped explain where he was going wrong. In sum, Pitter may not have injected Orwell with his gift for storytelling, but she taught him to compose those stories.

How to Write Like Tolstoy begins with how all books begin—the open-ing sentence, the opening paragraph, the whole question of starting off right. Thereafter the chapters are roughly organized according to the creative process. How characters are created seems paramount— most often, a character will stay with us long after the particular story has faded away—but how does one give them life? What names does one bestow, how much of a backstory should be included? Mark Twain agonized for months about one of his characters who played with matches while in a Southern prison, burning the prison down and himself to death—even though that character was eventually cut and doesn't appear in either *Tom Sawyer* or *Huckleberry Finn*. Twain laughed at his self-inflicted sense of guilt, but he couldn't prevent it. So I also look at what is meant by a character "taking over" a story— the notion, shared by writers from Jane Austen to Jane Smiley, that fictional characters can have an independent life, an existence above and beyond their authors' endeavours.

Then there is a subject rarely treated in books about writing: plagiarism. Every author "borrows," both from the work and from the lives of others. Shakespeare is applauded for building on Plutarch and Holinshed, while Doris Kearns Goodwin is pilloried for gathering up another writer's research without acknowledgement. What are the ethics of either of them doing what they did, and when might borrowing become a creative act in itself? Laurence Sterne rejoiced in being a plagiarist, while Malcolm Gladwell, finding himself plagiarized, went on to congratulate the perpetrator for having added value to what he first wrote. What does it mean to be "original"? Where do ideas come from? The authors and their liftings run the gamut from simple theft to the grey area of writing about people you know and the harm it can do. It is not a simple issue.

Every writer has to decide on a point of view to tell his or her story—whether it should be first person, or third, or multiple viewpoints, and if so how many, and when to switch from one narrator to another. Then there is the question of how close to the action the author stands, and not for the first time Tolstoy is a prime example of an author who orchestrates narrative distance as well as narrative voice. Some of the greatest novelists loved to experiment; from Jane Austen and Wilkie Collins through Faulkner and Kafka to Norman Mailer and Salman Rushdie (who has admitted that in *Midnight's Children* he deliberately made mistakes of fact and judgement, only later to discover there were some unintended mistakes too—which served his overall purpose in making his narrator unreliable).

Every great writer also has a particular voice, one different from those of his characters. "Voice" implies speech, and some authors (Ivy Compton-Burnett, famously) employ almost all dialogue, others very little. What does dialogue in a novel seek to accomplish? How much does one put in, how much leave out? What of direct speech, indirect speech, or internal dialogue? This leads on to the subject of irony. The word has come to imply so many different things over the decades, as fashions and meanings change, yet that evolution is fascinating in itself, for it is at the heart of all good writing, challenging the reader to respond to what cannot be said but which must be understood.

A question that has perplexed me for years is what is meant by story and how it differs from plot. Is the issue no more than semantics, or is it at the heart of the way novelists set about their business? When I first read Stephen King's *On Writing*, still the best book on the art of authorship, I found it extraordinary how he disagreed so vehemently with E. M. Forster, who had lectured on the subject over sixty years before—and who had felt just as passionately. Both of them were wrong to take such extreme positions, and setting the two off against each other helps explain why, and indeed what makes a good story in the first place.

Years ago, when my three children were much younger, their mother and I would take it in turns to read aloud to them. One evening I returned early from work because it was my turn to read, and we were on the very final pages of *Tom's Midnight Garden*, Philippa Pearce's classic story (a magical one, even) first published in 1958. As I mounted the stairs to the children's bedroom I could hear my wife's voice—she too had longed to read those final pages to them and to make her plan work had sent them to bed early! I sat on the stairs and listened, and as I did thrilled to the music of the words. So I have devoted a chapter to the subject of rhythm in prose writing, from Gustave Flaubert wandering the woods near his house, proclaiming his latest lines, to Charles Dickens and Thomas Mann, puffed up from their reading tours, devoting more and more attention in their later novels to how what they wrote actually *sounded*.

Another subject generally skirted by literary critics is sex. How does one write about it, or should one even try? The way novelists have handled the topic varies hugely, from Samuel Richardson's sup-

posed reticence to John Updike's calculated openness, either steering
clear of explicit description or trying to find a way around the censors of the day. In most good novels, sexual activity is not an end in
itself but tells us about the characters and their story. Physical intimacy, though, can be an embarrassing subject to write about effectively, and my conclusion is that one *should* try.

The subject of revising, whether done by oneself or responding to
the advice of others, is crucial. "Abridge, abridge! Begin on the second page," Chekhov advised his brother, who longed to be a writer
too. Yet while revision most often involves cutting, pruning, cleaning
up, at its best it is a *re-vision*. One needs to look with fresh eyes, not
just do carpentry (although it sometimes *is* just carpentry). Balzac
revised heavily, as did Norman Mailer. P. G. Wodehouse hated second drafts, while Jack Kerouac, William Golding, and John Cheever
over the years had to deal with editors good, interfering, and bad.

The final chapter is about—well, final chapters. How to bring a
story of any length to a conclusion. Dickens and Eliot both had
trouble with their endings, while Hemingway often found the whole
business impossible. Tolstoy could hardly let go of his characters,
particularly in *War and Peace*. I say a lot about Lev, one of my favourite authors, but plenty of others play important roles, not only the
great nineteenth-century exponents but also figures like Beckett and
Philip Roth and Updike, Jonathan Franzen and Elizabeth Strout.

In her guide *Reading Like a Writer* Francine Prose recalls how she
has heard fellow writers say that "they cannot read while working on
a book of their own for fear that Tolstoy or Shakespeare might influence them." Great writers can inhibit new writers, true—or maybe
one reads Scott Fitzgerald or Henry James and can't escape imitat-
ing them; but more often such writers are inspiring. They have certainly inspired me. The journey through their struggles and
achievements is the main thing, and although I don't expect readers
of this book to end up modern Tolstoys—who knows?

HOW TO WRITE LIKE
TOLSTOY

CHAPTER 1

Grab, Invite, Beguile:
Beginnings

LEONARD: So what were we talking about?
KATE: The first sentence.
LEONARD: Oh yeah, Christ.

THERESA REBECK, *SEMINAR,* 2011

Into the face of the young man who sat on the terrace of the Hotel Magnifique at Cannes there had crept a look of furtive shame, the shifty hangdog look which announces that an Englishman is about to speak French.

P. G. WODEHOUSE, OPENING OF
THE LUCK OF THE BODKINS, 1925

How to begin? I'm thinking of that moment when a writer stares at a sheet of blank paper (or, today, a screen) like a weightlifter assessing a massive dumbbell; the effort of setting down any mark seems beyond him. A cup of coffee is appealing—a second cup, a quick session of emailing, a short walk, even a phone call. After all such procrastinations, a final inspiration: focus instead on something completely different to what was planned, and likely *far* better. What was it Douglas Adams said? "I love deadlines. I love the whooshing sound they make as they fly by."

Gertrude Stein liked to look at cows in the intervals of her writing, and would be driven into the countryside to do so. Woody Allen takes constant showers to aid inspiration. Those *grandes dames* of postwar British fiction, Iris Murdoch and Muriel Spark, never set pen to paper until they had thought of a satisfactory opening. "A novel is a long job," Murdoch explained, "and if you get it wrong at the start you're going to be very unhappy later on." John Irving, on the other hand (I am deliberately packing in examples), begins each of his novels by writing the book's final sentence. Before he starts to write, George Steiner, the polymath and novelist, takes a page of "top prose" in the relevant language and reads it aloud, often until he knows it by heart. "But it will have nothing to do with the subject." In *The Plague* Albert Camus has his character Joseph Grand rewrite the first sentence of his novel eternally, with only minimal variations.

Beginnings are notoriously difficult. E. L. Doctorow tells of being asked by his daughter to give her an absence note for her schoolteacher. He started to write, then thought, "No, that's not it," and started again. The second version didn't hit the required note either. Further drafts followed, until his young daughter was in a state of panic and there was a pile of crumpled pages on the floor. Finally his wife came in and, with a look of disbelief, dashed off the required short letter. Doctorow concluded: "I had been trying to write the perfect absence note. It was a very illuminating experience. Writing is immensely difficult. The short forms especially."

He is hardly alone. The American wit of the interwar period, Robert Benchley, was at his typewriter at *The New Yorker* agonizing over how to begin. He got up, talked with some friends, and an hour later returned to his desk. He gathered his thoughts once more and typed out the single word "The." Then he left for a party that was in full flow down the hall, but conscience forced him back. He sat down, focused again, and typed three more words, ". . . hell with it." With that he returned to the revellers.

In A. A. Milne's *Winnie-the-Pooh,* Christopher Robin's unnamed narrator starts his tale with the words, "Once upon a time, a very long time ago now, about last Friday. . . ." When that time is, exactly, is not generally the issue: all that matters is that we are about to escape into a world of make-believe.

The phrase "Once upon a time" can be traced to as early as 1380; not until 1600 did it become a stock opening for oral narratives. It occurs in other languages too, from the familiar to the more obscure: in Estonian it's "Behind seven lands and seas there lived. . . ." In classical Arabic, it translates as "There was, oh what there was, in the oldest of days and ages and times. . . ." In Iraqw, a tongue used in Tanzania, it's "I remember something that our father told me. . . ."

That reliance is a storyteller's trope, a device to indicate that one is entering a land of make-believe, assuring the reader's passage from the real world to the fictional. (In the 1890s, Robert Graves's father would start any story he told to his children with "And so the old gardener blew his nose on a red pocket handkerchief. . . .") But where and when does the narrative proper begin? The difficulty of openings has haunted many authors, as if they need to clear the air (or their throats) before they get going. Graham Greene begins *The End of the Affair* (1951) with almost an apology: "A story has no beginning or end; arbitrarily one chooses that moment of experience from which to look back or from which to look ahead."

An additional burden is the thought of all those weightlifters who have gone before you. Early in his novel *The English Patient,* Michael Ondaatje argues: "Many books open with an author's assurance of order. One slipped into their waters with a silent paddle. . . . But [unlike works of non-fiction] novels commenced with hesitation or chaos. Readers were never fully in balance. A door a lock a weir opened and they rushed through, one hand holding a gunnel, the other a hat." Yet novels can begin slowly—from Oscar Wilde's *The Picture of Dorian Gray* in 1890 to Arundhati Roy's *The God of Small Things* (1997), we get openings all about the weather.*

Equally, non-fiction books can start with a bang or a memorable phrase—take the opening page of Isadora Duncan's autobiography, which contains the sentences "My first memory is of a fire. I remember being thrown into the arms of a policeman from an upper window." But a work of non-fiction is often specific—one knows, more or less, what one is getting; whereas a novel competes with all the other fictions that have ever been written.

Only one book could ever open: "In the beginning was the Word, and the Word was with God, and the Word was God." Around the first century A.D., the pagan sometimes known as "Pseudo-Longinus" wrote in *On the Sublime* of the (slightly different) opening in Genesis that this was a superb beginning, for its author "both understood and gave expression to the power of the divinity as it deserved." Another biblical scholar has judged "In the beginning" as "the most wholly satisfactory opening any story can have." But the question is not just how to begin a story, but how do you get someone's attention?

In *Laughing Gas* (1936), P. G. Wodehouse's farcical take on Hollywood, the entire opening scene is given up to . . . what an opening scene *should* be. Reggie Havershot, a Bertie Wooster-like character, is

---

* In 2006, I quoted some of the most famous opening sentences in literature during a university talk. "It is a truth universally acknowledged, that a single man in possession of a good fortune must be in want of a wife"; "It was the best of times, it was the worst of times"; "Happy families are all alike; every unhappy family is unhappy in its own way"; "It was a bright cold day in April, and the clocks were striking thirteen." Not a frisson of recognition ran across the crowded lecture hall. Then I read: "Mr. and Mrs. Dursley, of number four, Privet Drive, were proud to say that they were perfectly normal, thank you very much." A sudden, distinct murmur: the opening of Harry Potter's first adventure.

trying his first attempt at fiction when he comes across a friend (who he all too slowly realizes is suffering from the father of all hangovers), to whom he insists reading the start of his projected novel. After the friend has listened to a painfully awful rendering, he comments: "The first rule in telling a story is to make it thoroughly clear at the outset who's who, when, where, and why. You'd better start again at the beginning."

There's good sense in this, but does it force us to continue reading? The great Agatha Christie starts off *The Murder on the Links* (1923) by making that problem her solution:

> I believe that a well-known anecdote exists to the effect that a young writer, determined to make the commencement of his story forcible and original enough to catch and rivet the attention of the most blasé of editors, penned the following sentence:
>
> "'Hell!' said the Duchess."
>
> Strangely enough, this tale of mine opens in much the same fashion. Only the lady who gave utterance to the exclamation was not a duchess. . . .

And off she goes. With the very next paragraph who should enter but Hercule Poirot, and all's well with the world.

Individual authors must select which style suits their purpose to establish voice, range of vocabulary, syntactic habits, and so on; each opening also makes a promise about the story that is to come—it establishes expectations.

Christie's lightly swearing duchess belongs to a category of opening that I call "grabbers"—deliberate attempts to seize the reader with a first sentence or perhaps first paragraph. Typical of this would be the start of most Elmore Leonard thrillers—the wish to show, at once, that this story is going to *thrill*. His 1985 novel *Glitz* opens: "The night Vincent was shot he saw it coming." And again, three years later, *Freaky Deaky*:

> Chris Mankowski's last day on the job, two in the after-noon, two hours to go, he got a call to dispose of a bomb.

The next sentence introduces us to "a guy by the name of Booker, a twenty-five-year-old super-dude twice-convicted felon," who is in his Jacuzzi when the telephone rings, so he gets out and moves to his favourite seat, a green leather wingback chair, only to be told by the caller that he is sitting on a bomb, and getting up will set it off.

Not only suspense stories can begin with "grabbers." When Gabriel Garcia Márquez read *The Metamorphosis*, the first line of which runs: "As Gregor Samsa awoke that morning from uneasy dreams, he found himself transformed in his bed into a gigantic insect," the sentence "almost knocked me off the bed. I was so surprised. . . . I thought to myself that I didn't know anyone was allowed to write things like that."

A good opening sentence not only leads one on, it enables the author to introduce character, mood, setting. In *Brighton Rock* (1938), Graham Greene starts dramatically enough:

> Hale knew they meant to murder him before he had been in Brighton three hours.

The rest of the paragraph deftly sets the scene:

> With his inky fingers and his bitten nails, his manner cynical and nervous, anybody could tell he didn't belong—belong to the early summer sun, the cool Whitsun wind off

the sea, the holiday crowd. They came in by train from Victoria every five minutes, rocked down Queen's Road standing on the tops of the little local trams, stepped off in bewildered multitudes into fresh and glittering air: the new silver sparkled on the piers, the cream houses ran away into the west like a pale Victorian water-colour; a race in miniature motors, a band playing, flower gardens in bloom below the front, an aeroplane advertising something for the health in pale vanishing clouds across the sky.

In a sense, every good opening is a "grabber," in that its author wants the reader to keep turning the pages; as the garrulous shoemaker who narrates the Czech novelist Bohumil Hrabal's *Dancing Lessons for the Advanced in Age* (1964) says, "No book worth its salt is meant to put you to sleep, it's meant to make you jump out of bed in your underwear and run and beat the author's brains out."

The famous beginning of *David Copperfield* (1850)—"Whether I shall turn out to be the hero of my own life, or whether that station will be held by anybody else, these pages must show"—comes into a "grabber" sub-category, that of "Here I am!"

Something similar is true also of Ralph Ellison's "I am an invisible man" (1952), or the beginnings of *Robinson Crusoe* (1719), even *Huckleberry Finn* (1885), Saul Bellow's *Herzog* (1964), or Dodie Smith's *I Capture the Castle* (1948)—"I write this sitting in the kitchen sink"— or the opening to Harper Lee's *Go Set a Watchman:* "Since Atlanta, she had looked out the dining-car window with a delight almost physical." It's not a matter of the information given so much as the self-confidence of the narrator announcing him- or herself as the centre of the story.

If there is a danger here, it's of the reader identifying the narrator with the author. "I've had the misfortune," wrote Marcel Proust, "of beginning a book with the word 'I' and immediately it was thought that instead of attempting to discover general laws, I was analyzing myself in the individual and detestable sense of the word." However, it remains a powerful way of beginning a tale, and the use of a fictitious "I" does force the reader into a semblance of dialogue with the narrator.

Close to this approach but significantly different in intention and effect is the beginning that tries to shock. Tom Robbins starts *Villa Incognito* with: "It has been reported that Tanuki fell from the sky using his scrotum as a parachute." Iain Banks begins *The Crow Road* (1992): "It was the day my grandmother exploded."* These are examples of grandstanding, the writer as show-off. Authors can forget that they have to go on after the opening sentence, and anti-climax can result. Thomas Mann begins *Buddenbrooks,* his first novel, "And— and—what comes next?" and continues with a second character replying, "Oh, yes, yes, what the dickens does come next?" A rare Mann joke.

Stephen King starts *The Shining* with "Jack Torrance thought: *Officious little prick.*" In context, this is effective, but the opening to Victoria Glendinning's first novel, *The Grown Ups* (1989), runs: "There's more to loving than fucking." I was her editor and didn't question it; only after the book was published did we both agree that that first sentence drew the wrong attention to itself. Not that outrageous

* Over the years, the dying mother has become something of a first-sentence cliché. Reviewing Alice Sebold's novel *The Almost Moon* in 2007, *The Guardian* noted: "[It] begins with a shameless grabber of a sentence: 'When all is said and done, killing my mother came easily.'" See "Novel of the Week," *The Week,* November 3, 2007. In similar vein, Albert Camus opens *The Stranger* (1942) with "Mother died today," William Boyd *The New Confession* (1988) with "My first act on entering this world was to kill my mother." Jeffrey Archer's *A Matter of Honour* (2007) also has the narrator's mother die in the opening sentence.

openings can't work. Quirky can be good: Mikhail Bulgakov begins *The Heart of a Dog* (1925), "Ooow-ow-ooow-owow!" as if language itself has failed him, and Tom Wolfe, in *The Bonfire of the Vanities* (1987), early on the opening page gives us a long drawn-out cackle: "Heh-heggggggggggggggggggghhhhhhhhhhhhhhh."

Garrison Keillor put such attempts in fine context. "When someone gets in your face as a writer does, either you love him or you loathe him," he wrote, citing a memoir he was reading of two lesbians who had taken up farming sheep in Minnesota. It begins with them attending shepherd school and learning to assess the potency of a ram by holding his testicles. "A book that starts with a woman reaching up between a ram's hind legs is a book close to my heart."

In his introduction to a reissue of *Double Star,* the science fiction writer Robert Heinlein talks about "the narrative hook . . . not the annoying kind that shouts for attention, but the kind that engages your curiosity and makes you want to read the next line." This takes us to a clutch of beginnings that I group under the heading of "invitational," well rendered in the classic German beginning, "At the turn of the century, in the province of D——." Such openings do not attempt to seize our attention but slowly, courteously almost (*cortesia,* tact of heart, a welcome), invite us inside their world. *It's interesting, you'll find much to involve you here; please make the effort.*

Francine Prose once told a class to compare the first chapters of Balzac's *Eugénie Grandet* (1833) and *A Flag for Sunrise* (1981) by Robert Stone. The Balzac begins with a leisurely tour of a provincial town, while, near the start of the Stone, we get an obvious "grabber"— a hippie backpacker's corpse shows up in the freezer of an army lieutenant in a restive Central American country. Prose suggested to her students that comparing the two might reflect a vital difference between nineteenth- and twentieth-century fiction: "Perhaps these contrasting openings had something to do with the way our attention spans have been altered—for better or worse—by the bright gratifications of movies and the rhythm of television, which has schooled us to expect the 'hook' before the first commercial."

I agree with this, but would add that different fish require different bait. One can introduce the main character without fanfare and still be remarkably effective. *Moby-Dick* (1851)* is really an example of this; as Prose notes, it gives "a kind of authority . . . [it] makes us feel that the author is in control"—in control of *his experience*. After "Call me Ishmael" (in itself a small irony, as only one character in the novel thereafter ever does call the narrator by that name), Melville gives us Ishmael's life history, and from that a description of the whaling coastal city of the Manhattoes. We are invited in.

In *The Old Man and the Sea* (1952), one of Hemingway's best openings, the whole opening paragraph makes an impact:

> He was an old man who fished alone in a skiff in the Gulf Stream and he had gone eighty-four days now without taking a fish. In the first forty days a boy had been with him. But after forty days without a fish the boy's parents had told him that the old man was now definitely and finally *salao*, which is the worst form of unlucky, and the boy had gone at their orders in another boat which caught three good fish the first week. It made the boy sad to see the old man come in each day with his skiff empty and he always went down to help him carry either the coiled lines or the gaff and harpoon and the sail that was furled around the mast. The sail

---

* "Moby-Dick" appears on the title page and divisional title page of the original American edition, even though only one of the name's many occurrences in the text includes the hyphen. Hyphenated titles were conventional in mid-nineteenth-century American publishing.

was patched with flour sacks and, furled, it looked like the flag of permanent defeat.

A whole raft of relationships, of allegiances and betrayals, is provided, as well as the small details and a tone of voice that make one want to continue reading.*

The "invitational" first sentence has the advantage that, because the story begins at a more leisurely pace, the author is not required to continue with a fireworks display; the rewards are of a different kind. Take the opening of Forster's *A Passage to India:* "Except for the Marabar Caves—and they are twenty miles off—the city of Chandrapore presents nothing extraordinary." We could hardly be less grabbed, although we register that those caves are indeed extraordinary, and it is within them, of course, that the novel's most violent act is supposedly enacted: Forster's opening provides both a courteous introduction and a sinister foreboding.

Another well-used "invitational" opening has the reader come into the middle of a conversation—often between family members; thus the beginning of *Dombey and Son* (1848), several Anne Tyler novels, and, most effectively, *To the Lighthouse* (1927):

> "Yes, of course it's fine tomorrow," said Mrs. Ramsay, "But you'll have to be up with the lark," she added.

---

* However, beginnings were generally a problem for Hemingway. A new edition of *The Sun Also Rises*, his 1926 novel, shows that he dabbled with an entire alternate first chapter using third-person narration instead of the first-person that he eventually chose. Rather than the current opening sentence, "Robert Cohn was once middleweight boxing champion of Princeton," the discarded chapter begins by introducing the book's heroine, Brett Ashley, with: "This is a novel about a lady." Having completed his revised version, Hemingway then scribbled in pencil, as an epigraph, Gertrude Stein's judgement, "You are all a lost generation," thus immortalizing the phrase. See Patricia Cohen, "Edition Has Alternate Opening of 'The Sun Also Rises,'" *The New York Times,* July 5, 2014, p. C3.

> To her son these words conveyed an extraordinary joy, as if it were settled, the expedition were bound to take place, and the wonder to which he had looked forward, for years and years it seemed, was, after a night's darkness and a day's sail, within touch.

James Ramsay, six, longs to sail over to the lighthouse across the bay, and his father promises to take him. We learn this with only oblique help from the author, the technique making us work hard to keep up with the narrative of the characters' inner lives. The critic and novelist David Lodge, while in mid-discussion of another Virginia Woolf novel, *Mrs. Dalloway*, describes such a beginning as "this abrupt plunging of the reader into the middle of an ongoing life."

Woolf may have picked up this trick from Ford Madox Ford, an avowed modernist who liked to drop his readers into the middle of scenes and let them orient themselves. Ford's four linked novels, which comprise *Parade's End*, were all published between 1924 and 1928, the years directly before *To the Lighthouse* was written. Beginning a novel this way was hardly new: witness Laurence Sterne's *Tristram Shandy*. People have to begin somewhere, and as every novel is a kind of journey, *To the Lighthouse* observes another well-tried beginning: setting your characters off on an expedition. Only, of course, in Woolf's story Mrs. Ramsay's promise is never exactly kept.

Some writers are cavalier about their openings. The prodigious Rex Stout (1886–1975), creator of the much-loved detective Nero Wolfe, produced over seventy novels and short stories, and would regularly begin a new book with the doorbell to Wolfe's apartment ringing. At least four of his stories begin this way—*Golden Spiders* (1953), *Eeny Meeny Murder Mo* (1962), *The Mother Hunt* (1963), and *A Family Affair* (1975). A further novel is actually titled *The Doorbell Rang* (1965). Stout would have no idea what would happen next, after the door was opened: the plot would have to take off from there. Thomas

Mann was similarly unhappy about over-planning, confiding, "Certainly, to envisage too clearly beforehand all the difficulties of a task . . . would be enough to make one shudder and forgo it." But everyone plans differently.

A number of writers have a particular image that comes to them and sets off the whole story. Paul Scott wrote that the picture that came to him for the beginning of his Raj Quartet series of novels was of a young English woman running for her life at night, in an Indian village. It came, he says,

> as images always do, apparently by chance, unexpectedly —in the dark of a restless, sleepless night. Vaguely, one can trace the antecedents: the trauma of the Indian village experiences, the desire to get away, to run, the knowledge of the dangers that exist when you attempt to cross bridges, the whole feeling of the British in India, and the feeling of India itself—a vast, flat territory, strangely forbidding, somehow incalculable, ugly, beautiful. And there she was, my prime mystery, a girl in the dark, running, exhausted, hurt in some way, yet strangely of good heart—tough, resilient, her face and figure a sense rather than an observed condition. But she runs.
>
> From what? To where?

In the finished novel, the first paragraph has become:

> Imagine, then, a flat landscape, dark for the moment, but even so conveying to a girl running in the still deeper shadow cast by the wall of the Bibighar Gardens an idea of immensity, of distance, such as the years before Miss Crane had been conscious of standing where a lane ended and cultivation began: a different landscape but also in the al-

luvial plain between the mountains of the north and the
plateau of the south.

Again, the tone is invitational, even though the material is dramatic. Clearly, Scott later explained, the running girl and this Miss
Crane are not the same person, and clearly the reference to the wall,
which fixes locality, is not part of the original picture that came to
mind, but "If it is a good hard image it will stand. Nothing will erode
it." That said, it was not Scott's opening paragraph, even if it was the
first scene that occurred to him. "Between the originating image and
its pinning down on the page, there is often a terrible gap of time and
changing circumstance." Imagination is fused with knowledge:

> Images do not have exact time schedules. Names, locations,
> time schedules, plot references—these are what the images
> create. In the original image are the seeds of all your novel.
> See your image, feel it, work it out in all its complexity to
> the best of your ability, and then try to put it all on the page.

In August 2010 the celebrated film designer Robert Boyle died at
the age of one hundred. He had mainly worked with Alfred Hitch-
cock, so most of the films he designed had strong narratives. A movie,
he said, "starts with the locale, with the environment that people live
in, how they move within that environment." He recalled those film
openings where we see a spinning globe, then the camera zooms in
on a country, a city, a particular street and house, then on into a particular room—a method known as "telescoping." Some books work
like that (Balzac's 1835 novel *Le Père Goriot*, for instance). The invitation, as it were, has been delivered.

If one can't advance character and story together, does it matter?

In *The Wings of the Dove* (1902), Henry James invites us to find of interest Ms. Kate Croy, who is waiting for her father . . . and waiting, and waiting. By the end of the first page we are still enmeshed in the opening paragraph, waiting as well. We are given atmosphere and the inner state of the main character, but already life is squeezed out of the story. With the exception of *Waiting for Godot*, readers and audiences don't like to be held in this kind of suspense for too long. One has to get on with it.

Perhaps aware of this, some novelists jump straight into a simple narrative—the beginning of *Madame Bovary* (1857), say:

> We were at preparation, when the headmaster came in, followed by a new boy dressed in "civvies" and a school servant carrying a big desk. Those who were asleep woke up, and everyone got to his feet with an air of being interrupted at work.

There's little embroidery here—Flaubert is just setting off on his tale, and we are happy to go with him. Other examples of invitational openings—I'm choosing at random—are Mark Haddon's *The Curious Incident of the Dog in the Night-Time*, Tolstoy's *Childhood, Boyhood, Youth*, or Hilary Mantel's *A Place of Greater Safety*.

Another way of inviting the reader into your chosen fictional world is to make some grand declaration—It was the best of times, it was the worst of times, and so on. It can even be "semi-grand": Wilkie Collins's *The Woman in White* begins: "This is the story of what a Woman's patience can endure, and what a Man's resolution can achieve." The nineteenth-century German philosopher Friedrich Schlegel called such expressions "porcupines," arguing that a self-standing grand statement should be isolated from its surroundings and complete in itself, like a porcupine. But the dangers can be seen from the portentous opening to George Eliot's *Middlemarch*, or this, the starting paragraph to D. H. Lawrence's *Lady Chatterley's Lover* (1928):

> Ours is essentially a tragic age, so we refuse to take it tragically. The cataclysm has happened, we are among the ruins, we start to build up new little habitats, to have new little hopes. It is rather hard work: there is now no smooth road into the future: but we go round, or scramble over the obstacles. We've got to live, no matter how many skies have fallen.

It's not uninteresting, but to modern ears it's overblown, both a throat-clearing and a little pompous. Nowadays we're not prepared for being lectured to, so contemporary novelists rarely use this device, attempting instead a quieter summing-up, an emotional taking stock, such as Louise Erdrich gives us in *Tracks* (1988), the third in a tetralogy that explores the lives of four families living on a reservation in North Dakota: "We started dying before the snow, and like the snow, we continued to fall."

Another way of leading us into a tale is the "frame-story," in effect two beginnings, where a narrator explains how the main account was discovered. James's *The Turn of the Screw* (1898) consists of a deceased woman's journal, while Lionel Davidson's *The Rose of Tibet* (1962) starts with a description of how a certain manuscript comes to the attention of a publisher via an aged Latin instructor; and so on. It's a way of imparting a special authority to the story that follows, but it's also a distracting device, a soft sell, an invitation to step inside and see what's on offer.

One temptation of a general overview approach is to introduce too many characters at the start, so we don't know which ones we should be paying attention to—the first French translation of *The*

Brothers Karamazov omitted the opening chapter of the novel, "The History of a Family," entirely—and with it Dostoyevsky's overview of his characters—one presumes because it was thought to be confusing.

A notable satire on openings comes at the beginning of Woody Allen's film *Manhattan* (1979): we view nearly three minutes of shots of New York as the sun rises on a new day and hear Allen's voice-over, speaking as Isaac Davis, a forty-two-year-old comedy writer in agony about how to start his first novel:

> Chapter One. He adored New York City. He idolized it all out of proportion. [Errr, no, make that:] he romanticized it all out of proportion. [Better.] To him, no matter what the season was, this was still a town that existed in black and white, and pulsated to the great tunes of George Gershwin. [Arr, no, let me start this over. . . .]

Which is what he does. Two further attempts follow; then comes the fourth:

> Chapter One. He adored New York City—although to him it was a metaphor for the decay of contemporary culture. How hard it was to exist in a society desensitized by drugs, loud music, television, crime, garbage. . . . [No, too angry. I don't want to be angry. . . .]

And so on to the final version, a send-up of first novels, first pages, and being an incurable romantic:

> Chapter One. He was as tough and romantic as the city he loved. Behind his black-rimmed glasses was the coiled sexual power of a jungle cat. [I love this.] New York was his town, and it always would be. . . .

———

This leads neatly to my third category: first sentences intended to beguile, generally by tone of voice or originality of approach. Grabbers may also beguile, as can invitational openings; invitational openings may quicken our interest, but by definition they can never be grabbers.

From the very beginning of the novel, authors have looked for ways of sidestepping the business of a formal beginning. William Thackeray opens *Vanity Fair* (1847) not with a sweeping statement, a family conversation, or an appetizing hook but with a stage manager's note, "Before the Curtain," which summarizes what the reader is about to encounter:

> a great quantity of eating and drinking, making love and jilting, laughing and the contrary, smoking, cheating, fighting, dancing, and fiddling: there are bullies pushing about, bucks ogling the women, knaves picking pockets, policemen on the lookout, quacks (OTHER quacks, plague take them!) bawling in front of their booths, and yokels looking up at the tinselled dancers and poor old rouged tumblers, while the light-fingered folk are operating upon their pockets behind.

This not only gives a panoramic view of what lies in store but also provides a play-like quality—and an unusual first page, of course. Some forty years later, Mark Twain chose to open *The Adventures of Huckleberry Finn* (1884) with the "notice":

> Persons attempting to find a motive in this narrative will be prosecuted; persons attempting to find a moral in it will be banished; persons attempting to find a plot in it will be shot.

Twain not only sidestepped the problem of finding a suitable first paragraph by putting up a satirical defence of the whole novel, he also, crucially, was establishing a *voice*. He charms us into reading on.

There were still other games for authors to play. Kate Atkinson, whose first novel *Behind the Scenes at the Museum* (1995) won the Whitbread Book of the Year, starts her third, *Emotionally Weird* (2000), with three different openings. Philip Roth begins *Portnoy's Complaint* (1969), otherwise a continuous monologue, with a mock medical dictionary definition of the title. Modern novelists have played with opening their stories with letters (Stephen King's *'Salem's Lot*, for instance) or, as with Martin Amis's *Money*, a suicide note from the protagonist. The opening words of Toni Morrison's novel *Home* (2012), "Whose house is this?" are not even part of the main text but of the epigraph, which quotes a song cycle written by the author some twenty years before.

These are all authorial tricks, however, one-offs. More generally, the kind of first sentence I have in mind is where the authorial voice is at once established, making one want to read on. Almost an *un*-invitational opening, but certainly a beguiling one, is the famous beginning to *Catcher in the Rye*:

> If you really want to hear about it, the first thing you'll probably want to know is where I was born, and what my lousy childhood was like, and how my parents were occupied and all before they had me, and all that David Copperfield kind of crap, but I don't feel like going into it, if you want to know the truth. In the first place, that stuff bores me, and in the second place, my parents would have about two hemorrhages apiece if I told anything pretty personal about them.

The novel's voice is immediately established: non-conformist, defiant towards the expected, the bloody-minded teenager *in excelsis*, but also (unconsciously, as far as the story's narrator is concerned) very funny.

I could mention many other examples of this third category— Sabatini's *Scaramouche:* "He was born with a gift of laughter and a sense that the world was mad"; Daphne du Maurier's *Rebecca:* "Last night, I dreamed I went to Manderley again"; or Nabokov, almost my archetype of what a beguiling start can achieve:

> Lolita, light of my life, fire of my loins. My sin, my soul. Lo-lee-ta: the tip of the tongue taking a trip of three steps down the palate to tap, at three, on the teeth. Lo. Lee. Ta.
>
> She was Lo, plain Lo, in the morning, standing four feet ten in one sock. She was Lola in slacks. She was Dolly at school. She was Dolores on the dotted line. But in my arms she was always Lolita.
>
> Did she have a precursor? She did, indeed she did. In point of fact, there might have been no Lolita at all had I not loved, one summer, a certain initial girl-child. In a princedom by the sea. Oh when? About as many years before Lolita was born as my age was that summer. You can always count on a murderer for a fancy prose style.

As the novelist Mohsin Hamid has confessed, Humbert Humbert is hardly a likeable narrator—"But that voice. Ah. That voice had me at 'fire of my loins.'" Nor is it just Nabokovian charm. Francine Prose points out that "in the midst of all that flighty exhibitionism, Nabokov has nonetheless managed to give us some hard information. Already we have learned that the narrator's relationship with Lolita . . . is sexual ('fire of my loins'), that she is little more than a child (a four-foot-ten-inch schoolgirl), that the narrator is capable of not merely quoting but also playing upon the poetry of Edgar Allan Poe ('in a princedom by the sea') and finally, that he has committed a murder." If there has been a beginning more suitable to its creator's purpose, I can't think of it.

Tone is important, but it's like the colour of paint on the walls, not the walls themselves. And whatever the first line, it has to link with what follows. In the same *Paris Review* where Marquez talks about Kafka's *Metamorphosis,* he considers what must resonate beyond just the opening sentence. "One of the most difficult things is the first paragraph," he writes.

> I have spent many months on a first paragraph, and once I get it, the rest just comes out very easily. In the first paragraph you solve most of the problems with your book. The theme is defined, the style, the tone. At least in my case, the first paragraph is a kind of sample of what the rest of the book is going to be.

Joan Didion had her own take on this: "What's so hard about that first sentence is that you're stuck with it. Everything else is going to flow out of that sentence. And by the time you've laid down the first *two* sentences, your options are all gone." More happily, according to the Canadian writer Mavis Gallant, authorship "is like a love affair: the beginning is the best part."

The Artful Dodger introduces Oliver Twist to Fagin;
George Cruikshank, 1838.

CHAPTER 2

Circular Ruins:
Creating Character

The color of Fanny Price's eyes in *Mansfield Park* and the furnishing of her cold little room are important.

VLADIMIR NABOKOV, 1948

I feel sorry for novelists when they have to mention women's eyes: there's so little choice. . . . Her eyes are blue: innocence and honesty. Her eyes are black: passion and depth. Her eyes are green: wildness and jealousy. Her eyes are brown: reliability and common sense. Her eyes are violet: the novel is by Raymond Chandler.

JULIAN BARNES, 1984

Some time in the late 1850s, Ivan Turgenev visited Leo Tolstoy at his estate Yasnaya Polyana ("Bright Glade") and was escorted by his host to a large barn full of animals. It took only a few minutes before Turgenev was storming back to the main house. He later complained to a friend how Tolstoy would go up to each animal—be it horse, cow, or duck—and explain its character, its love life, its family connections. "It was intolerable! He knows I can't create characters like him, and here he was doing it with a whole menagerie!"*

That memorable characters be intrinsic to storytelling seems a given, but the very term *characterization*, suggesting flexibility and range, was actually a mid-nineteenth-century idea. The word derives from the ancient Greek for a stamping tool that creates a distinctive mark: from there it came to mean the particular mark of an individual, similar to his signature, but no more than that. Another Greek word, *ethos*, from which we get "ethics," more specifically meant character. Aristotle, while perfectly aware of the importance of personality, believed in the primacy of plot-driven narrative over characters, arguing in his *Poetics* that tragedy was "a representation, not of men, but of action and life."

The novel rises in late antiquity, fades away into romance, re-emerges in Japan and Spain, then settles down in France and England during the eighteenth century. The shift from the stress on the outer life to the inner arrived with what has been dubbed "the petty-bourgeois realist novel"—and was later reinforced by the development of analytic psychology, so that we generally now believe that character is the most important single component of a work of fiction. We gorge on Becky Sharp and Tess D'Urberville; Fagin and Ebenezer Scrooge; Anna Karenina and Prince Myshkin; Sherlock

---

* The two men later quarrelled furiously, and for a while it seemed they might even duel; for years they didn't speak. Then in 1878, when Tolstoy was fifty and Turgenev sixty, the latter again visited the count's home. After Turgenev had read the family a tale he had written (received politely but without enthusiasm) the novelists went for a walk. "They came across a seesaw. Looking at the seesaw and then at each other, they were aware of a subtle challenge that each found irresistible. Turgenev mounted one end and Tolstoy the other, and then they were at it, up and down, up and down, faster and faster—one moment Turgenev and *his* ideas in the ascendant, the next Tolstoy. Of course the Tolstoy children were delighted." See Paul Scott, *On Writing and the Novel* (New York: Morrow, 1987), p. 97.

Holmes and Count Dracula; the Mad Hatter and Winnie-the-Pooh. They stay with us over time, and we can reinterpret them or come to new understandings as we get older. Of all people, Karl Marx said that many of Balzac's characters gained their full growth only after the author was dead. Indeed, when Balzac himself was dying he cried out that the only person who could save him was Bianchon, the doctor from *Le Père Goriot.* Joseph Conrad, while writing *Under Western Eyes,* suffered a weeks-long breakdown, during which he conversed with the novel's characters in Polish.

Even before we have learned to read, our lives are peopled with figures from unreal worlds. Other forms and other media tell stories, but nothing equals the novel in richness and psychological depth. The major characters of fiction belong to us, and we are deeply connected to them. Dickens fans were so anxious over the fate of Little Nell in *The Old Curiosity Shop* that in 1841 six thousand of them stormed the piers in New York City, shouting to arriving sailors, who were thought to have already read the final chapters available in Britain, "Is Little Nell alive?" More recently, lines have stretched down the streets outside bookshops on the days when a new Harry Potter adventure has been published.

Even unsympathetic or unpleasant characters have important places in our hearts. They may be stalking horses for private angers or repositories of childhood memories, but an Iago or a Moriarty can exert a hold over our imaginative life, and it is one of the odder truths of fiction that a major villain requires a major death—or at least several sentences devoted to their leaving us: witness Count Dracula, Bill Sykes, or Captain Hook. Plato remarks in *The Republic* that bad characters are volatile and interesting, whereas uncomplicated good characters are dull and always the same. Through the centuries, novelists have found it difficult to portray goodness, but we scarcely mind so long as we can hiss the villain.

When our most-loved characters, good or evil, are given physical

form in film or on stage, we become outraged when the chosen actors do not conform to how we have imagined them; that is not *our*
Emma Woodhouse, *our* Rochester. Sometimes we accept the casting,
however inexact: Susannah York portrayed Sophie Western in the
1967 film of *Tom Jones* as a tall, almost tomboyish blonde, even
though Fielding's Sophie is a fine-boned brunette: "Her shape was
not only exact, but extremely delicate: and . . . her hair, which was
black, was so luxuriant that it reached her middle. . . ." But most
people accept her, just as they accept the diminutive, popeyed Peter
Lorre playing Raskolnikov in Josef von Sternberg's film of *Crime and
Punishment* (1935), even though the tortured protagonist is described
in the novel as "quite an extraordinarily handsome young man, with
beautiful dark eyes, dark brown hair, over medium height, slim, and
well built." Lorre catches the essence of his character's turmoil, and
that is enough.

It is the closeness we feel that charges the voltage of our response.
Partly this is because novels allow access to secret thoughts denied to
the historian, the biographer, or even the psychoanalyst. "The
novel," argues David Lodge, "can offer us more or less convincing
models of how and why people act as they do." His own favourite is
Leopold Bloom, the hero of *Ulysses*, "in whom most of us can recognize universal human traits, follies, desires and fears. Through his
creator's stream of consciousness we get to know him more intimately than perhaps any other fictional character before or since."

This has never been better put than in the following passage from
Swann's Way, where Proust's narrator asks himself why he is so drawn
to the creations of fiction. How does a character in a novel improve
on someone in real life?

> A real person, profoundly as we may sympathize with him,
> is in a great measure perceptible only through our senses,
> that is to say, he remains opaque, offers a dead weight that

our sensibilities have not the strength to lift. If some misfortune comes to him, it is only in one small section of the complete idea we have of him that we are capable of feeling any emotion.

Novelists can substitute for those "opaque sections" their equivalent in what Proust calls "immaterial sections." By such knowledge we make these characters our own, since "it is in ourselves that they are happening, that they are holding in thrall, while we turn feverishly the pages of the book, our quickened breath and staring eyes." Every emotion is multiplied tenfold, and we experience the most intense feelings that would never in day-to-day existence have been revealed to us.

Fictional and real people do the same things—they fall in love, deceive one another, murder, feel guilt, steal, run away, betray, make things up, sacrifice themselves, are cowardly, go mad, take revenge, end up killing themselves (not to mention, are bored, have indigestion, fill in their tax returns). But once again, even in such specific actions, the invented characters are the ones we get to know the best. Proust's contemporary, D. H. Lawrence, had his own take: "The novel, properly handled, can reveal the most secret places of life: for it is in the *passional* secret places of life, above all, that the tide of sensitive awareness needs to ebb and flow." Perhaps that is just a more flowery version of what Henry James believed: that the best way to get to know characters is to upset them.

To return to Turgenev: in two further letters to friends, after saying that he found Tolstoy's descriptions of hunts, sleigh rides at night, and similar scenes "first rate, marvellous . . . the work of a master beyond compare," he complains that the historical passages, "which the readers adore, are absolutely farcical, a charlatan's tricks." Tolstoy delights the reader with "the pointed tip of Alexander's boot," or "Speransky's laugh . . . in order to make him think that he knows *everything* about the matter since he goes into such detail, whereas all he knows are only these small trifles—a trick and no more, but the public falls for it."

Turgenev goes on: "There is no development of character . . . just an immense amount of the old psychological business ('What do I think? What is thought about me? Do I love or detest?')." He complains of Tolstoy's repeated resort to "vibration and oscillation of feeling" as just a writerly device, like the repeated mention of small traits, "the down on Princess Volkonsky's upper lip," and the like.

The truth is, what Turgenev labelled "tricks" can be an economical way of conveying aspects of character and are part of a novelist's skill set. In Tolstoy's case, a steward twiddling his fingers behind his back or the set of Vronsky's teeth signal something about them (as do—despite Julian Barnes's clever comment in the epigraph that heads this chapter—Anna's "shining grey eyes") and stop short of being contrivances because they work at an appropriate level of tension and power. Their author's energy prevents such details becoming stagnant. We don't know what Anna looks like besides the odd detail, nor Karenin, but consider this description of the latter as seen by his wife:

> At Petersburg, so soon as the train stopped and she got out, the first person that attracted her attention was her husband. "Oh mercy! Why do his ears look like that?" she thought, looking at his frigid and imposing figure, and especially the ears that struck her at the moment as propping up the brim of his round hat. . . .

We take in something of Karenin's cold, authoritative posture, but more how his ears grow in proportion to his wife's disaffection with him—they tell us a little about how Karenin looks but a great deal about Anna's feelings. Tolstoy had his own take on the power of description:

> Do you remember . . . the way Homer conveys Helen's beauty? With these simple words: "When Helen walked in, at the sight of her beauty old men rose to their feet." One pictures the radiance of that beauty right away. No need to describe her eyes, her mouth, her lips. Everyone is left free to imagine Helen in his own way, but everyone is struck by this beauty that draws old men to their feet at the mere sight of it.

Rather than take Turgenev's comments as criticism, it's more useful to turn his words around—and see Tolstoy, as the critic Janet Malcolm describes him, as "one of literature's greatest masters of manipulative techniques." And he manipulates us over both his main characters and those who may be only incidental to his story.

Creative writing manuals talk about stereotypes—characters who possess the expected traits of a group rather than being a developed individual. To this they add the central character, the protagonist; the antagonist, with whom the main character is in conflict; and the character foil, whose traits contrast with the main character. These are useful headings but may not necessarily help. Dr. Watson and Sherlock Holmes, for example, over fifty-six short stories and four novels, don't develop at all (with the possible exception of Holmes in "The Last Bow," in which the great detective looks forward to retirement and total immersion in the world of beekeeping), but that is part of the genre of early detective-story writing. Dorothy L. Sayers bucked the trend when she transformed Lord Peter Wimsey from a man traumatized by the suffering he had witnessed in the Great War into a still compassionate but disciplined professional.

We think of characterization as being at the heart of fiction, but this is only partly true. Nabokov claimed that all great novels were great fairy tales. But as Philip Pullman notes in his introduction to *Fairy Tales from the Brothers Grimm*, "There is no psychology in a fairy tale. The characters have little interior life; their motives are clear and obvious." Other works of fiction besides fairy tales can be memorable without psychological detailing. In yet another introduction, this time to *The Castle*, Kafka's literary executor Max Brod wrote:

> Kafka's characters tend to be stripped to generic being, with but rudimentary physical descriptions and very little psychological analysis. ("Never again psychology," he wrote.) It is precisely this mode of characterization that enables readers to supply multiple interpretations of the action, as if, in part, they too are "writing" the story. It is true that the mere fact of narrative presupposes a certain minimal psychology, but only seldom does Kafka "enter" a character. What matters about the Kafka protagonists is not their "intrinsic being" but rather the role they must perform in narratives of enigma.

Kafka's characters, however, as with those of fairy stories, are more about narrative function than "intrinsic being." Most fictions require a greater profiling.

Although the simplest way to introduce a character, common in older fiction, is to give a physical description and biographical summary, some writers avoid giving lengthy descriptions so as not to influence the reader unduly. Jane Austen, for one, expended little energy on the appearance of her leading romantic players. Her characters are "handsome" or "pleasing" or "not at all handsome," leaving her readers to conjure up the rest. In *Jane Eyre*, the tyrannical Mrs. Reed, whom we meet on page 1, is not given any physical description until page 43. It is up to the individual author to decide how much information to give. Some like to provide as much as possible as soon as possible, which is not necessarily wrong but can clog up the narrative.

Other authors begin with names, going on to body language, voices, their characters' desires and secrets. V. S. Pritchett used bodies as emotional pointers: McDowell, in "The Vice-Consul," has "an unreasonable chin and emotional knees," while Mr. Ferney, in "Tea with Mrs. Bittell," has "two reproachful chins and a loud flourishing voice." Both Anthony Trollope and Thomas Mann, echoing Tolstoy, focused on the teeth of their females as a pointer to character, Thomas Hardy on their lips,* although he generally fussed over naming his creations, his most famous heroine progressing from Love Woodrow to Cis Woodrow, then Sue Troublewell, then Tess Woodrow, then Rose-Mary Troublefield, before coming to rest as Tess D'Urberville. Conan Doyle wanted to call his detective "Sherrinford Hope" (and Dr. Watson "Ormond Sacker"), "Hope" being the title of a whaling ship on which he had served as a doctor in 1880; he changed the name only because his wife Louisa hated it.

The right appellation can be a complicated business. Interviewed about the choice of Lolita, Vladimir Nabokov was expansive:

> For my nymphet I needed a diminutive with a lyrical lilt to it. One of the most limpid and luminous letters is "L." The

---

* Not just to character, but to sexuality. His own notes on his life are filled with such observations as, "Met Miss—, . . . Smokes: handsome girl: cruel small mouth: she's of the class of interesting women one would be afraid to marry"; "A Cleopatra in the railway carriage . . . a good-natured amative creature by her voice, and her heavy moist lips"; "Called on 'Lucas Malet.' A striking woman: full, slightly voluptuous mouth, red lips." Thomas Hardy, *The Life and Work of Thomas Hardy*, ed. Michael Millgate (Athens: University of Georgia Press, 1985), pp. 221, 240, 258.

suffix "-ita" has a lot of Latin tenderness, and this I required too. Hence: Lolita. However, it should not be pronounced as . . . most Americans pronounce it. Low-lee-ta,
with a heavy, clammy "L" and a long "o." No, the first syllable should be as in "lollipop," the "L" liquid and delicate,
the "lee" not too sharp. Spaniards and Italians pronounce
it, of course, with exactly the necessary note of archness
and caress. Another consideration was the welcome murmur of its source name, the fountain name: those roses and
tears in "Dolores." My little girl's heartrending fate had to
be taken into account together with the cuteness and lim-
pidity.

Through the ages, writers have agonized over what to call their
characters. Balzac believed that invented names "did not give life to
imaginary beings," and only those that really belonged to someone
were endowed with vitality; he once dragged a friend over half Paris
in search of a suitable name for the hero of a story, eventually discovering "Marcas" over a tailor's shop, to which he added, as "a flame,
a plume, a star," the initial "Z." "Z. Marcas," he said, conveyed to
him the idea of a great, if unknown, philosopher or poet. Charles
Dickens would pore over the Transactions of the Privy Council lists
looking for unusual names, while "Copperfield" came from a sign he
noticed on a shop in a London slum. He and Anthony Trollope are
famous for making their choices to underline what their characters
were like: Thomas Gradgrind, Scrooge, Sir Orlando Drought, Uriah
Heep, Lord Decimus Tite Barnacle, the Artful Dodger, Dr. Pessimist
Anticant, Wackford Squeers, Sarah Gamp (surprisingly, one of William Faulkner's favourite characters in all fiction). Modern novelists
are no less focused. Allan Gurganus prowls graveyards (they provide
"excellent fictitious names").

The American writer Hilma Wolitzer has confessed that she is uncertain whether to continue with a novel until she is happy with her main characters' names. Paul Auster, the author of sixteen books, was asked during a public lecture how he came up with his names, which are frequently strange, almost surreal, and often symbolize what their owners are like. He explained that his people came to him "already christened"; just as he knew their fates and foibles, so he knew what they were called. The majority of writers, however, do not have such epiphanies and need to work hard to find what is fitting.

On her website, the teacher and romance author Carolyn Jewel says that these appellations have to work on three levels. "You must consider how the name looks on the page, how it sounds in your head and how it sounds if said out loud. All three count." Common names can create notable characters, from Elizabeth Bennet and Isabel Archer to Philip Marlowe and James Bond (of contemporary authors, David Mitchell is particularly good here), but the out of the ordinary can be effective: Huckleberry Finn, Atticus Finch, Jay Gatsby are not only memorable—they identify an era, a mood.

The unusual, allied to alliteration, can call special attention to a character: thus Phineas Finn, Bilbo Baggins, Nicholas Nickleby, Ratso Rizzo, Severus Snape. Even Major Major Major Major in *Catch-22*—although that is an exception, as silly names rarely work. Dickens, over a lifetime of frantic activity, invented, it is estimated, *thirteen thousand* characters, including 318 orphans, and was happy to sacrifice psychological detail to a universal type. After he named a character in *Hard Times* Mr. M'Choakumchild, Bernard Shaw called it "almost an insult to the serious reader." In *Our Gang* (1971), a grimly unfunny satire of the Nixon administration, Philip Roth creates a Trick E. Dixon; John Cheever's third novel, *Bullet Park*, provides as protagonists Mr. Hammer and Mr. Nailles; Don DeLillo gave the name Bucky Wunderlick to the central character of *Great Jones Street* (1973): all attempts to be funny that aren't. But then in much of his fiction William Faulkner gave or made allusions to names current in widely syndicated comic strips, and no one objected.*

The naming of characters can be an opportunity for settling old scores. Dickens, it is said, modelled the physical characteristics and possibly some of the personality traits of his *David Copperfield* villain, Uriah Heep, on Hans Christian Andersen, who had been a guest at the Dickens home and outstayed his welcome. Evelyn Waugh frequently introduced into his early fictions a marginal, ridiculous character called Cruttwell, named after the unpopular principal of Hertford, the Oxford college he attended; and H. G. Wells pastiches Winston Churchill in *Men Like Gods*. A most mischievous example is by Dylan Thomas, who in his radio play *Under Milk Wood* created the fictional village of Llareggub, which everyone thought was authentically Welsh—until, after the play had been broadcast, someone recited the name backwards.†

When I first became an editor, one of the authors I inherited was the Scottish adventure writer Alistair MacLean. At that stage of his career, each book he wrote shot to the top of the bestseller lists, and he had become slipshod. Commenting on the typescript of his latest novel, *Circus,* I pointed out timorously (MacLean's rages were legendary) that the central villain had henchmen called Johnson, Johnstone, and Jackson. They were pretty interchangeable as characters, all being summarily dispatched by the hero, but all the same. . . .

---

* Even great authors slip up. As David Lodge notes, "One of the great mysteries of literary history is what exactly the supremely respectable Henry James meant by calling one of his characters Fanny Assingham." *The Art of Fiction*, p. 36.

† In October 2014, it was announced that seventeen authors, including Margaret Atwood, Julian Barnes, Robert Harris, Tracy Chevalier, and Alan Hollinghurst, would sell the right to name characters in their coming novels as part of a charity auction. Ms. Chevalier asked for a name for a "tough-talking landlady of a boarding-house in 1850s Gold Rush–era San Francisco." It may yet start a trend. Lee Child has already woven some twenty players' names from his favourite football team, Aston Villa, into his books.

"Change it if you like," MacLean told me. "Just don't show me the proofs." So I inserted instead the names of fencers who had recently beaten me in competition. No one noticed.

One can purposely play to or against type when naming characters. Will the names work as well at the end of a story as they do at the beginning? Maybe he or she has grown into it, or out of it? Dickens wrote that he "had found a good name" in Pip for *Great Expectations*, and it does indeed work for his protagonist as he changes through the course of the novel. Plantagenet Palliser (a word that originally meant "carpenter," thus a "smoother-outer") is a minor actor in Trollope's *The Small House at Allington*, then in a later sequence of novels becomes a major figure and is memorably raised to a new standing, the Duke of Omnium.*

Some fictional names reveal unusual care by their creators. In *Crime and Punishment* (originally called *The Drunkards*), "Raskolnikov" translates as "schismatic," which seems to add little, but the word's meaning embraces "to be rent asunder," like a stone split in two—which Rodion (ironically, "hero's ode") Raskolnikov surely is. Further yet, Raskolnikov is an extension of *raskolnik,* a non-conformist or a dissenter. Dostoyevsky deliberately chose names that describe a mood or a character in broad terms. Thus Devushin, from *deva,* a maid; Karamazov, from the Tartar *kara,* black; Karmazinov, from the French, *cramoisy,* crimson; Shatov, from *shatkiy,* unsteady; Smerdyakov, from *smerdyet,* to stink; and many more.

---

* When Philip Roth was writing *Portnoy's Complaint* (1969), the novel that made his name, sparking a storm of controversy over its explicit depictions of masturbation, he selected the surname of his protagonist from the Jewish/Russian "портной," "tailor." In 2013, the *New Yorker* writer David Denby wrote to Roth commenting acerbically on *The Collaboration: Hollywood's Pact with Hitler,* a book about Hollywood and Nazism by Ben Urwand. Roth immediately replied that it was a fabulous name; "I should really have called Portnoy Urwand." Private correspondence, September 29, 2013.

Names should not only match the character in terms of strengths or weaknesses, they should fit era and gender. Shakespeare, in *Antony and Cleopatra,* designates the latter's maidservant "Charmian"— Greek for "delight" or "little joy," but which in this neuter, diminutive form is a sign that she is no entitled lady-in-waiting but an ex-slave, thus a one-time human chattel, whose function in Cleopatra's court crucially depends on a personal relationship with her mistress.

There are other boxes to check off. One shouldn't choose rhyming names unless for a purpose, as they annoy readers. (A real-life seventeenth-century pirate went by the name Aristotle Tottle; he did not prosper.) It seems obvious, but one should avoid the names of the famous, both from life and in literature. Kingsley Amis, so often critical of his son's work, revealed that, after encountering a character named Martin Amis in *Money,* he threw the manuscript across the room.

What holds for names applies to nicknames too (often an indication of one character's power over another)* and also to a character's mannerisms or distinguishing features. In Kipling's tale "Mrs. Bathurst" (1904), a British sailor called Vickery is known as "Click Vickery" because of his ill-fitting false teeth. It is virtually all we learn about him, but since he is incidental to the story, it is enough. Maxwell Perkins (1884–1947), the famous editor at Scribners, wrote how J. M. Barrie once described Thomas Carlyle walking along the street in a broad-brimmed hat with a thick stick: "He didn't make any description of him or say anything brilliant . . . (but) Carlyle was always more visible to me after that, and realer." In the cinema, this is called

---

* In *David Copperfield,* David's great-aunt Betsey insists on calling him "Trotwood" (her surname), then just "Trot," as a condition of his being accepted into her household; later David allows the self-regarding, amoral Steerforth to call him "Daisy," a name that underlines the inequality and ambiguity of their relationship. See Tim Parks, "How Does He Come to Be Mine?" *London Review of Books,* August 8, 2013, p. 11.

"the master shot," an establishing image, a single detail that defines a character. Films have continued to provide language to describe what the novelist does. An early biographer of Dostoyevsky wrote, "There is a sense in which he invented the close-up. . . . From a flicker of a brilliantly enlarged eyelid we deduce the movements of a soul."

A writer can tell his or her readers what a character is like (via the narrator, or another character, or directly from the character) or leave it to the reader to infer such information from the character's thoughts, actions, and speech. The publisher and novelist Sol Stein in *Stein on Writing* quotes the sentence, "She always stood sideways so people could see how thin she was." The description does double duty, letting the reader see the character's attitudes, while at the same time we learn that she is lean. I recently read a sharp comparison between two Daisies—Daisy Buchanan in *The Great Gatsby* and the chorus-girl heroine of Edmund Wilson's first novel *I Thought of Daisy* (1929). Wilson's Daisy is leadenly described as "interesting, attractive, amusing and profoundly sympathetic," whereas at our first meeting with Gatsby's Daisy she is portrayed as looking as if she "had just been blown back in after a short flight around the house," a phrase that instantly conveys the foolish, sad, and beguiling creature she is. Thus—and here Shakespeare's phrase is particularly apt—is Daisy Buchanan "bodied forth."

E. M. Forster said famously that novels require "flat" people as well as "round," the test for the latter being whether he or she is "capable of surprising in a convincing way." Whereas flat characters (called "humours" in the seventeenth century) are made up of a single idea or quality, round characters must adjust, grow, and react to the people around them. Hemingway tends to have round male characters and flat female characters, while Iris Murdoch has it in reverse. But how round is "round"? When in 1944 a young Saul Bellow sent a manuscript to *Partisan Review*, one of its editors cautioned him against a tendency to "excess elaboration and center-less facility." Bellow replied:

> What I find heartbreakingly difficult in these times is fathoming the reader's imagination. . . . I find myself perpetually asking: "How far shall I take this character? Have I made such and such a point clear? Will the actions of X be understood? Shall I destroy a subtlety by hammering it?"

At some point one has to trust one's readers as well as one's own judgement in observing how people act. Victor Hugo constantly made notes about everything—even in mid-conversation he would turn aside and scribble down something he'd just said, or heard, as something he might be able to use. Agatha Christie came up with Hercule Poirot in 1916 after recollecting Belgian refugees she had seen two years before. Iris Murdoch relied more on imagination: "You think about a certain situation and then some quite extraordinary aspect of it suddenly appears. The deep things that the work is about declare themselves and connect. Somehow things fly together and generate other things, and characters invent other characters, as if they were all doing it themselves."

When the Australian novelist Peter Carey was asked whether he discovered his characters as he wrote, he replied: "The big question for me is, What sort of person would do that thing—not just because it suits a story or suits something symbolically, but who would really, *really* do that? When I continue to ask myself that question and I don't take the easy answer, complicated characters are born."

A friend of mine, Betsy Carter, has written three well-received novels; her approach is to interview her characters, imagining them sitting before her, talking about their lives. (Recently, she demoted a leading female to a support role: she must have failed the interview.) Betsy referred me to Anne Lamott's *Bird by Bird*. There I read:

You may only know your characters' externals instead of their essences. Don't worry about it. More will be revealed over time. In the meantime, can you see what your people look like? What sort of first impression do they make? What does each one care most about, want more than anything in the world? What are their secrets? How do they move, how do they smell? Everyone is walking around as an advertisement for who he or she is—so who is this person? Show us. . . .

You also want to ask yourself how they stand, what they carry in their pockets or purses, what happens in their faces and to their posture when they are thinking, or bored, or afraid. Whom would they have voted for last time? Why should we care about them anyway? What would be the first thing they stopped doing if they found out they had six months to live? Would they start smoking again? Would they keep flossing?

This is useful advice, and can help a novelist lay out "the twists and turns in the landscape of the characters' minds," but the process can be taken too far and lead to the error of thinking that conquest of detail can of itself produce good characterization. Jorge Luis Borges was listening to a story by Robert Louis Stevenson when he heard a character described as "dressed and painted to represent a person connected with the Press in reduced circumstances," and in a fit of laughter halted his reader, exclaiming, "How can someone be dressed like that, eh? What do you think Stevenson had in mind? Being impossibly precise, eh?" Impossible precision: a useful bogey-phrase.

Four years ago, I was invited to join a reading group. We meet only about six times a year, which is just as well, as the books chosen are mainly nineteenth-century classics and are rarely short. The group, about ten of us, revolves round Ilja Wachs, a German-Jewish immigrant who has been teaching English literature at Sarah Lawrence College for almost half a century. Tall and still with a swimmer's grace, with his snow-white hair flying out from his head in great loops that seem to have a life of their own, Ilja presides over our gatherings with courtliness, good humour, great knowledge, and the kind of love for literature that lights up a whole room.

Early in 2013, he asked me to read a draft memoir he had put together, a series of interviews he had recorded which he planned to shape into a book. In one passage, he wrote:

> Imagination is fundamentally moral, in its operations and functions in human life, and when we imagine other lives, either as writers or as readers, that itself is in some way a moral function. . . .
>
> George Eliot is key here, because one of the ways literature works is that it allows us identification, and one of the problems that it poses to the moral imagination is that often the process of identification is with one person, and we merge imaginatively with that person, and share with that person's conceits, and don't so much experience the rest of the world.
>
> Eliot knows that, so she makes a deliberate effort to keep us from that kind of primitive identification by continually interrupting us; we merge with Dorothea, we feel with Dorothea, we hiss at Casaubon, and then Eliot stops the action and starts saying to us, "No, no, no, you really have to understand Casaubon, and if you understand him you'd realize how much like you he is, in spite of his seeming flatness, his bureaucratic dead scholarship," and she works that very carefully. . . . It's a constant process of merging and then withdrawing, then of merging again and withdrawing. A very sophisticated technique of dealing with something

that's necessary to literature—the felt experience of relating to other human beings in a deep way.

This seems to me profoundly true, and the case he makes about minor characters is important. In his book about writing, another great teacher of literature, John Gardner, makes a similar point about John Steinbeck's *The Grapes of Wrath* (1939). It should have been one of America's great books, he says. But while Steinbeck had been scrupulous in his research about Okies and the miserable conditions they endured during their migration to California to find work during the Depression, he never bothered to find out about the California ranchers who employed them; he had no interest in why they acted as they did, and so wrote a melodrama in which complex good is pitted against unmitigated, unbelievable evil. Steinbeck, concludes Gardner, was "guilty of simplification."

Against this, there is the criticism that Henry James made of George Eliot, that she knew her characters too well, "hemmed them in with her knowing essayism."* He wanted the people of his fictions to be "*seen*, in the plastic irresponsible way," more like in real life, when someone's character has "to be inferred by the reader." But that is different from short-changing the kind of people you are creating. I was recently reminded by Sebastian Faulks of an exchange we had when he was revising his 1989 novel *The Girl at the Lion d'Or.*

RC: You should give an extra scene to the minor character here to give her some closure.

---

* In his preface to *The Portrait of a Lady,* James actually quotes Eliot's defence of the "smaller female fry" who are the prototypes for Isabel: "In these frail vessels is borne onward through the ages the treasure of human affection." He wasn't criticizing Eliot's interest in "smaller" or less sympathetic characters, only how she presented them.

sf: That means being like Tolstoy.

rc: Be more like Tolstoy.

A surprising number of novelists believe that somehow a fictional creation exists independently of their own authorship—Iris Murdoch's "characters invent other characters, as if they were all doing it themselves." Many writers say their creations "take over and develop lives of their own." Thus the title of this chapter, "Circular Ruins," which recalls a story by Borges that refers to a moment in *Through the Looking-Glass* where Tweedledee points out the sleeping Red King to Alice, and explains to her that she herself is no more than someone in his dream. Alice, like all characters in fiction, has just that much reality.*

Yet writers' blogs are full of comments like, "A character I thought was going to be a blip on the page suddenly turned into a major driving factor to the story. Sure caught me by surprise!" Harold Pinter helps explain this in an early account of his inspirations: "My characters tell me so much and no more." Asked about her novel *Falling in Place* (1991), Ann Beattie contributed this revealing recollection:

> **INTERVIEWER [LARRY MCCAFFERY]:** *Falling in Place* seems to me to have a much greater sense of structure or "plot" [. . .]

---

* In the story, Borges's protagonist arrives in a primitive jungle village. "The purpose which guided him was not impossible, though supernatural. He wanted to dream a man; he wanted to dream him in minute entirety and impose him on reality." Later, "the stranger dreamed that he was in the center of a circular amphitheater which was more or less the burnt temple." At the story's end, "with relief, with humiliation, with terror, he understood that he also was an illusion, that someone else was dreaming him." Writers, Borges suggests, are creators who engender one another and whose existence and originality would be impossible without their predecessors. Jorge Luis Borges, *Ficciones* (New York: Grove, 1994).

that is, it seems to be working towards that climax, the shooting of Mary by John Joel.

BEATTIE: I was so surprised when that shooting happened.

LM: How far in advance had you realized that this was where the book was heading?

AB: Never. I was totally amazed to find the gun in the kid's hands. But then I remembered there had been that odd box which belonged to Parker's grandfather.

SECOND INTERVIEWER [SINDA GREGORY]: So you hadn't planted that box there with the gun in it?

AB: No, in fact, after the shooting happened, I thought, "Oh, my God, we're only three weeks into the book and here Mary is dead on the ground—what am I going to do to resurrect her?" So I resurrected her. Really, I was very upset when that shooting happened.

Something odd is going on here, but also very important to do with the way characters are created. P. D. James, exercised about how one of her leading suspects would behave, went to bed uncertain, then the next morning "woke up and realized exactly what he'd do." This isn't a character taking on an independent life but rather the author's subconscious providing an answer that would not come in normal waking hours. One can understand why Pascal wrote (albeit in a religious context), "If I had not known you, I would not have found you." In his autobiography, Mark Twain writes of the drunken tramp who, he recalls, is mentioned in *Tom Sawyer* and *Huckleberry Finn* and who burns to death in the village jail that he

lay upon my conscience a hundred nights afterward and
filled them with hideous dreams—dreams in which I saw
his appealing face as I had seen it in the pathetic reality,
pressed against the window-bars, with the red hell glowing
behind him—a face which seemed to say to me, "If you
had not given me the matches, this would not have happened; you are responsible for my death." I was *not* responsible for it, for I had meant him no harm, but only good. . . .
The tramp—who was to blame—suffered ten minutes; I,
who was not to blame, suffered three months.*

This is different from an author having a proper respect for his
actors, recognizing that his creations are meant to be fully realized
human beings and not ciphers or like some ventriloquist's doll. When
Nikolai Gogol suddenly breaks off from describing a character's motives to tell us that "there is no creeping into a man's soul and finding
out all that he thinks," he is demonstrating, if in a somewhat intru-
sive way, just that respect. Only it isn't a man—it's a fiction, a com-
pound of words on a page. One has to keep a balance.

In his *Life* of George Eliot, her widower, John Cross, reflected on
her writing method: "In all that she considered her best writing,
there was a 'not herself' which took possession of her, and that she
felt her own personality to be merely the instrument through which
this spirit, as it were, was acting." Thomas Mann had a similar experience. "Things," he wrote, "have a will of their own, and shape
themselves accordingly." When writing *Death in Venice*, he says, "I had

---

* Although the point about Twain's approach remains valid, the burning to death
of the tramp, Muff Potter, does not occur in either book, although there is an
opaque allusion to it in chapter 23 of *Tom Sawyer*, where Tom and Huck give some
matches to Potter when he is in jail. However, *Life on the Mississippi* (chapter 56)
contains a dramatic account of the tramp's death and Twain's consequent struggle with his conscience.

at moments the clearest feeling of transcendence, a sovereign sense of being borne up, such as I had never before experienced." Proust too had what he called "privileged moments" in the throes of composition. Faulkner had something close to it, where time is suspended and a kind of ecstasy possessed him. As his biographer described it, Faulkner's "description of the state when he wrote has within it qualities usually associated with a religious or spiritual experience. Possessed by something, he moved beyond himself—thus 'ecstasy.' "*

Such stories are close to the notion of "free association," a method of treating patients that Sigmund Freud developed between 1892 and 1895, in which patients were allowed to say whatever occurred to them, without being guided by the analyst. In *The Interpretation of Dreams*, Freud cites a letter from Friedrich Schiller that maintains that, "where there is a creative mind, Reason . . . relaxes its watch upon the gates, and the ideas rush in pell-mell." Freud also admitted that he was influenced by an essay by Karl Ludwig Börne (1786–1837), "The Art of Becoming an Original Writer," which suggests that to foster creativity you "write down, without any falsification or hypocrisy, everything that comes into your head." This is but a short step to an author exclaiming of a morning, "You'll never believe what one of my characters has just done!"

In some sense with each character in a novel a real person is created (with Tess, Thomas Hardy was to fall in love with his own heroine), but more accurately, each author is creating an *illusion* of a person, because they are telling a tale, and all they need is for that illusion to be convincing, for that fictional person to seem real for the

---

* This is different from, though links with, a tennis player or other athlete said to be "in the zone," when writing comes easily and in a rush. Balzac had written eighty-five novels in his *Comédie humaine* series with another fifty already planned by the time he died at the age of 51. In his mid-thirties, he confided in a letter that in a fit of creative energy he had just spent twenty-six days without once leaving his study: "Sometimes it seems to me that my very brain is on fire."

reader. "It is not improbabilities of incident but improbabilities of character that matter," wrote Hardy in his diary. Characters exist on the page, not in another world. A complete backstory (apart from being impossible) is not necessary.

The act of writing can release thoughts that have not been on the conscious level, so a character may *seem* to take control, and that may even be to the story's benefit. By contrast, Anthony Trollope overheard two clergymen complaining that the appalling Mrs. Proudie, one of the recurring characters in his serialized Chronicles of Barsetshire, had become boring; he killed her off in the next instalment. George Eliot interrupts her novels to ask her readers if they agree with her about her characters, although—as one critic recently commented—"to anyone on the receiving end of Eliot's sympathy, one wants to say, 'Duck!'" (Her favourite women in particular always seem to find themselves imprisoned in one way or another.) D. H. Lawrence objected to authors who "put their thumb in the pan," meaning that a work of fiction has an autonomous life of its own, and a novelist should not disturb this delicate equilibrium by forcing his or her own purposes upon it.

In some respects, fictional characters resemble children. The author is the parent, one might argue, and although they are created by him or her at a certain point they take on autonomous life, and the wise parent does not attempt to control them. It's here that the comparison breaks down, because children are indeed autonomous, whereas the people in a work of fiction are not. In 1967, Vladimir Nabokov was interviewed for *The Paris Review*. His autocratic responses are funny (if harsh) and make a vital point:

INTERVIEWER: E. M. Forster speaks of his major characters sometimes taking over and dictating the course of his novels. Has this ever been a problem for you, or are you in complete command?

NABOKOV: My knowledge of Mr. Forster's works is limited to one novel, which I dislike; and anyway, it was not he who fathered that trite little whimsy about characters getting out of hand; it is as old as the quills, although of course one sympathizes with *his* people if they try to wriggle out of that trip to India or wherever he takes them. My characters are galley slaves.*

Nabokov's characters obey his every wish because they have no independent life outside his imagination. In an essay about *The Corrections,* Jonathan Franzen takes on Forster's notion of characters "taking over" and Nabokov's infuriated response. "When a writer makes a claim like Forster's," Franzen says,

> the best-case scenario is that he's mistaken. More often, unfortunately, I catch a whiff of self-aggrandizement, as if the writer were trying to distance his work from the mechanistic plotting of genre novels. The writer would like us to believe that, unlike those hacks who can tell you in advance how their books are going to end, *his* imagination is so powerful, and *his* characters so real and vivid, that he has no control over them. The best case here, again, is that it isn't true, because the notion presupposes a loss of authorial will, an abdication of intent.

But what, then, does a writer mean when he claims to be the servant of his characters? For Franzen, once a character has been fleshed out enough to begin to form a coherent whole, a kind of inevitability has been set in motion:

---

* One might add that his interlocutors were manacled too: Nabokov gave only written interviews, requiring all questions to be written out and presented to him in advance.

A character dies on the page if you can't hear his or her voice. In a very limited sense, I suppose, this amounts to "taking over" and "telling you" what the character will and won't do. But the reason the character can't do something is that *you* can't. The task then becomes to figure out what the character *can* do—to try to stretch the narrative as far as possible, to be sure not to overlook exciting possibilities in yourself, while continuing to bend the narrative in the direction of meaning.

Kate Atkinson obviously feels the same pressure. "It's the nearest we'll ever get to playing God," she says, "to suddenly produce these fully formed creatures. It is a bit odd. Other aspects you work out more—you rework sentences, you rework imagery. But not characters. They're not deciding their own fates, clearly, but once you have them, that unconscious process is at work." One lets down a bucket into one's subconscious and draws up what is normally beyond reach. Marilynne Robinson, asked to reflect on her classic 1980 novel *Housekeeping*, commented: "Writers always say characters surprise their authors, and I thought that would be likelier to happen if I had not judged them at the outset and would not judge them at any point in the story."

It seems clear that novelists (maybe all writers) can enter a state, if not of ecstasy, then connecting to a subconscious or partly conscious part of themselves where their characters act in a way they had never intended in their fully conscious moments. That is not lack of discipline or self-indulgence; it is a crucial part of the act of writing. But after that privileged moment come the fully conscious times of revision and control. Thus John Joel may come to shoot Mary, but Mary gets to live again.

———

Where does one put in the backstory (a word that came into the English language only in 1984), and just how much should one use? Exposition is ammunition—you fire it off when you need it. You make your characters as interesting as possible, and in respect of the leading players keep them developing. Character, wrote George Eliot of Tertius Lydgate in *Middlemarch*, "is a process and an unfolding." That at least is one tradition, a particularly nineteenth-century notion. From the 1920s on, novelists like Joyce or Woolf or dramatists like Brecht or Beckett held that human beings do not have that much consistency or continuity. For them, character is not unified or coherent, so "development" is a chimera. Which view one subscribes to is a matter of individual belief, and for most modern writers shifts in personality can be slight and still be effective. Still, when contemplating whether a character is being "true" to his or her nature, one should remember Oscar Wilde's definition of truth: "one's latest mood."

Again, each actor in a story should contribute in some way. Sometimes characters are just fillers. Can they be cut or combined with another? First-time writers often have twins, or two brothers, who can be reduced to one, with double the complexity; by putting more than one function or role into a character, it's possible to make them that much more interesting. Each person should have some universally found quality that provides the reader with a shock of recognition (think Miss Havisham in *Great Expectations*, or Sethe, the tormented mother of Toni Morrison's *Beloved*), but the most successful characters should not be predictable, and it can pay to have a person run against the personality traits he or she has been given. This is particularly true of the most sympathetic, heroic creations: they need that little drop of poison that the bee puts into honey to stop it going bad.

———

In a *Paris Review* interview, Kingsley Amis talks of how the world of *Lucky Jim* was based not on his time as a young lecturer at Swansea (as often supposed) but from what he saw when he visited Philip Larkin, then on the library staff at the University of Leicester. This raises the question about the rights and wrongs of creating characters based on the people in one's own life.

In one sense, nearly all novelists base their creations on what they have personally experienced, but it is a matter of degree, and some writers put people they have known into their fictions with little or no attempt to disguise the borrowing: it is said that all Tolstoy's characters in *War and Peace* were members of his own family, and Tolstoy himself said that he never invented a single person—everyone was based on someone he knew. Again, Fitzgerald never attempted to deny that the leading women in *The Great Gatsby*, Daisy Buchanan and Jordan Baker, were based on his early girlfriend, Ginevra King, and her classmate at the Westover School in Connecticut, Edith Cummings.

Such an approach has become more public over the years. Sheila Heti's 2012 novel *How Should a Person Be?* carries the subtitle "A Novel from Life," and uses "transcribed conversations, real emails, plus heavy doses of fiction" in taking what can be borrowed from life to its ultimate point. In an interview, Heti explained: "Increasingly I'm less interested in writing about fictional people, because it seems so tiresome to make up a fake person and put them through the paces of a fake story. I just—I can't do it."

All the same, one should be careful in separating art from life. For most writers, it takes considerable hard work before they can extract what is most valuable from their life stories. "People tend to underestimate the power of my imagination," declared Nabokov, "and my capacity of evolving serial selves in my writings." John Cheever would say repeatedly, "Fiction is not crypto-autobiography." But the issue is not resolved so easily. Gail Godwin, in her essay-memoir *The Making of a Writer*, describes her struggle to translate her own life experiences into fiction:

> Fact and fiction, fiction and fact. Which stops where, and how much to put in of each? At what point does regurgitated autobiography graduate into memory shaped by art? How do you know when to stop telling it as it is, or was, and make it into what it ought to be—or what would make a better story?

After the publication of *Portnoy's Complaint*, Philip Roth read newspaper reports of his own nervous breakdown ("all that masturbation catching up on him," as Martin Amis remarked sharply, adding, "the pulp novelist Jacqueline Susann said on a chat-show that she would like to meet Philip Roth but wouldn't like to shake his hand"). His artistic pride hurt, years later Roth had his fictional alter ego, Nathan Zuckerman, explain in *The Counterlife* (1986) that they "had mistaken impersonation for confession, and were calling out to a character who lived in a book." In a 2014 interview, he spelled this out further: whoever reckons that the words and thoughts of a writer's characters are the author's own is "looking in the wrong direction." Instead the writer's thoughts lie "in the plight he has invented for his characters, in the juxtaposition of those characters and in the lifelike ramifications of the ensemble they make—their density, their substantiality, their lived existence actualized in all its nuanced particulars."

That, in sum, is what creating character is all about.

CHAPTER 3

Stolen Words: Three Forms of Plagiarism

Plagiarize, plagiarize, plagiarize!
Only be sure always to call it please "research."

TOM LEHRER, "LOBACHEVSKY," 1953

Not every imitation ought to be stigmatized as plagiarism.
The adoption of a noble sentiment, or the insertion of a borrowed ornament, may sometimes display so much judgment
as will almost compensate for invention.

SAMUEL JOHNSON, *THE RAMBLER,* 1751

The previous chapter has sixty-six notes referring to sources. How far can I say that the chapter is my own work? To what extent is it acceptable for me to borrow the words or thoughts of another person or even use that person's life and character as the raw material for what I might write? Today we look unkindly on what a friend of mine calls "heavy lifting," but what goes by the general name of plagiarism is far more complicated than one might think.

Disgust at plagiarism has a long history. For instance, from c. 200 to 185 B.C. the director of the famous library at Alexandria was one Aristophanes of Byzantium, who during his time in charge served as a judge in a competition of poets held before the king. Working daily with the utmost drive and diligence, Aristophanes systematically read through each of the books, then disqualified all but one of the poets on the grounds of plagiarism. When called on by the king to prove his charges, he rushed back to the library and, "relying just on memory, from certain bookcases produced an armful of rolls." The poets' disqualifications stood.

Yet through the centuries, artists of all kinds—not just writers—have glorified in using the works of others. Ramses III, who ruled Egypt from 1186 till 1155 B.C., had the names of previous pharaohs chipped off major monuments and substituted his own. Despite Aristophanes the Librarian, plagiarism, in the ancient classical world, was not thought reprehensible, and sources were rarely cited. In ancient Rome, writers saw their role as emulating and reworking earlier masterpieces; *imitatio,* if not a virtue, was a valued skill. Fortune favours the brave, wrote Virgil—blithely ignoring the fact that Terence had written the same line some years earlier.

One look at the cultural landscape shows how much using other artists' work has been at the centre of artistic production. Bill Bryson has aptly commented that "Shakespeare was a wonderful teller of stories so long as someone else had told them first." He borrowed plots, characters, and titles; plays, poems, and novels by other writers were reworked; and whole passages of text were lifted without attribution. Such wholesale plagiarism was not only tolerated, Shakespeare's audiences appreciated and expected it. The description of Cleopatra in her barge is wholly drawn from Plutarch, but burnished by genius.

In the *Rambler* essay that heads this chapter, Dr. Johnson quotes Virgil, Horace (who plagiarized voraciously), Ovid, and Cicero, as well as Pope and Dryden, to illustrate how often they borrowed, and generally eighteenth-century authors treated originality with suspicion. Laurence Sterne incorporated into *Tristram Shandy* many passages taken almost word for word from Robert Burton's *The Anatomy of Melancholy,* Francis Bacon's "Of Death," *Gargantua* by Rabelais (a favourite source), and several others, rearranging them to serve his purpose. *Tristram Shandy* was published between 1759 and 1767. Almost at once, Oliver Goldsmith defended its borrowings:

> Sterne's Writings, in which it is clearly shewn, that he, whose manner and style were so long thought original, was, in fact, the most unhesitating plagiarist who ever cribbed from his predecessors in order to garnish his own pages. It must be owned, at the same time, that Sterne selects the materials of his mosaic work with so much art, places them so well, and polishes them so highly, that in most cases we are disposed to pardon the want of originality, in consideration of the exquisite talent with which the borrowed materials are wrought up into the new form.

In volume 4 of his great novel, Sterne takes to task a clergyman, Dr. Homenas, who plagiarizes ineptly, delivering one of the most eloquent denunciations of the practice in literature. "Shall we forever make new books, as apothecaries make new mixtures, by pouring only out of one vessel into another? Are we forever to be twisting and untwisting the same rope?" Yet this very passage was itself taken from Burton's attack on imitators in *The Anatomy of Melancholy:* Sterne goes on to acknowledge his borrowings from writers such as Montaigne (who in turn refers to Plutarch as "my breviary," frequently quoting him without acknowledgement) but was silent about his many thefts from Burton—although I suspect he knew perfectly well what he was doing when he plagiarized to condemn plagiarism and enjoyed every moment. In his personal life, Sterne even plagiarized himself, plundering love letters penned years before to his wife for billets-doux to his mistress.

Plagiarism has always had its critics: William Hazlitt wrote in 1820, "If an author is once detected in borrowing, he will be suspected of plagiarism ever after." But by others it has been met by smiles of acceptance. In 1885, H. Rider Haggard was accused of taking passages from a travel book for *King Solomon's Mines;* he shrugged off the charges, saying that he was drawing on a reality common to all. Across the English Channel, Émile Zola, accused of heavily plagiarizing for his naturalist novel about dipsomania, *L'Assommoir,* replied: "All my novels are written in this way; I surround myself with a library and a mountain of notes, before taking up the pen. Look for plagiarisms in my preceding works, Monsieur, and you will make some wonderful discoveries."

"'Originality' is only plagiarizing from a great many," remarked Rupert Brooke, stealing the line from Voltaire. Pablo Picasso said plagiarism was merely stealing from thieves—and promptly stole from others (including from his own work) to prove his point. Plagiarists continue to thrive. The celebrity interviewer David Frost first rose to prominence after he was spotted in a nightclub act that he had "borrowed" from his university contemporary Peter Cook— quickly earning himself the sobriquet the "Bubonic plagiarist." Eric Clapton sometimes lifts whole phrases from Robert Johnson or Muddy Waters, with little complaint. And when it was revealed in May 2014 that Bob Dylan had taken more than a thousand phrases from other authors, a Harvard classics professor who has written papers on Dylan's use of Virgil defended him, saying, "That's something that poets have been doing forever. It's a way of alluding to or correcting or parodying what came before." Well, it *can* be, but it isn't necessarily so.

Mark Twain, one of those from whom Dylan "borrowed," him-

self wrote to Helen Keller after she had been accused of plagiarism
in one of her early stories:

> Oh, dear me, how unspeakably funny and owlishly idiotic
> and grotesque was that "plagiarism" farce! As if there was
> much of anything in any human utterance, oral or written,
> *except* plagiarism! The kernel, the soul—let us go further
> and say the substance, the bulk, the actual and valuable ma-
> terial of *all* human utterances—is plagiarism. . . . Ninety-
> nine parts of all things that proceed from the intellect are
> plagiarisms, pure and simple.

This is wrong-headed—Twain was being kind, as if there were no
such thing as original expression or research or thought. Yet by the
late nineteenth century, "plagiarism-hunting" was frowned upon
and the "hyper-valuation" of originality much debated, while the
most memorable defence of borrowing from other writers had to
wait until T. S. Eliot's famous essay in *The Sacred Wood,* first published
in 1920. In an attack on the Jacobean playwright Philip Massinger
and his colourless borrowings from Shakespeare, Eliot wrote:

> One of the surest of tests is the way in which a poet bor-
> rows. Immature poets imitate; mature poets steal; bad poets
> deface what they take, and good poets make it into some-
> thing better, or at least something different. The good poet
> welds his theft into a whole of feeling which is unique, ut-
> terly different from that from which it was torn; the bad
> poet throws it into something which has no cohesion.

Massinger has never recovered. Yet *The Waste Land,* published two
years later, is basically a tissue of quotations, and many of its footnotes are inaccurate; Eliot admitted that he put them in so the pub-

lisher would be forced into another printing, with corrections. One cannot help feeling: *people in glass houses.* . . .

In the years since Eliot's pronouncement, views against plagiarism have hardened. When in 2005 I started teaching at Kingston University, I was given a form handed to every student. "Plagiarism," it read, "amounts to presenting someone else's ideas as your own without proper acknowledgement." Among the examples that followed:

> Copying out paragraphs from a book without giving full reference;

> Cutting and pasting text from a website and attempting to pass it off as your own work;

> Borrowing another student's essay and copying all or part of it.

I am not sure about the last category: that suggests blatant cheating, like looking over someone's shoulder during an exam. But the consequences of such behaviour were spelled out clearly. "DO NOT do any of these things under any circumstances. Plagiarism may result in severe penalties, which will affect your final degree result. To avoid any suspicion of plagiarism, make sure all work you quote is fully referenced."*

---

* Most academic institutions still define plagiarism as if it applies only to the written word. Stanford sees it as the "use, without giving reasonable and appropriate credit to or acknowledging the author or source, of another person's original work, whether such work is made up of code, formulas, ideas, language, research, strategies, writing or other form(s)." Yale views it as the "use of another's work, words, or ideas without attribution" which includes "using a source's language without quoting, using information from a source without attribution, and para-

In the summer of 2010, an article appeared in *The New York Times* about a spate of plagiarism on American campuses. This led to a flurry of indignant letters to the editor. A typical one read: "To put one's name to language crafted by others is public acknowledgement that the perpetrator lacks all sense of pride and self-worth. Such a thief will never know the deep pleasure, the joys, of creativity and deserves only our pity and contempt."

A professor of English at Kean University described his approach on the first day of class: he would distribute a plagiarism "quiz" designed to define academic dishonesty. It reviewed the guidelines for citing sources properly, addressed the reasons students plagiarize, explained why it was a serious offence, and pointed out how easy it was to get caught.*

Plagiarism has been called "a table-manners violation," but today it is seen as an ethical and an aesthetic infringement, one even open to a civic action. There may be no deliberate attempt to deceive. Much plagiarism is accidental: students often mix their own ideas and those of their sources when they take sloppy notes or are careless about writing down bibliographical information. It is not always easy

---

phrasing a source in a form that stays too close to the original"; and Oxford characterizes it as the use of "a writer's ideas or phraseology without giving due credit." Picasso would have been most put out.

* Several online sites explain plagiarism and how to avoid it. The Plagiarism Advisory Service (jiscpas.ac.uk) helps writers of all kinds; similarly, plagiarism.org (which lists *eleven* different offences); owl.english.purdue.edu/owl/resource/930/010 and grammarly.com (an automated proofreader and plagiarism-checker— "Check your texts against over 8 billion documents; corrects up to ten times as many mistakes as other word processors"). Most of these describe how one might unintentionally plagiarize: not knowing the proper forms of citation, or thinking that one is paraphrasing when one is plagiarizing. (It is acceptable to retain the essential ideas of the original, but one must significantly change its style and grammatical structure, and even then one can't look something up, change a few words, and call it original research. These resources spell out what "significantly" implies.)

to distinguish between "common knowledge," which one is free to use, and original ideas (despite what Mark Twain wrote) that are the intellectual property of others.

To detect plagiarism, universities now use sophisticated electronic systems (such as Turnitin, produced by a company called iParadigms), and most teachers simply type into Google or similar search engines any suspect phrase or passage and usually find the original author within seconds. Still, a 2001 survey showed that over 40 percent of U.S. university students admitted to copying from the Internet. In Britain, there are more than eighty thousand law students, of whom a whopping three hundred a year are caught using other people's material without acknowledgement. In a survey of fifty thousand applications in 2007, many for medical science courses and for Oxford and Cambridge, it was found that 234 applicants for medicine began their personal statements with an identical anecdote about setting fire to their pyjamas at the age of eight. One wonders where the original story came from and why so many applicants thought it would benefit their case. . . .

The discovered plagiarist often has to pay a heavy price: humiliation, disgrace, ostracism. As Judge Richard Posner comments in his excellent short study, *The Little Book of Plagiarism*, plagiarism is "a chump's crime." He also notes that when the University of Oregon published a pamphlet on the dangers of plagiarism it lifted an entire section from Stanford's teaching assistant handbook—without acknowledgement.

Well-known authors can be the most blatant offenders. In 2001, Stephen Ambrose (whose more than twenty books include *Band of Brothers*, from which the hugely successful HBO series was made) published *The Wild Blue: The Men and Boys Who Flew the B-24s over Germany*. The first printing was half a million copies, and the book reached twelfth on the *New York Times* bestseller list. But whole passages turned out to be almost identical to those in a 1995 book, *Wings of Morning: The Story of the Last American Bomber Shot Down over Germany in World War II*, by Thomas Childers, a history professor at the University of Pennsylvania. Key passages are lifted and repeated without proper attribution: while Childers is mentioned in the bibliography of Ambrose's book and in four footnotes, these give no indication that entire paragraphs have been copied.

In the weeks that followed it was shown that Ambrose had plagiarized from six additional books and had been lifting material from other people's work from as far back as 1975, in his *Crazy Horse and Custer*. Ambrose tried to defend himself, arguing that he had published "hundreds of thousands of sentences," of which only a few, maybe "ten pages out of a total work of some 15,000 pages," were taken from others. But his reputation could never recover, and, already sick before the controversy, he died of lung cancer in October 2002, unredeemed.

That same year, Doris Kearns Goodwin was said to have used several earlier works by other historians without attribution in writing her 1987 study, *The Fitzgeralds and the Kennedys*. Professor Goodwin explained that she had mixed up quotations from the books mentioned with her own notes, and that she had never intended to pass off the writing of others as her own. She hired a high-powered political consultant, Robert Shrum, to orchestrate media support, and a group of prominent historians, headed by Arthur Schlesinger, Jr., signed a letter to *The New York Times* proclaiming that Goodwin "did not, she does not, cheat or plagiarize. In fact, her character and work symbolize the highest standards of moral integrity." This prompted a pointed article in *The New York Times Book Review* by Bruce McCall, "The Dog Wrote It":

> Evidence suggests that writers may be unusually accident-prone. "An encyclopedia fell on my head." "I slipped leaving Elaine's." "The Red Sox lost again, I banged my head

against the wall in frustration, and next thing I knew I was transcribing Nabokov."

Small wonder, he concludes, that reported incidents of amnesia among writers "have recently multiplied in exact proportion to the number of plagiarism lawsuits filed."

Eventually it came out that soon after *The Fitzgeralds and the Kennedys* was published Lynne McTaggart, the principal author whose work was plagiarized (there were several), had accepted a large sum of money from Goodwin's representatives not to reveal the theft; new endnotes were added to Goodwin's paperback, as well as a paragraph to its preface declaring McTaggart's study the "definitive" biography of Kathleen Kennedy. But Goodwin never admitted that she had plagiarized anything; only after the thefts came to light did McTaggart announce, "I felt vindicated. [Goodwin] was properly chastised." She now added (fifteen years late): "There is a moral issue in general that needs to be examined."

There is indeed a moral issue here, but it is still unclear how serious the ethical infringement is. In an article in *The New York Times Book Review,* the poet Sandra Beasley has written about how she felt when a serial plagiarizer, Christian Ward, published her poems under his own name. "Where would Dante send a plagiarist?" she asked rhetorically. "The Eighth Circle of Hell is reserved for the fraudulent and requires a descent down a cliff on the back of Geryon [the Monster of Fraud, a winged beast with the face of an honest man], within waving distance of Mordred [the notorious traitor who opposed King Arthur] and Count Ugolino [the thirteenth-century political turncoat] in their pit of treachery." A beat, then: "That seems a tad excessive."

In recent years, by far the most interesting case of alleged plagiarism arose in the autumn of 2006, when *The Mail on Sunday* published a long article attacking Ian McEwan for having wrongly used another writer's work for his 2001 novel *Atonement.* This came just as a film of the book starring Keira Knightley was in production. In a further article, its sister paper the *Daily Mail* described the "plundering" of a 1977 memoir, *No Time for Romance,* by an ex-nurse and author of romantic novels named Lucille Andrews. McEwan's use of her material came at a time when Andrews was widowed and stuck for funds, making his action "all the more cruel." Other journalists were soon recalling the controversy over McEwan's 1978 debut novel, *The Cement Garden,* noting that key elements of the plot closely mirrored some of those of a 1963 novel by the British author Julian Gloag.

In fact all McEwan had done was use Andrews's autobiography for authentic details of nursing and hospital conditions in wartime Britain. The end of his novel included, at first publication, a note to acknowledge *No Time for Romance,* among several other works. Only a handful of words were the same in the two books. But then came the follow-up. Letters from a number of other authors rained in (all coming to McEwan's defence), among them Margaret Atwood, John Updike, Peter Carey, Colm Tóibín, Zadie Smith, and Martin Amis—a particularly generous act on Amis's part, as *The Rachel Papers* had been plagiarized in 1979 by Jacob Epstein in his novel *Wild Oats.**

---

* Incredibly, Epstein's hero spends much of his time researching a case of plagiarism. There is even a second case of plagiarism in the novel, when a minor character is caught stealing from *Winnie-the-Pooh!* The book won plaudits from Lillian Hellman, John Gregory Dunne, Anne Tyler, and Darryl Pinckney, among others. *Wild Oats* was published in 1980, when Epstein was twenty-three; Amis's own debut novel, *The Rachel Papers,* had appeared in 1974, when he was twenty-four. When Amis finally went on the record, in *The Observer* (October 19, 1980), he noted fifty-three cases of outright borrowings and concluded that, "Epstein wasn't 'influenced' by *The Rachel Papers,* he had it flattened out by his typewriter." For Amis, Epstein was committing literary suicide, and he even had some sympathy for him. Plagiarism "risks, or invites, a deep shame, and there must be something of the death-wish in it." Amis admitted having lifted an occasional line himself—specifically a description in *Our Mutual Friend* and a whole paragraph from J. G. Ballard's *The Drowned World.* But these were lapses, not wholesale lift-

Rose Tremain wrote that her book *Music and Silence* depended "to a shocking extent on one extremely small illustrated book, *Christian IV,* by Birger Mikkelson." Kazuo Ishiguro said that were McEwan guilty of plagiarism, "at least four of my own novels will have to be marked down as plagiarized."

The most surprising letter was from the reclusive Thomas Pynchon:

> Oddly enough, most of us who write historical fiction do feel some obligation to accuracy. It is that Ruskin business about "a capacity responsive to the claims of fact, but unoppressed by them." Unless we were actually there, we must turn to people who were, or to letters, contemporary reporting, the encyclopedia, the Internet, until, with luck, at some point, we can begin to make a few things of our own up. To discover in the course of research some engaging detail we know can be put into a story where it will do some good can hardly be classed as a felonious act—it is simply what we do.

French theorists like Barthes and Foucault have long argued that in the strictest sense there is no such thing as an "author," because all writing is collaborative and produced by a kind of cultural collective.* But I prefer the Australian novelist Thomas Keneally's take on

---

ings. In reply, Epstein told *The New York Times*: "I've been dreading this for months. It is the most awful mistake, which happened because I made notes from various books as I went along and then lost the notebook telling me where they came from." Ah, the lost or confusing notebook. Amis, who never took the matter further, comes out of the affair very well. See Thomas Mallon, *Stolen Words: Forays into the Origins and Ravages of Plagiarism* (New York: Ticknor and Fields, 1989), pp. 89–143.

* As long ago as 1879 George Eliot was calling for "communistic principles" of authorship: the disposal "to treat the distinction between Mine and Thine in

the debate. "Fiction," he wrote, "depends on a certain value-added quality created on top of the raw material, and that McEwan has added value beyond the original will, I believe, be richly demonstrated."

In November 2004, Malcolm Gladwell explained this notion of "value-added quality" in a useful, if controversial, way. Writing in *The New Yorker,* he told of being contacted in the spring of that year by a psychiatrist named Dorothy Lewis, about whom he had written some eight years before, detailing her extensive experience studying serial killers. Lewis now told Gladwell that, tipped off by a friend, she had read the script of a Broadway production, *Frozen,* by the British playwright Bryony Lavery, in which one of the main characters is a New York psychiatrist suspiciously like Lewis. It was not only damaging (it made up a sexual relationship between the psychiatrist and the killer she visits professionally) but it also plagiarized extensively from the Gladwell article. She had marked line after line of identical passages. "I was sitting at home," Gladwell quotes her as saying, "and I realized that it was I. I felt robbed and violated in some peculiar way. It was as if someone had stolen—I don't believe in the soul, but, if there is such a thing, it was as if someone had stolen my essence." She compiled a chart of overlaps between her own life and the play:

---

original authorship as egoistic, narrowing, and low" (*The Impressions of Theophrastus Such,* ed. Nancy Henry [London: William Pickering, 1994], p. 58). More recently, in 2010, a teenage German novelist, Helene Hegemann, was criticized by a fellow novelist for having incorporated chunks of his own writing into hers. Far from apologizing, she declared that this had been her deliberate intention. She was the child of the remix age, she said, and "there's no such thing as originality anyway, just authenticity." Amid the controversy that followed, David Shields published *Reality Hunger,* a feisty literary "manifesto" constructed almost entirely of quotations from other writers and thinkers. Expressive writing, he declared, was lagging behind the other arts in using appropriation as a tool. See Randy Kennedy, "The Free-Appropriation Writer," *The New York Times,* February 28, 2010, p. 3.

fifteen pages long, listing twelve instances of almost verbatim similarities, some 675 words, between *Frozen* and Gladwell's profile.

Initially he too felt outraged. To have lifted his material without his approval was "theft," plain and simple. Only, as the article stretched on, Gladwell found the issue was not so simple. "Instead of feeling that my words had been taken from me, I felt that they had become part of some grander cause. . . . Intellectual-property doctrine isn't a straightforward application of the ethical principle 'Thou shalt not steal.' At its core is the notion that there are certain situations when you *can* steal." His conclusion was that while Lavery had copied his work, her plagiarism had served a larger purpose. She "wasn't writing another profile of Dorothy Lewis. She was writing a play about something entirely new—about what would happen if a mother met the man who killed her daughter." She had then used Gladwell's descriptions of Lewis's work and the outline of her life "as a building block in making that confrontation plausible. Isn't that the way creativity is supposed to work? . . . Plagiarism . . . is not merely extremist. It has also become disconnected from the broader question of what does and does not inhibit creativity."

Even Bryony Lavery lamely admitted to Gladwell, "I thought it was O.K. to use it. It never occurred to me to ask you, I thought it was *news*." Plagiarism—particularly at the undergraduate or academic thesis level—has no "added value"; it is plainly wrong by any criterion, both deceitful and fraudulent, and deserves to be punished. But should there be one rule for the gifted, another for the also-rans? In an essay on the "appropriation artist" David Salle ("nothing . . . is new; everything has had a previous life elsewhere"), Janet Malcolm describes his borrowings as "immediate freshening." Gladwell is surely right in drawing distinctions; the only problem is who is to decide when the "added value" makes using another's work an acceptable thing to do.

———

Plagiarism in many instances should be shunned and punished; at the same time, it has been at the heart of cultural life for centuries, bringing much good and much pleasure. The great plagiarists have committed no crime. And, in the Gladwell example, there is the "added value" argument, which many find persuasive. But there is a further question to raise, and in many ways it is the most interesting.

The word *plagiarism* comes from the Latin for kidnapping, literally "going out with a net." It was used first in something like its modern sense in A.D. 1 by the Roman poet Martial. A *plagiarius* was, in his view, someone who stole someone else's slave or enslaved a free person. In epigram No. 32, he applies the term metaphorically to another poet, whom he accuses of having claimed authorship of verses Martial had written. Later, in epigram No. 53, he uses not *plagiarius* but the word for thief (*fur*) to apply to someone whom we would call a plagiarist. As Martial was to put it, a plagiarist doesn't just steal a person's body; he kidnaps his person, her inner life.

This develops into an altogether different literary theft. For both the memoirist and the novelist are inevitably inspired by the people they have met, and will make use of them to suit their purposes. This may not strictly be plagiarism, but it is similar territory. "Writing is an act of thievery," admits Khalid Hosseini, author of the autobiographical novel *The Kite Runner*. "You adapt experiences and anecdotes for your own purposes." John Cheever put it more gently: "Fiction is a force of memory improperly understood."

It can also cut close to non-fiction, and the lines of demarcation become blurred. In a recent essay, Alexander Stille, himself a memoirist, has written: "Within this kind of work there is inherent conflict. The characters in a memoir are not real people, but inevitably feed on the blood of the living like vampires. And so it is entirely natural for those real people to defend their identities as if they were fighting for their lives."

Such "kidnappings" can cause as much pain as, if not more than, someone whose work is plagiarized may feel. During the mid-1960s, Michael Holroyd was researching his two-volume biography of Lytton Strachey when he took time out to complete a short novel, his first and, as it turned out, his only. "It would be some fifty thousand words long and cover the happenings of a family over twenty-four hours," wrote Holroyd many years later. The book was accepted for publication by Heinemann in Britain and by Holt, Rinehart in the United States. "During the long wait for publication I had given the typescript to my father to read—and he was horrified. For him the book was not a novel at all but a hostile caricature of the family. 'You go out of your way to avoid any redeeming features in anyone's characters,' he wrote. . . . 'The formula is evident. Take the weakest side of each character—the skeleton in every cupboard—& magnify these out of proportion so as they appear to become the whole and not only part of the picture. Please understand the whole family are together in their dislike of this distorted picture you have drawn of them.'"

The family had not in fact read the book, but Holroyd's father's reaction was enough. In a special introduction to the novel, finally reissued in 2014 after years out of print, Holroyd explains how he in turn felt. "I was nonplussed by this awful reaction. I had borrowed certain traits, gestures, tricks of speech and various mannerisms from members of the family, but had fixed them on to characters with very different careers and past lives."

Whatever his son's motives, Holroyd the father was determined to stop publication. There may have been breaches of trust, but none of copyright, and certainly no plagiarism of an actionable kind, so instead he threatened to sue for libel. In Britain, where libel laws are strict, Heinemann was concerned, but Holroyd was aghast. "The intensity of his grief and anger . . . shocked me. So I withdrew the novel and returned my advance." Holt, however, having taken legal advice, went ahead, and the book was published in the United States in 1969. "No copies reached my family and I was able to help my father, who was sliding towards bankruptcy, with my advance."

Something very different happened over the publication of Salman Rushdie's novel *Midnight's Children*. When his father first read the book, in 1980, he was convinced that Ahmed Sinai, the novel's drunken patriarch, was a satirical portrait based on him. He was furious. Salman Rushdie did not deny that the character was a fictionalized version of his parent—"In my young, pissed-off way," he later explained, "I responded that I'd left all the nasty stuff out"—but he objected to his father's wounded reaction, which he thought betrayed a crude understanding of how novels worked. "My father had studied literature at Cambridge so I expected him to have a sophisticated response to the book." But in Rushdie's case he never rescinded his "kidnapping."

This making use of—even making off with—someone else's life seems to me to be what a *plagiarius* does. But it is, simply, what writers do. In an endnote essay in *The New York Times Book Review* the novelist and playwright Roger Rosenblatt put this well:

> For the wolf of a writer, the family is a crowd of sitting ducks. There they assemble at the Thanksgiving table, poor dears—blithering uncles, drugged-out siblings, warring couples—posing for a painting, though they do not know it.

The objects of a writer's scrutiny may be entirely blameless, but the writer will infuse his family with whatever characteristics suit his purpose, because "defects make for better reading than virtues."

Literature is littered with stories of how novelists have taken the lives of people they have met and used them for their fictions. The family is just the nearest ammunition to hand. Friends and enemies, lovers and ex-lovers, all are grist to the artist's mill. The celebrated society hostess Lady Ottoline Morrell (1873–1938) was the inspiration for Mrs. Bidlake in Aldous Huxley's *Point Counter Point*, for Hermione Roddice in D. H. Lawrence's *Women in Love*, for Lady Caroline Bury in Graham Greene's *It's a Battlefield*, and for Lady Sybilline Quarrell in Alan Bennett's *Forty Years On*. (In the first two instances at least, she felt betrayed by authors she regarded as friends.) Zelda Fitzgerald complained of her husband that in *The Beautiful and Damned* she could "recognize a portion of an old diary of mine which mysteriously disappeared shortly after my marriage, and also scraps of letters which sound vaguely familiar. Mr. Fitzgerald seems to believe that plagiarism begins at home." A novelist I edited wrote of a main character whose father had murdered her mother—a situation taken from real life by the novelist from the pillow talk of a onetime lover, whose own family had experienced exactly that tragedy. Only when the book was in proof did he show it to her, and she was outraged. Chastened, he rewrote the novel. Many writers do not behave as well—or, if they do, not as late.

In 1872 a neighbour of Tolstoy's cast off his mistress, Anna Pirogova. The railroad had recently been extended into the province, and in her despair Anna rushed down to the tracks and threw herself under a train. The corpse was taken to a nearby engine shed, and Tolstoy, hearing of the tragedy, rode over to view the remains, even though he had never known the woman. We do not object when we learn that he used Anna Pirogova as the inspiration for Anna Karenina, or when an otherwise anonymous Madame Delphine Delamare, after numerous adulteries as the wife of an inattentive country doctor, in 1850 poisons herself and becomes the model for Emma Bovary. When, in *The Magic Mountain*, Thomas Mann, for his portrait of Mynheer Peeperkorn, borrowed some of the features of Gerhart Hauptmann, at that time Germany's foremost dramatist, a scandal ensued, and Mann was forced to appeal to Hauptmann directly: "I have sinned against you. I was in need, was led into temptation, and yielded to it. The need was artistic." And there the matter rested. These are just three examples, when in truth hardly any imaginative writer doesn't borrow from people they know. Even so, when the instances come closer to home, we may justifiably feel that our person has been kidnapped.*

Most writers acknowledge the destructive, even self-destructive element in their chosen profession. "As a younger man," admitted Peter Carey, "if anything was worth stealing I would steal it." Whether it is in fiction or non-fiction, most writers take that "right" for granted. "The novelist destroys the house of his life and uses its stones to build the house of his novel," Milan Kundera wrote in *Art of the Novel,* not as apology but as a description of the way things are.†

John Updike confessed that fiction is "a dirty business." His art had "a shabby side. . . . The artist who works in words and anecdotes, images and facts wants to share with us nothing less than his digested life." In his book *Self-Consciousness*, he exempts himself from

---

* This leaves plenty of room for error. Around 1999, a woman librarian brought a case against Joe Klein and Random House since she believed that she was the model for a character who has an affair with the Clintonesque presidential candidate in Klein's *Primary Colors* and was thus defamed. It was said that the woman cited as evidence the description of her character's shapely legs in the novel being an exact description of her own. In fact, Klein had used as inspiration the legs of his literary agent, Kathy Robbins (my wife). When Kathy was required to make a formal deposition, she made sure she wore a short skirt and high heels. The claim duly failed, a New York court ruling that a depiction "must be so closely akin" to the real person claiming to be defamed that "a reader of the book, knowing the real person, would have no difficulty linking the two."

† In an extreme case, David Graham Phillips, early hailed by H. L. Mencken as "the leading American novelist" of his day, was fatally shot in 1911 by a man overcome by rage at what he believed was the depiction of his family in one of Phillips's fictions. The author, on his way to the hospital, said that he had no knowledge of his assailant or his family. See Peter Duffy, "Character Assassination," *The New York Times Book Review,* January 16, 2011, p. 23.

"normal intra-familial courtesy," adding that "the nearer and dearer they are the more mercilessly they are served up." Interviewed for a 1982 TV documentary, he bluntly states: "My duty as a writer is to make the best record I can of life as I understand it, and that duty takes precedence for me over all these other considerations." After Updike and his first wife told their children they planned to divorce, he composed a story about the episode ("Separating") a mere two weeks later, a "way of hiding," he put it in a 1968 interview, "of too instantly transforming pain into honey."*

The Norwegian writer Karl Ove Knausgård, whose six-part memoir/novel *My Struggle* is extremely revealing about his close relatives, has said that the question of whether a writer ought to use his family as material is like asking: would you save the cat or the Rembrandt from a burning house? His answer is that we must save the cat, choosing life over art—but he portrays his own family in intimate, hurtful detail.

Graham Greene has famously written about the "ice chip in the heart" that allows novelists to plagiarize the lives of friends—an image he took from Hans Anderson's *The Snow Queen*, in which a sliver of glass from a shattered magic mirror lodges in the heart of a young boy, Kai. For Greene, that chip of ice is essential equipment. Nearly all writers have to ask whether they possess such a splinter, and to what degree.

---

* Updike's novel detailing a lengthy affair, *Marry Me*, written in 1962, stayed locked in a safe-deposit box in a local bank for over a decade; he then had it published in 1976, when his first wife was still alive but after they had divorced.

Five-Way Portrait of Marcel Duchamp;
unidentified photographer, 1917.

CHAPTER 4

The Trick of It:
Points of View

Remember that writing is translation. And the opus to be translated is yourself.

E. B. WHITE, IN A LETTER TO A STUDENT

"And who are you?" said he.
"Don't puzzle me," said I.

LAURENCE STERNE, *TRISTRAM SHANDY*, 1759–67

It's more than forty years ago now since I first read about the Argentinian businessman whose daughter Sylvia had fallen in love with Klaus Clement, the son of a German immigrant to Argentina. The businessman, a German half-Jew named Lothar Hermann, had also immigrated to Buenos Aires after the Second World War, having survived the horrors of a concentration camp, although in the years since the war he had lost his sight. Sylvia announced that she wanted to marry Klaus, and perhaps as an initial step the two fathers could talk? Klaus's father was based in San Fernando, an industrial community twelve miles north of the centre of Buenos Aires, where he was a department head at Mercedes-Benz, so a phone conversation was the practical thing.

The call was arranged, but when Hermann heard Klaus's father over the airways he almost dropped the receiver in horror—for he recognized immediately his long-time tormentor, Otto Adolf Eichmann, who from 1942 on had been responsible for managing the mass deportation of Jews to extermination camps in German-occupied Eastern Europe. Hermann had often heard his voice. In the weeks to come it was the information from Hermann and his daughter that would lead to the kidnapping of Eichmann by Mossad agents and Eichmann's eventual trial and execution in Israel in 1962.

This story, initially gleaned from a short news report in a British paper, stayed with me through the years. Some time in 1988, the Scottish novelist Allan Massie was talking to me about how he wished to take on a subject that would bring him readers from well beyond British territories, and I suggested my chilling tale. Mightn't Allan view the events through the perspectives of the blinded father, the war criminal, and each of the two young lovers? He was taken by the idea, but asked if I had really kept it to myself over some two decades. I assured him that I had. Allan went off to cogitate and a month later produced an outline of the novel he would write. Hutchinson, my publishing home at the time, offered him a contract, and he set to work.

A few months on, I was at a book party when Bernice Rubens, a friend of mine who had won the Booker Prize in 1970, came up and said excitedly that she was well into a new novel "based on that idea of yours—the one about Jewish persecution." I was mortified. Had I really forgotten that I had told her about the Hermann family tragedy? I started to babble about Allan Massie, but she quickly cut me short. "No, no," she said, laughing. "Your idea for me was a novel called *I, Dreyfus*."*

This is a circuitous way into a quite different subject, that of narrative point of view. I remembered then how I had told Bernice about all the many books concerning the Dreyfus affair, but what if a novelist recounted that much-persecuted man's story from within—using the first person? We talked about the advantages of writing from that perspective.

For a start, first person can give an authenticity, even a greater intensity to the story. And if we see events through a single perspective, receiving directly only that person's opinions, thoughts, and feelings, the author has opportunities for limiting what that character experiences or understands and can play with our responses accordingly. A novel doesn't have to have the same person telling events all the way through, of course: first-person narrative can be singular, plural, or multiple (various people recounting the tale in their own voices—as turned out to be the case with Allan's novel). A difficulty with this approach is that first-person voices tend to sound alike the closer they come to transcribed speech, and one wants characters not only to see things differently but to "sound" differently too.

First-person narratives can appear in several forms, including dramatic monologue, as in Camus's *The Fall* or Twain's *The Adventures of Huckleberry Finn*, or interior monologue, as in Proust's *Remembrance of Things Past* or Dostoyevsky's *Notes from Underground*. Flaubert's *Madame Bovary* begins from the perspective of a classmate of Emma's future husband, a narrator from whom we never hear again; Gertrude Stein's *The Autobiography of Alice B. Toklas* is a first-person narra-

---

* Bernice Rubens's account, bearing that title, took some time to be completed, and was published only in 1999. Allan Massie's retelling of the Eichmann-Hermann story, *The Sins of the Father*, appeared in 1991. A Booker Prize judge named Nicholas Mosley resigned from the panel when Massie's novel failed to make the shortlist.

tive disguised as someone else's memoir. Among other notable examples is Styron's *The Confessions of Nat Turner,* based on a historical account left by a rebel slave awaiting execution, a kind of racial ventriloquism. In each case, the chosen point of view serves a definite purpose.

This is particularly true in *Anna Karenina,* when early on in the novel Kitty Scherbetskaya attends the grand ball where she expects Vronsky, the object of her love, to propose to her. Instead, she watches aghast as he and Anna show the first signs that they are in love, and she recognizes that Vronsky has no interest in her at all. Rather than having Tolstoy describe the scene as the objective narrator, we see, through a rival's eyes, the full force of Anna's magnetism, and although Kitty is filled with jealousy as Anna and Vronsky dance the mazurka (leaving her partnerless) she cannot help be witness to the radiant beauty of Anna in her simple black gown, all the more powerful because for Kitty what she is seeing is a nightmare.

That is one example. The whole of a narrative can itself be presented as a document, such as a diary, in which the narrator makes explicit reference to the fact that he or she is writing or telling a story. This is the case in Bram Stoker's *Dracula,* although in addition to first-person accounts the narrative includes letters and newspaper reports. In *The Divorce Papers* (2014), first-time author Susan Rieger presents the entire tale in the form of emails, letters, court transcripts, psychiatric evaluation forms, lawyers' worksheets, to-do lists, recordings, formal dinner invitations, and newspaper articles. Rieger quotes from Stoker in her opening epigraph: "How these papers have been placed in sequence will be made manifest in the reading of them. All needless matters have been eliminated, so that a history . . . may stand forth as simple fact."

The first-person narrator may also be one who closely observes the principal character, as in *The Great Gatsby.* After Fitzgerald had completed his initial draft his editor, Maxwell Perkins, wrote to him:

You adopted exactly the right method of telling it, that of employing a narrator who is more of a spectator than an actor: this puts the reader upon a point of observation on a higher level than that on which the character stands and at a distance that gives perspective. In no other way could your irony have been so immensely effective.

This holds true for, among others, several fictions by Joseph Conrad. Joan Didion, interviewed in 2006, picked out his 1915 novel *Victory* because of the way the plot unfolds:

The story is told third-hand. . . . So there's this fantastic distancing of the narrative, except that when you're in the middle of it, it remains very immediate. It's incredibly skillful. . . . It opens up the possibilities of the novel.

Since the narrator has a role within the story (whether participating or not), he or she may not have knowledge of all the events. For this reason, the first-person approach is often used for detective fiction, so that reader and narrator learn about the case at the same time. One traditional method in such stories is to employ the main detective's principal assistant as the narrator: Dr. Watson plays this role in the Sherlock Holmes mysteries,[*] as does Captain Arthur Hastings, O.B.E., who appears in nine Hercule Poirot cases. This has the advantage that the assistant can't get inside the lead detective's head, so that while Holmes or Poirot may get ahead of us, we don't get ahead of ourselves.

In his preface to *Best Detective Stories 1928–9*, Ronald Knox (1888–

---

[*] In her short book about detective fiction, P. D. James made the point that "writers who create a serial character inevitably endow him or her with their own interests and preoccupations" (P. D. James, *Talking About Detective Fiction* [New York: Vintage, 2011], p. 32). This may be generally true, but it is not easy to see many affinities between Conan Doyle and Holmes beyond a doctor's interest in forensic analysis.

1957), a twice-ordained priest and an obsessive writer and reader of mysteries, magisterially laid down the rules for the genre as he saw them: among them that the stupid friend of the detective should be slightly, but no more than slightly, less intelligent than the average reader and that his thoughts should not be concealed. He is both the foil to the main detective and the reader's companion. We may be a step or two in front of him, but generally he sets the pace. One final rule, Knox declared: the narrator himself should never be the one who commits the crime.

This last "rule" was brilliantly ignored by Agatha Christie in *The Murder of Roger Ackroyd* (1926), in which Dr. James Sheppard, who becomes Poirot's helpmate and who recounts the case, turns out to be the murderer. There is a story that Christie was almost kicked out of the Detection Club because of it, and was saved only by the final vote of the president, Dorothy Sayers, but the trick was repeated in the lesser-known *Endless Night* (1967).* Christie was rightly unrepentant, and the unreliable narrator has become a staple of all kinds of fiction, not just when murder is afoot.

---

* This select society, sometimes called the London Detection Club, was founded in 1928 and would become the social centre for England's crime writers. The club met regularly for dinners to discuss their work and as a means of establishing a set of standards for their field. The swearing-in ceremony, as promulgated in 1929, demanded assent to the following questions: "Do you promise that your detectives shall well and truly detect the crimes presented to them, using those wits which it may please you to bestow upon them and not placing reliance on, nor making use of Divine Revelation, Feminine Intuition, Mumbo-Jumbo, Jiggery-Pokery, Coincidence or the Act of God? Do you solemnly swear never to conceal a vital clue from the reader? Do you promise to observe a seemly moderation in the use of Gangs, Conspiracies, Death-Rays, Ghosts, Hypnotism, Trap-Doors, Chinamen, Super-Criminals and Lunatics; and utterly and forever to forswear Mysterious Poisons unknown to Science?" And finally: "Will you honour the King's English?" One author who would never have made the club, had it been instituted in his day, was Anton Chekhov, who in 1884 employed a narrator who turns out to be the murderer in a 180-page melodrama, *The Shooting Party,* his one novel.

As Peter Carey notes of Herbert Badgery, the 139-year-old protagonist of his 1985 novel *Illywhacker* (the title is Australian slang for
a con artist), "A lying first-person narrator allowed me to use the immediacy of first person, but also the third person, because he's a
liar—he will tell you everything. He didn't have to be there. There's
a great thing to be had from the energy of first person."

Such narrators may be unreliable for any number of reasons.
How much are we to trust the "I" voice in *Lolita* (an obsessed scholar-
murderer), *The Catcher in the Rye* (an angst-ridden and alienated teenager), *Rebecca* (a naïve young woman almost brainwashed into
suicide), Flann O'Brien's *The Third Policeman* (where the narrator has
been dead for most of the novel), or William Golding's *Pincher Martin*
(in which the narrator is drowned on the very first page)?

In an essay of 1992, printed eleven years after *Midnight's Children*
was published, Salman Rushdie discusses the unreliable narrator at
the heart of that novel. "I hope," he writes, "that *Midnight's Children* is
far from being an authoritative guide to the history of post-
independence India." The years after colonial rule are seen through
the eyes of Saleem Sinai, who makes various mistakes of reporting
during the course of the book.

Rushdie points out that, although he did make some errors unintentionally (in his description of the Amritsar massacre, for example,
he describes the "fifty white troops" who opened fire, when in fact
they were not white), he went to some trouble to get things wrong.
His intention, he says, was "Proustian," because what interested him
was the process of filtration itself. In shaping the way that Saleem
tells his tale, Rushdie wanted to show that Saleem

> is no dispassionate, disinterested chronicler. He wants so to
> shape his material that the reader will be forced to concede
> his central role. He is cutting up history to suit himself. . . .
> The small errors in the text can be read as clues, as indica-

tions that Saleem is capable of distortions both great and small. He is an interested party in the events he narrates.

This is subtly done and shows how carefully Rushdie chose his main protagonist. A friend of mine, an excellent editor, recently wrote to an author client: "The 'unreliable narrator' device is probably the hardest of any to pull off. The author has to be 100 percent reliable, in control, and totally aware of the difference between truth and not-truth at all times. Any looseness of 'grip' on the part of the author is going to translate itself into blurring and confusion on the page and therefore in the mind of the reader, and no amount of last-minute clarification will set it right."

Ann Beattie, who besides her fiction also teaches creative writing, says, "You have to figure out who the right person is to tell the story. And often, people who are very self-aware will only sound as if they are pontificating." Thus it may serve for the narrator to be tellingly biased like Saleem; impaired like Benjy in *The Sound and the Fury* or the fifteen-year-old autistic narrator of *The Curious Incident of the Dog in the Night-Time;* insane (the governess who narrates Henry James's *The Turn of the Screw*);* a congenital liar (such as Thomas Fowler, the cynical journalist in *The Quiet American*); or plain stupid (Jonathan

---

* I admit this is my interpretation. Is the governess in fact mad, or is she correct in thinking that her two young charges are consorting with a pair of malevolent spirits? The reader becomes a jury of one, and must determine her guilt or innocence.

In a 2015 issue of *Publishers Weekly,* two authors of books with unreliable narrators—Colin Winnette with *Coyote,* which features a possibly unhinged mother, and Jeremy M. Davies, whose *Fancy* is about a man looking for a cat-sitter—discuss their greatest unreliable narrators in literature. Among those chosen was Henry James's *The Sacred Fount* (1901), his least-read major novel, in which the narrator spends the entire book concocting elaborate deductions about fellow partygoers based on next to no evidence. *Publishers Weekly,* February 27, 2015.

Swift's Gulliver). In Julian Barnes's 2011 Booker-winning *The Sense of an Ending*, the unreliable narrator is a mystery to himself, making the novel a puzzle to solve.

Saleem is not the only narrator in classic fiction to manipulate his memories, intentionally or otherwise: Ken Kesey tries something similar in *One Flew over the Cuckoo's Nest*. Kesey, who polished his prose style as a young member of the Stanford creative writing programme of 1946, noted (while imputing to himself an undeserved originality) that:

> The book I have been doing . . . is a third-person work but something was lacking; I was not free to impose my perception and bizarre eye on the god-author who is supposed to be viewing the scene, so I tried something that will be extremely difficult to pull off, and, to my knowledge, has never been tried before—the narrator is going to be a character. He will not take part in the action or ever speak as I, but he will be a character to be influenced by the events that take place, he will have a position and a personality.

Thus we get a story told by "Chief" Bromden, the gigantic half–Native American inmate of a psychiatric hospital. Again, for narrators who are children or mentally impaired, their limited vision means they cannot always make sense of their experience, thus hiding or confusing elements of the plot for the reader.

In other narratives, a framing device—a story within a story—presents the narrator as a character who begins to recount his own tale. This technique has a long history, dating back at least to the beginning section of *The Odyssey*, and even before that, to the Sanskrit epics of India in the tenth century B.C. This form gradually spread west from Asia and became popular, encouraging such frame collections as *The Decameron* and *The Canterbury Tales*.

Wuthering Heights uses the same device to tell not only the story of Heathcliff and Catherine but also various subplots. Mary Shelley's *Frankenstein*, too, has multiple framed narratives, so that the explorer Captain Robert Walton writes letters to his sister describing the story told to him by the much put-upon scientist Victor Frankenstein. Frankenstein's account contains the creature's story, and the creature's story even briefly contains an account of a family among whom he had been living. Thus a series of reflecting states of consciousness, belonging to people outside the story but accidentally drawn into it, become the spies and eavesdroppers to events. The whole is like a set of Chinese boxes.

Whether to use first person or third person or a variety of different voices can be one of the most difficult technical questions for a novelist to resolve. Over my years in book publishing, I used at regular intervals to be sent the latest script by Norman Mailer, which his agent would submit to a raft of publishers hoping to drum up a large advance to help his client with his various alimony payments. The scripts were often in an unruly state, suggesting that Mailer was lazy over what he wrote, and was content for publishers to take it or leave it. In fact, he was fascinated by his craft (while writing his first, great book, *The Naked and the Dead*, he would constantly re-read *Anna Karenina* for inspiration), and late in his career produced an excellent, if typically idiosyncratic, book about writing, *The Spooky Art*.

At one point, he notes that when it came to planning *Tough Guys Don't Dance* (2002), with a protagonist who is an "alcoholic sexual sleaze-bag," he had to decide whether to write in the first person or third. "First person is always more hospitable in the beginning," he says. "You can give a sense of the immediate almost at once." But while in the first person you gain immediacy you lose insight, "because you can hardly move into other people's heads without using a few devices, usually dubious."

Even with non-fiction, he believes, "Nothing is more difficult than to become comfortable writing about yourself in the first person. It's highly unnatural, because 'I' makes up only about a third of the consciousness of any human being. 'I' may be the prow of the ego, but you do get into all sorts of other places where you want 'one' to talk about different aspects of yourself." This is well put.

Not just inexperienced novelists waver. Hemingway had to suffer this put-down from the eminent critic Edmund Wilson: "For reasons I cannot attempt to explain, something dreadful seems to happen to Hemingway as soon as he begins to write in the first person. . . . He seems to lose all capacity for self-criticism."

The journey can work either way. E. L. Doctorow wrote the first draft of his 1971 novel *The Book of Daniel*, inspired by the case of Julius and Ethel Rosenberg, the couple executed as Russian spies in 1953, in the third person, but felt that the result was lifeless. He then rewrote it from the point of view of the couple's son looking back on events in adulthood.

Kafka began *The Castle* as a first-person narrative, and was several chapters in before he switched to a third-person narrator, Josef K. In an introduction to the work, Irving Howe explained:

> K.'s desire to reach and then go beyond the Castle—but what can there be beyond?—was, I believe, shared by Kafka himself, though with a keener scepticism and a sharper humor regarding the risks of the enterprise. It is this evident kinship between author and protagonist . . . that prompts the opinion that of all Kafka's fiction this is the most personal.

Possibly Kafka changed from first person to avoid being too closely identified with his protagonist; just as Evelyn Waugh felt it necessary to add this epigraph to a first-person account in *Brideshead Revisited*: "I am not I; thou are not he or she; they are not they."*

In February 2014 I travelled to Norwich to talk with Rose Tremain, whose prize-winning novel *Restoration* (1989) is told in the first person. During the eleventh century, Norwich was the largest city in England after London, but now has just over 210,000 inhabitants, including the University of East Anglia, of which Rose is the current chancellor. We met in her light-filled home a few minutes' drive from the university. Back in 1987, she was over fifty pages into *Restoration*, writing in the third person, when she concluded that "it felt very underpowered and lifeless," and decided to start again, but in the first person.

"I am, I discover, a very untidy man," the novel begins. The year is 1664, the voice that of Robert Merivel, a pleasure-seeking, ambitious doctor in the court of Charles II. This was hardly an autobiographical portrait. "It takes a while to find a voice," Rose told me. "Only once you have, it can serve you endlessly. There are so many tricks and shortcuts—although you're asking yourself many more questions. I couldn't go where he couldn't go—I probably had to revise more than with third-person.

"The change to first person was quite unsettling. The act of projection I needed to do was huge—how to describe Merivel's experience of the Fire of London, for instance: how can one have the

---

* Jeffrey Archer has generally employed the third person in his novels, but when in the late 1980s I was editing *As the Crow Flies*, in which the protagonist rises from East London barrow-boy to become Lord Mayor of London (a post that Archer himself coveted), I frequently had to cross out "I" when the author had meant to write "he": Archer had identified with his hero.

feelings of terror and remorse he has? And how to write without just repeating what Pepys recorded? But I know Merivel well enough by now I could send an email in his voice. First person helped define the book and also stopped it sprawling. I feel so alive following somebody else."

This feeling "so alive following somebody else" can bring a wonderful freedom, but it involves responsibilities too. One consideration when using a single viewpoint is whether one is being fair to all the characters in a fiction. George Eliot upbraided herself for forgetting this. Well on in *Middlemarch*, she writes: "One morning, some weeks after her arrival at Lowick, Dorothea—but why always Dorothea? Was her point of view the only possible one with regard to this marriage?" She then tries to be fair to Casaubon, but with mixed results.

Edith Wharton, in her guide to writing fiction, warns that every novelist should ask: "Who saw this thing I am going to tell about? By whom do I mean that it shall be reported? Who is listening? On what occasion is the story being told, and why?" In her view, it had to wait until Henry James and the long ruminative introductions he wrote to his fictions to pose such enquiries. James held that a "center of consciousness" had to preside over any scene; he loved the first-person form, feeling that this "post of observation," as he called it, let him explore issues relating to consciousness and perception and use interior monologues and unreliable narrators to deepen the story.

In his preface to *The Ambassadors*—which is told in the first person throughout—James discusses his concerns about "the romantic privilege of the first person," calling it "the darkest abyss of romance." What he values, he says, is "the terrible *fluidity* of self-revelation," but at the same time, in *The Ambassadors* at least, he deliberately sets up his narrator with "a confidant or two, to wave away with energy the custom of the seated mass of explanation after the fact, the inserted block of explanation after the fact." Ah, those James prefaces!

First-person narrative can tend toward stream of consciousness, a phrase coined in *The Principles of Psychology* (1890) by James's brother, William, to characterize a person's day-to-day flow of thought and sensation: "Consciousness, then, does not appear to itself as chopped up in bits. . . . It is nothing jointed; it flows. A 'river' or a 'stream' are the metaphors by which it is most naturally described." Literary critics soon took up the phrase to describe any author's attempts to imitate that process, naming Molly Bloom's soliloquy or Mrs. Dalloway's thoughts as early examples, but also going back to Edgar Allan Poe and even Laurence Sterne. In each case, the intensity of being part of a private world, without interruption from other characters or from the author himself, can give a narrative special intimacy.

First-person narrators may be multiple, as in Ryūnosuke Akutagawa's 1915 short story "Rashōmon," which gives sharply contradictory accounts of the same event from the points of view of four first-person narrators; or Robert Browning's *The Ring and the Book* (1868), a fictional account in verse based on a real-life murder trial, in which the crime is described ten times through twelve different "books," ten of which are monologues by different people involved in the case, while the first and last books are recounted by the author. The depth of psychological insight this allowed Browning made the poem easily his most successful work.

In the first-person-plural point of view, on the other hand, narrators tell the story using "we." No individual speaker is identified; the narrator is acting as a member of a group. William Faulkner, an avid experimenter in points of view, employs third person plural both in "A Rose for Emily" (1930), a short story in which the residents of a Southern town collectively try to make sense of the life—and death—of Emily Grierson, an eccentric elderly spinster, and in his novella *Spotted Horses* (1931). Jeffrey Eugenides's novel *The Virgin Sui-*

cides (1993) is written from the perspective of an anonymous group of teenage boys who become infatuated with five sisters living in Grosse Pointe, Michigan. This form is also used by the chorus in Greek tragedy, although there a visible group speaks together— sometimes as "we," sometimes "I."

What is to be gained by this point of view? Steven Millhauser, who won the Pulitzer Prize in 1997 for his novel *Martin Dressler* and who uses the first person plural in several of his fictions, most notably in his remarkable story "The Knife Thrower," provides interesting insights in a 2003 interview:

> I found myself increasingly drawn to this pronoun, partly because it allowed me to enact the drama of an entire community set against a person or group that threatens it, and partly because the pronoun felt new and exciting, a pronoun that didn't drag in its wake one hundred billion stories, as in the case of an "I" or a "he." It strikes me as a barely explored pronoun, full of possibilities, and I'm certainly not done with it.

Millhauser then gives an unusual rationale for what the "we" form can achieve:

> What interests me is the way moral indecisiveness or questioning may be given more weight or significance by attaching itself to a multiple being. A single narrator might have multiple interpretations of an event, or might try to evade moral choice in numerous ways, but the same kind of uncertainty in an entire community becomes public, societal, even political, and carries a different weight. . . . The moral wavering of the "we" in "The Knife Thrower" is more dis-

turbing than the moral wavering of an "I" would have been, or disturbing in a different way.

Millhauser is right to stress how a group of people who share a moral wavering can give weight to a story, but many stories don't allow this: *Crime and Punishment,* for instance, requires a solitary figure at its centre. It all depends on the tale one has to tell.

Such variations lead back to Norman Mailer and the most popular narrative voice in fiction. He writes:

> With a full use of the third person, you are God—well, of course, not quite, but, one way or another, you are ready to see into everyone's mind. . . . This Olympian third person, this Tolstoyan presence, needs experience, confidence, irony, insight, and lordly detachment. When it can be done, hurrah.

Mailer recognizes that there are different forms of third-person narrative—what is called "limited omniscient," where we are told the thoughts and feelings of only one character, and "omniscient," where we are told everything about the story, including the thoughts and feelings of everyone who has something to add, even (a complicated distinction) information in the narrator's mind to which none of the characters is privy.

And yet variety, even uncertainty, of viewpoint can yield surprising dividends. What has come to be called *style indirect libre,* or free indirect speech, is where the narrative seems to tell the truth plain and simple—to have all the certainty that third-person point of view provides, but where something more complex is being attempted, some of the characteristics of third person being mixed (usually) with another voice or voices. Austen, Goethe, and Flaubert were early practitioners. The critic Michael Wood gives a good example from *Mansfield Park:*

> About thirty years ago, Miss Maria Ward, of Huntingdon, with only seven thousand pounds, had the good luck to captivate Sir Thomas Bertram, of Mansfield Park, in the county of Northampton. . . .

This appears to be neutral third person, but as Wood notes, "'only,' 'good luck' and 'captivate' seem to have crept in from neighbourhood chatter, and if 'captivate' means something other than 'be married to,' it's slightly at odds with good luck." Other voices are making themselves heard; the social world of the story has invaded the language of the narrator.

When first-person narrative is interrupted in this way it can be even more effective—when we think we are standing alongside the protagonist, but we are not, "he or she is just a grammatical spot, a place to tell the story from." We think we are within first or third person, but the author is weaving in other points of view. And it is the mark of *style indirect libre* that it usually gives no obvious sign whether it is being deployed or not. It can catch us by surprise, and sometimes the synthesis fails and we flounder among the interpretations, but when successfully used, by Austen or Flaubert or Woolf, for instance, it can be a highly effective mix. Not only in fiction: David Nokes used it in his biography of Samuel Johnson to enter the consciousness of Johnson and many of his friends.

There are other ways in which authors get inside a maximum number of their book's characters. William Faulkner's *The Sound and the Fury* (1929) is concerned not only with how things appear to three very different brothers and their novelist creator but also with how they express themselves, using four different narratives (and con siderable retelling): the wayward moaning of Benjamin "Benjy" Compson, a cognitively disabled thirty-three-year-old, the stream of consciousness of Quentin, the more logical telling of Jason, and the "objective" point of view of the narrator for the final Dilsey section.

In *Absalom, Absalom!* (1936), Faulkner focused on the transformation of his main character, Thomas Sutpen, who became not only a matter of narration but the story: Faulkner wanted to embed the narrative, the act of transmission, into the story itself. The tale, about three families of the American South before, during, and after the Civil War, including the Compsons again, is told entirely in flashbacks narrated mostly by Quentin Compson to his university roommate, Shreve, who frequently contributes his own suggestions. The accounts of Rosa Coldfield and of Quentin's father and grandfather are also included and reinterpreted by Shreve and Quentin, events unfolding in non-chronological order and often with differing details. This results in a peeling-back-the-onion way of revealing the family's true history. Rosa initially tells the story, with long digressions and a biased memory, to Quentin, whose father then fills in some details. Finally, Quentin relates his version to his roommate. By the end, the reader is more certain about the attitudes and biases of the characters than about the facts.

Another example of a convoluted, multi-level structure is Conrad's short novel *Heart of Darkness*, which has a double framework: an unidentified "I" narrator relates a boating trip during which another character, Marlow, tells the main story. Even within this framing device, we are told that another character, Kurtz, has told Marlow a lengthy tale of his own. Thus we have an "I" narrator introducing a storyteller as "he" (Marlow), who talks about himself as "I" and introduces another storyteller as "he" (Kurtz), who in turn presumably told his story from the perspective of "I." No wonder this has been dubbed a "hall of mirrors" approach.

More recently, Damon Galgut's remarkable *In a Strange Room*

(2010) contains three interconnected stories examining three kinds of relationships (a power struggle, an erotic dalliance, and a friendship in which one party is caregiver and warden) and shifts from first to third person, often in the same sentence, apparently as a way of distinguishing immediate experience from remembered experience. In his review of the book, William Skidelsky observed that this device achieves two paradoxical things. On the one hand, the use of the personal, authorial voice suggests that what we are reading actually happened—that *In a Strange Room* is a form of memoir—but at the same time it chips away at the narrator's reliability, since Galgut uses these interjections to express doubt about what he is describing: "I can't remember," "I forget his name," and so on. The first person simultaneously implicates the author in what he is describing while reinforcing his distance from it, positioning *In a Strange Room* somewhere between memoir and fiction.

Such disturbance is less likely in the last point of view used by novelists: addressing the reader as "you." This form has most often been employed in letters, from the early epistolary fictions of Samuel Richardson, *Pamela, or Virtue Rewarded* (1740–41) and *Clarissa, or The History of a Young Lady* (1748).

Letters have the advantage that they chronicle an ongoing process. As Richardson put it: "*Much more* lively and affecting . . . must be the style of those who write in the height of a *present* distress, the mind tortured by the pangs of uncertainty . . . *than* the dry, narrative, unanimated style of a person relating difficulties and dangers surmounted can be. . . ." (He had learned his skills early, from the age of thirteen having helped three young women he knew to write responses to the love letters they received.) During the weeks that the enormously long *Clarissa* was being published (it eventually ran to seven volumes), Richardson was besieged by readers who begged him not to allow his heroine to die, and many followers of *Pamela* supposed it to be an actual correspondence, with Richardson merely the editor.*

In the eighteenth century (which even went through a phase of "it-narratives," where stories were told from the point of view of money, corkscrews, lapdogs, or the like), epistolary novels were immensely popular. Jane Austen's first draft of *Sense and Sensibility* was in letter form, but her revised version was prophetic of the decline of the epistolary novel in the century to follow, and in the age of the phone it became rarer still.

The 1980s, perhaps due to Jay McInerney's success with *Bright Lights, Big City*, ushered in a brief revival of the second person. Short stories particularly took this form: Donald Barthelme's "The Sandman," many of the stories in Lorrie Moore's collection *Self-Help*, Mavis Gallant's "Mlle. Dias de Corta," and Junot Díaz's "Drown" are all told by one person addressing a particular individual, in effect like a long letter, while Nicholson Baker's *Vox* (2004) consists entirely of a conversation between strangers on a phone sex line. Paul Auster eschews second-person narration in all but one of his sixteen novels, though his two memoirs *Winter Journal* and *Report from the Interior* both use it.†

---

* When the heroine triumphs in the end, it is said that in Slough "enraptured villagers rang the church bells for joy." The same happened in Preston, where a maid had to explain the ringing bells to a passer-by: "Why, madam, poor Pamela's married at last; the news came down to us in the morning's paper." See Robert Hendrickson, *The Literary Life and Other Curiosities* (New York: Viking, 1981), p. 23.

† So does Italo Calvino's 1979 novel *If on a Winter's Night a Traveller*. Each chapter is divided into two sections, the first of which is in the second person and describes the process the reader goes through in attempting to read the next chapter of the book he is reading. The second half is the first part of a new book that the reader ("you") finds. The book's opening chapter is on the art and nature of reading, and what follows is divided into twenty-two sections, the odd-numbered passages and the final passage narrated in the second person. The ending exposes a

The playwright and novelist Michael Frayn also tried his hand at the epistolary form in *The Trick of It* (1989), where his protagonist is a university professor who specializes in the work of a contemporary woman novelist, and the book is written as a series of letters to a colleague. The tale ends with the academic vainly attempting to acquire "the trick of it" (that is, of writing fiction). But if there is any trick to be learned from these recent excursions, it is that the "you" form is best used sparingly, as a minor part of a novel's exposition.

I, thou, he, she, we, you, they. Steven Millhauser even recalls, "One of Beckett's narrators reports that as a child he learned the names of the days of the week. And the child thinks: 'Only seven!' I sometimes feel the same way about the personal pronouns. . . . Only three!—or perhaps: only six! I'd invent a fourth person, if I could. . . ."

Important though it is to decide who is to tell the story, such a question is part of the larger issue touched on earlier—what Joan Didion called "the distancing of the narrative." This slightly forbidding phrase concerns the space that exists between a reader and a story. At the most basic level, standing apart from one's characters creates detachment, while a more intimate distance promotes empathy and identification. In film, we are accustomed to seeing a camera used in wide-angle or in close-up; the same applies, through many shifts, to the written word.

Two years ago, I was alerted to an online group of writers who would email one another answers to common problems, early drafts, hints on agents and publishers, and much else. One of their number,

---

hidden element to the entire book, where the actual first-chapter titles make up a single coherent sentence, in itself the start of another, totally different book. The novel made Calvino's reputation, and in 2009 one prominent newspaper placed it 69th in a list of "100 novels everyone should read," describing it as a "playful postmodernist puzzle." It is certainly that.

an (as of this writing) unpublished novelist, Wendy Roberts, had written a paper called "The Art of Narrative Distance: The Sun Tzu Approach for Writers," and kindly sent me a copy. It is wise and well written, and says more about point of view than a score of books by established critics.

She begins by asking how we know when to opt for distance versus intimacy. There are no hard and fast rules; each writer must decide what works best for the story at issue. Roberts looks at the way four novelists writing about war have approached the problem. Her first example is Tolstoy, who in *War and Peace* employs wide distances to establish the fluctuating order in battles. The opening chapter of Book II begins:

> In October 1805 Russian troops were occupying villages and towns in the archduchy of Austria, and more new regiments kept arriving from Russia to be stationed by the fortress of Braunau, burdening the local inhabitants with their billeting. In Braunau the commander in chief, Kutuzov, had his headquarters.

The camera, as it were, has zoomed out to maximum distance, summarizing the state of the Russian army. Over the next few paragraphs, however, the focus narrows to one specific day in October and a specific regiment, and we read of one place, one evening, and one commander:

> . . . an elderly, sanguine general with grizzled eyebrows and side-whiskers, stocky and broader from chest to back than from shoulder to shoulder. He was wearing a brand-new uniform with creases from being packed away, with thick gold epaulettes which seemed not to weigh down but to lift up his massive shoulders. [. . .] It was clear that the regi-

mental commander admired his regiment, was happy with it, and that all his inner forces were taken up only with the regiment: but, in spite of that, his bouncing gait seemed to say that, besides military interests, no small part of his soul was taken up by the interests of social life and the female sex.

Only after this description does Tolstoy finally launch into "real-time" action and dialogue:

"Well, Mikhailo Mitrich, old boy," he addressed one of the battalion commanders (the battalion commander, smiling, moved forward; it was clear that both men were happy), "we were hard put to it last night. However, it seems the regiment's not such a bad one . . . Eh?"

What we are first given is the larger picture beyond what the characters can perceive individually, then we travel in careful increments from the broad overview to the close perspective of a single commander. As Roberts notes, balancing distance and intimacy depends on a writer's overall aims for a scene and the story as a whole. Sometimes intimacy must be sacrificed for the sake of clarity, especially in a novel like *War and Peace*, with its large time period, vast cast, and complex range of themes.

Another distancing technique, she says, is called "dramatic reporting." This documents only what can be seen or heard, thus excluding unexpressed thoughts and emotions. In the three excerpts I have given, Tolstoy employs generalizations, summary, omniscience, and the lack of individual narrative focus from a close third character to help place the scene, and even though we zoom in on the commander in the second passage, words like "it was clear that," or "it seems" keep us at one remove from his inner workings; the literary lens has been brought up close, but the language still provokes apart-ness. We are aware that someone is recounting this story, whether Tolstoy or some fictional approximation to him, and in a voice that does not belong to any of the characters in it.

Using this disembodied narrative voice, or "center of conscious-ness," as it has been called, suggests an unacknowledged, implied author (as opposed to an identifiable first- or third-person voice) through whom the story is filtered. Roberts takes three other war novels—*The Good Soldier Švejk* (1923) by Jaroslav Hašek, *Three Soldiers* (1921) by John Dos Passos, and *Going After Cacciato* (1978) by Tim O'Brien—to develop her theme, but the main point is clear. How close do you want the camera? In this respect narrative distance can be even more important than choice of narrator. Henry James no-ticed the effect that broad summarization had on his characters and altered his own techniques by pushing "all summary back into the minds of the characters" so that, as he put it, he could keep "it all within my hero's compass."

Dostoyevsky initially envisaged *Crime and Punishment* as a novella with four first-person tellings: a memoir written by Raskolnikov; his confession recorded eight days after the murder; his diary begun five days afterwards; and a mixed form in which the first half was a mem-oir and the second a diary. In the end, he chose to sacrifice many of a novelist's conventional prerogatives to the principle of uncertainty, and his most far-reaching sacrifice was that of omniscience. Through-out the novel, the narrator enjoys no consistent perceptual advan-tage: he sees the world through the same haze of subjective doubt as Raskolnikov.

Francine Prose, who with Norman Mailer has provided some of the best insights into how a novelist chooses a point of view, gives this gloss: "Ultimately he [Dostoyevsky] realized that, given the problems caused by the fact that his hero was to be semi-delirious for signifi-cant portions of the narrative, he could maintain the same intensity by sticking to a close third-person narration that, at critical junctures, merges with the consciousness of the protagonist." It is also likely that Raskolnikov began to develop beyond the boundaries within which he had first been conceived. The notebooks indicate that Dostoyevsky was aware of the emergence of new aspects of Raskolnikov's character as the plot proceeded, and he structured the novel in conformity with this "metamorphosis."

It wasn't until the third and final draft when a new approach occurred to him: "Narration from point of view of author, a sort of invisible but omniscient being who does not leave his hero for a moment." Although he used a third-person narrator, his ability to know everything is open to doubt. Complete omniscience would have robbed the novel of its haunting uncertainty and permanent nightmarish quality and given the reader too clear an insight into Raskolnikov's motivation. As it was, Dostoyevsky achieved the perfect distance and the perfect point of view.

Frontispiece from Galileo's
Dialogue on the Two Chief World Systems (1632).

CHAPTER 5

Says You: The Art and Craft of Dialogue

CLOV: What is there to keep me here?
HAMM: The dialogue.

SAMUEL BECKETT, *ENDGAME*

It's puzzling work, talking is.

MR. TULLIVER IN *THE MILL ON THE FLOSS*

I began by not saying a word. I just stared at my audience, and sixty pairs of student eyes stared back. Then I pretended to have lost my glasses, which turned out to be on the top of my head. Next, I took a photo of the whole class—all this must have taken a good two minutes, a long time. Finally I asked—"Dialogue?"—the point being that what had passed between us *was* a form of communication.

As far back as 1589, dialogue was defined as "a conversation be-

tween two or more persons, a literary composition." But such inter-
change embraces silences and pauses, and both can result from many
factors. Samuel Beckett characterized writer's block as "agonies of
galloping speechlessness," but he of all people knew what could be
achieved by the intentional failure to utter.

His friend and great admirer Harold Pinter is even more famous
for exploring "the noise within silence," as one admiring critic put it.
In 1994, the Abbey Theatre in Dublin was putting on six of Pinter's
plays, including his one-act *Landscape*. Pinter, who could labour all
day over a comma, told the director Di Trevis just before the first
rehearsal, "I've added a pause." The cast read through the play.
Afterwards, Trevis admitted to Pinter that she hadn't spotted anything new. Pinter, in all seriousness, replied: "I took it out."

Words dominated Pinter's life, yet he believed they concealed the
truth as much as revealed it. They acted, he said, as "a masquerade,
a veil, a web," and were "weapons to undermine or to terrorize." All
his plays are about what his characters are unable to express, or
choose not to, and he employed silence to indicate significant things
not being said, often to suggest the prospect of imminent violence.

Even so, the spoken word is the thing. As Alice famously wondered, "What is the use of a book without pictures or conversations?"
In an article in the trade magazine for British writers, *The Author,* the
playwright and novelist Nell Leyshon recently admitted that in her
early reading years, "If I picked up a book with no dialogue, I felt
unable to breathe, as though I was choking in words. I learned to
look at pages to see whether there was white down the right-hand
side. I learned that the sculptural shape on a page bears a relationship to the reading experience. I realized that when there is space
and air in the prose, I am able to interpret and draw conclusions.
When I hit dialogue in a piece of writing, I am released from authorial judgement; I can bring myself and my experience to the text."

Dialogue is crucial to the novel. It makes a story more lifelike and less "told," by conveying character, dramatizing an incident, and giving a sense of immediacy in a way that straight exposition may not do. It can also set the scene—it helps us visualize. It can provide pattern and tone. It can give the point of view of the author or of the characters; can provide suspense, flow; can control the story; and to some degree can make the reader work.

As so often, Jane Austen helps show the way. Azar Nafisi is a professor of English who started up a secret reading group in Ayatollah-dominated Iran, where her students would study forbidden Western classics. In her remarkable book *Reading Lolita in Tehran*, she writes of their reading Austen:

> The centrality of dialogue in *Pride and Prejudice* fits well into the dancelike structure of the novel. It seems that in almost every scene there is an ongoing dialogue between Elizabeth and Darcy. This dialogue is either real or imagined, but it is a constant preoccupation, leading from exchanges with the other to exchanges with the self.

The exchange of information is just the starting point for what dialogue can give us. As Oliver Sacks has said, "Speech—natural speech—does not consist of words alone. . . . It consists of utterance—an uttering-forth of one's whole meaning with one's whole being—the understanding of which involves infinitely more than mere word-recognition." However, one can sometimes speak lazily, lackadaisically, holding back "one's whole being," just as one can also be easily tempted to employ dialogue to deliver information that would be an unlikely part of normal conversation.

There are other quicksands. In his book of literary criticism, Sebastian Faulks notes about the Sherlock Holmes stories:

Too much of the action is given in speech. [. . .] The danger is that it can put the action at arm's length. With Holmes, it is necessary for the client who comes panting up the stairs at Baker Street to give a summary of his or her problem, but it seems to me there are too many pages in which the paragraphs begin with inverted commas. Watson, you feel, could easily have summarized the salient points. Holmes often then relates to Watson what happens on a preliminary solo expedition; sometimes this contains a second lengthy testimony, so that we have inverted commas within Holmes's inverted commas. [. . .] The best stories tend to be those in which the majority of the action is witnessed, not related.

The writer of fiction has to choose what he wants his characters to say and how what they say fits with his or her overall intentions. In *How Fiction Works*, James Wood, the best literary critic now writing regularly in both book form and magazines (and no relation to Michael Wood, quoted earlier), analyzes how to write dialogue either directly or indirectly. He uses a made-up series of examples; I have adapted his commentary to a short extract from *War and Peace*:

Pierre sees that everyone, everyone is smiling at him and Hélène. "Well, so what if you all know," he says to himself. "Well, so what? It's true," and he smiles his meek, child-like smile.

This is direct or quoted speech ("'Well, so what if you all know,' he says to himself"), the notion of a character's thought as a speech made to himself. A slight variation might run:

Pierre sees that everyone, everyone is smiling at him and Hélène. Well, so what if you all know, he thinks. So what? What you're seeing is true—and he smiles his meek, child-like smile.

Pierre's internal speech is reported by the author and flagged as such ("he thought"). This reported or indirect speech is the most recognizable, and the most regularly used, of all the codes of standard realist narrative. A third version might go:

Pierre sees that everyone, everyone is smiling at him and Hélène. So what if they all knew? It was true. And he smiles his meek, child-like smile.

This is free indirect speech or style: Pierre's thought has been freed of its authorial flagging, and there is an immediate gain in flexibility. The narrative seems to float away from the novelist and take on the properties of the character, who now seems to "own" the words. Tolstoy is free to inflect the reported thought, to bend it around the character's own words ("So what if they all knew?"). We are close to stream of consciousness, and that is the direction that free indirect style takes in the nineteenth and early twentieth centuries:

Everyone, everyone is smiling at him and Hélène. So what if they all knew? It was true. He could play their game easily enough—give them his meek, child-like smile.

In a later chapter, "Dialogue and Meaning," Wood writes about Henry Green, a leading British novelist from the 1920s into the 1950s. Green was obsessively concerned with the elimination of "those vulgar spoors of presence whereby authors communicate themselves to readers"; and argued that nothing killed "life" so much as "explanation." In 1950, during a talk on dialogue for the BBC, he imagined a husband and wife, long married, sitting at home one evening. At 9:30 P.M., the husband says he is going across the road to the pub. Green noted that the wife's first response, "Will you be long?" could be rendered in various different ways. ("Back soon?" "When will you be back?" "Off for long?" "How long will it take before you are back?"), each capable of a distinct resonance of meaning. The crucial point was not to hedge the dialogue with explanation, setting out motives or his characters' thoughts. Green considered such authorial assistance overbearing, because in life we don't know what people are like. Even so, if everyone obeyed his rule, fulsome explainers like George Eliot, James, Proust, Woolf, Philip Roth, and many others would have had to retire. I sympathize with Green in that many authors obtrude upon their characters, denying them a degree of independence they need in order to be convincing creations for us, but he takes his case too far. However, dialogue should carry multiple meanings, and if possible imply different things to different readers at the same time.

If ever one writer favoured dialogue in her novels, it was the British author Ivy Compton-Burnett (1884–1969). Little read now, her stories—which focus on late Victorian and Edwardian upper-middle-class families—are masterpieces about the undercurrents of family life and garnered her a unique reputation. Elizabeth Bowen said of *Parents and Children* (1941; the title is typical of her work): "To read in these days a page of Compton-Burnett dialogue is to think of the sound of glass being swept up, one of these London mornings after a blitz."

The clipped, precise interchanges Compton-Burnett gives us are extraordinarily flexible and usurp almost completely the functions of exposition, narrative, and description. In her introduction to *A House and Its Head* (1935), Francine Prose provides the best overview of what this highly gifted, highly eccentric author can achieve:

> She drops us—as if from a great height—into her opening scene. Thus *A House and Its Head* . . . starts with a seemingly offhand question—one that, like so much of Compton-Burnett's dialogue, barely conceals the bloodcurdlingly normal, human desire to have its speaker's existence acknowledged. "So the children are not down yet?" inquires Ellen Edgeworth, a query that will be repeated (nervily, for what other novel dares begin with a character saying the same thing again and again?) four times, with minor alterations, until at last Ellen's husband, Duncan, deigns to reply.

From these first lines on, nearly every exchange (and the book is constructed almost entirely of such exchanges) will resemble this one: dismissive, abusive, ironic, double-edged, more or less sadistic, devastatingly revealing, often extremely funny, and consistently entertaining.

It is, we discover, Christmas morning. All the characters are (and will be, up until the novel's final scenes) consciously or unconsciously trying to navigate the increasingly treacherous narrows that divide truth-telling from lying. All will be defined by the degree to which they resist or concede to the demands exerted by the despotic Duncan and by the forces he represents—family, privilege, money, order, entitlement, reputation.

This way of telling a story has several points in its favour—

literalness, a sharp definition of issues, acute penetration into the thoughts of the characters—but it requires concentration. Compton-Burnett's use of punctuation is deliberately perfunctory: there are no colons or semi-colons, no exclamation marks, no italics. All her characters talk alike, irrespective of age, sex, or class; every one of them seems cut from the same cloth: the children have the same awareness of evil, and the parents and grandparents are marked by the same predatory expedience. There is no "background filler" to help readers understand what is happening. The almost total reliance on dialogue makes people appear without substance except what their words give them.

Compton-Burnett is not alone in her reliance on conversation. Henry James attempted a novel written almost entirely in dialogue. Published in serial form in 1898–99, *The Awkward Age* has been praised as one of his best books, yet it often strings out scenes to great length and mind-numbing complexity. Edith Wharton, normally a great supporter of James, held that this tale of eighteen-year-old Nanda Brookenham and her social circle "lost more than it gained by being powdered into dialogue, and that, had it been treated as a novel instead of a kind of hybrid play, the obligation of 'straight' narrative might have compelled [James] to face and elucidate the central problem instead of suffering it to lose itself in a tangle of talk. [. . .] Dialogue, that precious adjunct, should never be more than an adjunct, and one to be used as skillfully and sparingly as the drop of condiment which flavors a whole dish."

Successful dialogue is not just what is said but how the author frames it. Many novelists fear that they aren't getting across what their characters are feeling, so they push the envelope. This can be either the simple but unconvincing versions of, "Gosh, I'm upset!" or getting adverb-disease. Stephen King, who calls this "the attribution verb," gives some examples from pulp fiction and paperback originals:

"Put down the gun, Utterson!" Jekyll grated.

"Never stop kissing me!" Shayna gasped.

"You damned tease!" Bill jerked out.

Even the greatest writers can fall into this trap. At the beginning of *Nicholas Nickleby* the young Nicholas is being interviewed by his evil uncle Ralph. It is our first meeting with both of them. In a single exchange we get:

"Oh," growled Ralph.

"Well, ma'am," said Ralph impatiently.

"I say," repeated Ralph, tartly.

"Ah, to be sure!" sneered Ralph.

"Who indeed!" snarled Ralph.

I would add in mitigation that Dickens was writing *Nicholas Nickleby* and *Oliver Twist* simultaneously, delivering 7,500-word instalments of each every month to his magazine editors (he was paid by the word), but one can understand why both Henry James and Joseph Conrad will happily employ the simple "he said" six times or more in a single piece of dialogue, with ne'er an adverb in sight. Jane Austen is equally parsimonious, but when she does alter her wording she does it with a point to make—so that in a family discussion in *Mansfield Park,* when the appalling Mrs. Norris doesn't simply *say* something but *cries* it, one takes it as a sign that she is upping the emotional temperature and attempting to control the conversation.

It is also a temptation to let a conversation go on too long; one can literally lose the plot. Anthony Trollope puts this well:

> The unconscious critical acumen of a reader is both just and severe. When long dialogue on extraneous matter reaches his mind, he at once feels that he is being cheated into taking something which he did not bargain to accept when he took up that novel.

More succinct is a line in *Get Shorty* by that master of dialogue, Elmore Leonard. Chili Palmer, the über-cool protagonist (played by John Travolta in the film version), is asked how long an assignment will take. "Don't worry about it," he slides out. "I won't say any more than I have to, if that." Some writers hardly bother with dialogue at all—take the bestselling *Miss Smilla's Feeling for Snow* by Peter Høeg: it has hardly any conversation, so mirroring the main character, who seems to like ice more than she does people. Lewis Carroll's Alice would not have approved; nor, generally, do I.

Then there is the matter of inner dialogue. In 2011, the novelist and translator Tim Parks, reviewing Graham Swift's novel *Wish You Were Here* in *The London Review of Books*, suggested that there was a discrepancy between Swift's description of his main character as "poor with words" and the constant and sometimes highly nuanced internal monologue the protagonist is given. A reader wrote in to complain that "part of what a good novelist does" is to "bring to the surface" thoughts that the character entertains but cannot express. This provoked a letter from Parks expanding on the problem. "The question is a fascinating one," he began. "Is thought that is expressed in words in an interior monologue the same as thought which finds no words and perhaps doesn't look for them or want them? Can certain ideas . . . be entertained at all without words?" If they can, is it possible in a novel to evoke those ideas without confusing the intelligence and articulacy of the author and "the equally complex figure whose mental life is perhaps largely free from language?"

D. H. Lawrence was one author, Parks says, who excelled at portraying characters with limited ability to express their feelings but with intense inner worlds. "The temptation for the novelist, who lives so much in language, is to imagine that all thought is expressed in words, words like his or her own, and indeed that word-driven consciousness is somehow superior." This is an important point, and each fiction-writer has to resolve the issue as suits him or her best.

There is a further temptation, known as information-dumping. In 1968 Tom Stoppard wrote *The Real Inspector Hound*, a pastiche of the Agatha Christie country house murder mystery. The play opens in the drawing room of Muldoon Manor. A man's body lies on the floor. Enter Mrs. Drudge, the cleaner. She circles the phone, as if expecting it to ring, and it does, right on cue. She picks up the receiver:

MRS. DRUDGE: Hello, the drawing room of Lady Muldoon's country residence one morning in early spring? . . . He*llo!*— the draw—Who? Who did you wish to speak to? I'm afraid there's no one of that name here, this is all very mysterious and I'm sure it's leading up to something, I hope nothing is amiss for we, that is Lady Muldoon and her houseguests, are here cut off from the world, including Magnus, the wheelchair-ridden half-brother of her ladyship's husband Lord Albert Muldoon who ten years ago went out for a walk on the cliffs and was never seen again—and all alone, for they had no children. . . . Should a stranger enter our midst, which I very much doubt, I will tell him you called. Good-bye.

She puts down the phone. A moment later, a stranger duly enters her midst.

A friend of mine, a novelist who teaches creative writing in New York, commented on this passage (which I confess I love): "In my experience, students struggle with getting the dialogue to sound natural, but they also struggle to learn how to incorporate dialogue into a prose piece: where to include action and interpretation, how to build in subtext, how to suggest that the speaker does or does not mean what he says, etc. (Where the adverbs go!) A playwright can depend on actors to convey much of this (or at least to offer an interpretation), whereas a novelist has to nail much more down. I've encountered this disconnect quite often when a gifted playwright takes a fiction course as an elective and discovers that the rules have changed." Even so, what is surprising is how many of the rules apply to both stories in performance (theatre, opera, film) and stories on the page.

In all forms of narrative, characters must not say what they couldn't possibly know or use words that weren't around at the time they are meant to be living—in *Julius Caesar,* for example, one of the characters says "Count the clock," centuries before the invention of clocks. And they must speak in their native tongue—a New York Jewish accent (Woody Allen, say) is syntactically different from a New York Italian accent (*The Godfather*). "When people talk," Hemingway advised a young writer, "listen completely. Most people never listen." Mailer chimes in with "Good dialogue depends on your ear."

Stephen King will study dialects from various parts of the United States, looking for syntactic differences or how sentences are structured. He gives an example of the negative positive in Boston English: "Let's go see if we can't get your car fixed," the sentence structure alone going a long way towards making the voice distinctive.

After publishing *On Beauty* in 2005, Zadie Smith had critics telling her that she didn't know how Americans spoke. She is another writer who leaves out quotation marks. James Joyce called such marks "perverted commas," while E. L. Doctorow has virtually no punctuation—he thinks it "over-literary," as people don't punctuate when they talk. But then Samuel Beckett punctuates to the last dot. A character in Zadie Smith's 2012 novel *NW* thinks of a cherry tree, and her thoughts are set on the page in the shape of a cherry tree. When she looks at a colleague's mouth, a ring of words, "tooth gold tooth tooth gap" is laid out in an oval round the word "tongue." Both Joyce and Sterne have a lot to answer for, but there's no absolute rule, beyond perhaps: help your reader, don't hamstring him or her, or show off to no purpose.

Much of writing good dialogue comes down to one important principle: trust the reader. When you write dialogue you are giving signals that make the reader, or the member of the audience, believe they are hearing authentic speech; you are not only saying, "This is how he or she talks," you are saying, "Take this in about their character, take this in about the story, or my theme, or this relationship." You want to do several things at the same time.

When it comes to conversation, how true to the way people speak should a novel be? For instance, written dialogue usually makes people sound more intelligent than they are. When someone really speaks without the *umms, errs,* and repetitions of real life and does so in well-formed sentences, it is immediately striking (Barack Obama, for instance). Everyone has had the experience of hearing him- or herself on tape: *do I really sound like that?* We would prefer it if our voices, and what we say, could be retouched by some sympathetic omnipotence.

Let us eavesdrop for a moment on some real-life dialogue:

HE: Shut up. Take your baby (*baby is crying*) . . .

WIFE, SOBBING: Don't look at me that way—nobody is afraid of you. Go to hell, you bastard!

HE: You're very good!

WIFE: You can go to your America without me, and I hope you die on the way.

This comes from a KGB transcript of a bugged conversation between John F. Kennedy's assassin Lee Harvey Oswald and his wife, and unlike the typical transcript of a random conversation is full of subtext. Among other points, it shows both Oswald and his wife reacting childishly—that in moments of stress our inner emotional child is likely to break out of hiding and dominate our adult self. A novelist must capture that.

Interestingly, much of writing dialogue in non-fiction shares the same rules as fiction, except that of course you're not supposed to be making it up—you're reporting it and so have a responsibility to accuracy and to truth. But you're allowed to "package" what has been said. I asked two novelist friends, Joe Klein, who as "Anonymous" wrote the bestseller *Primary Colors* (among other books in both fiction and non-fiction) and is now a political columnist for *Time*; and John Darnton, the author of five novels and also winner of a Pulitzer Prize for his dispatches from Poland for *The New York Times* in the early 1970s. Both agreed that, when reporting what someone's said, you *tidy it up*—you smooth it by cutting out repetitions, the ums and ers, the silly mannerisms—most of them, anyway. Is this ethical? Yes. Dangerous? Yes too, because you must use your judgement on whether the tidying-up is minor or whether you might be over-tidying and therefore misrepresenting. Thus the novelist writes dialogue to be convincing; the non-fiction author so that he or she is true to the intentions of the persons quoted.

In his novel *Infinite Jest* (1996) David Foster Wallace emphasizes that what he concentrated on was the authentic rhythms of speech and thought, even when doing so went against the received rules of writing. That is why Elmore Leonard is so much more than a mystery writer and why having an ear for how people speak is so vital to being a good novelist.

This is not to say, although some novelists are natural mimics, that dialogue should be a faithful version of talk in real life. Dialogue in fiction is a very special kind; the representation of speech, and still more of non-verbal events, is highly artificial, and has to be. As David Lodge points out, "A narrative style that faithfully imitated actual speech would be virtually unintelligible, as are transcripts of actual conversations."

Lodge takes a passage from *The Catcher in the Rye*, where the narrator is the teenager Holden Caulfield and where the prose has to sound like speech rather than writing, so Salinger uses a lot of repetition and exaggeration, short and uncomplicated sentences, even grammatical mistakes. But it is a balance between sounding like actual speech enough to convince and being so true to real life that it simply irritates. Lodge concludes: "There is a sense in which all dialogue in prose fiction is like telephonic dialogue, because (unlike drama) it must make do without the physical presence of the speakers. Indeed, fictional dialogue is still more deprived, in being denied the expressive timbre and intonation of the human voice."

Mark Twain struggled in his early fiction to capture the authentic voice of blacks in the American South. Of one piece, "A True Story, Repeated Word for Word as I Heard It" (1874), he told his friend William Dean Howells, "I amend dialect stuff by talking and talking and *talking* till it sounds right—and I had difficulty with this negro talk." Howells, then editor of *The Atlantic*, made sure that Twain was paid twice the going rate for all the work he put into the story, his first appearance in an elite Northern magazine. And yet, "racial mimicry, one way or the other," Twain scholar Andrew Levy writes astutely, "reinforced the idea that whites *knew* blacks. Twain seemed to be

creating a kind of mimicry in which he acknowledged they didn't."
He was, first and foremost, a *reporter*—he wanted readers to feel that
he'd got things right.

Henry James and Joseph Conrad were good friends, and in mid-
career both agreed that in their future books, none of their characters
would reply to a question directly, but only comment obliquely—
which would add tension. The psychologist William James is said to
have told his brother, "No one talks the way people do in your novels." To which Henry reputedly replied, "Maybe they should." Nobody talks like Philip Roth's characters, either. Or Proust's, or
Tolstoy's, or indeed many of the novelists who have created worlds to
which we happily surrender ourselves. Iris Murdoch was often ridi-
culed for making her characters spout the most unbelievable lines,
but she wrote several bestsellers, and her *The Sea, the Sea* won the
Booker Prize in 1978. This 2010 pastiche is all the funnier because it
is not unrepresentative of the real Murdoch:

> I followed Hartley to her home. "You may now be old, fat
> and ugly," I observed, "but I have always loved you, darling
> Hartley."
>   "Be still," she begged, "for I must remain unhappily
> married to the violent Ben, and together we must mourn
> the disappearance of our adopted son, Titus."

Murdoch got away with similar dialogue because she created her
own worlds, much as Compton-Burnett and possibly Twain did; in a
list of possible traps in having one's characters talk to one another,
however, straining credulity takes pride of place.

What about a character who lisps? Or stutters? Or swears the
whole time? Again, one can't just repeat "real life." One uttered
"fuck" on the page is like ten in conversation and immediately seems
off-putting. Paul Scott, who before he concentrated on writing novels

was a literary agent in London, recalls: "Asked, by one of our more distinguished publishers, who had made free with a blue pencil, to remove the last word of this kind [that is, "fuck": even in the mid-1960s British writers were coy about such words] from his otherwise promising first novel, a young writer, his eyes filling with unmanly tears, begged to be allowed to rescue this one last poor wretched refugee, saying, 'If my book comes out without even one of them, how can I face my friends?'"

James Wood would disagree. He recently penned an appreciation of the Glaswegian writer James Kelman (born 1946), whose novel *How Late It Was, How Late* won the Booker Prize in 1994. Wood picks up on Kelman's distinctive approach to language, in particular his habit of using and reusing "a relatively small register of words, as, for instance, in the way he repeats and refines 'fuck' and 'fucking'":

> A single sentence will deploy the same word differently. "If it was me I'd just tell them to fuck off; away and fuck I'd tell them, that's what I'd say if it was me," the narrator thinks in [the short story] "The One with the Dog." There is also "fucking" as a kind of midsentence punctuation (functioning like "but"): "She would just fucking, she would laugh at him." And also as impacted repetition: "Fuck sake, of course she would; what was the fucking point of fucking, trying to fucking keep it away; of course she'd be fucking worrying about him," Ronnie thinks in the story "Greyhound for Breakfast."

This is a good defence of constant word repetition, but it is like praising a musician for how many sounds he can get out of a single instrument; the result is impressive but quickly palls.

The same is true with all speech mannerisms. When in 1964 Norman Mailer, who hated books that prettified the speech of ordinary life, for instance rendering "motherfucking" as "mother-loving," published his fourth novel, *An American Dream*, in *Esquire*, he had a scene where a black man says "shit" some twenty times. Years later he reflected: "I really didn't need all twenty. Twelve would have done better, but I also knew that if I put in twelve, the editors would take out five, so I put in twenty. And the editors screamed, but I ended up with my twelve. They were happy and I was happy."

The Chilean novelist Isabel Allende, on the other hand, believes just one word that's foreign is enough to establish a character's background. Sebastian Faulks, in *Human Traces*, introduces us in the opening chapter to a protagonist who stutters. The character does so twice early on—then, in a book of 793 pages, just one other time, and that's enough. The story can now proceed, no longer weighed down by some need to tell the reader "This character stutters!" at every turn.

A caveat, however. In his study of how we speak, *Um . . . : Slips, Stumbles, and Verbal Blunders, and What They Mean*, Michael Erard argues that interruptions and mistakes provide clues to the way we render thought with sound, and what is stilted or stuttered illuminates how we retrieve words from memory, how we plan ahead of speech, how we unite meaning and intonation in real time, and how we acquire language in the first place.

The controversial American writer Jonah Lehrer* has written about how good ideas come to us, about the left and right hemispheres of the brain, and how one side, the right, will excel at what he calls "denotation"—storing the primary meaning of a word—while the left understands linguistic nuance, deals with "connota-

---

* In 2012, two of the three books that Lehrer has published, *Imagine: How Creativity Works* and *How We Decide*, were withdrawn from sale after it became known that he had fabricated quotations. That same year, he ran into further trouble over his contributions to both *The New Yorker* and *Wired* and was forced to admit to recycling content and plagiarism. Nevertheless, the information here is almost certainly sound.

tion," everything that gets left out of a dictionary definition, such as the emotional charge of a sentence or a metaphor. Language is so complex that "the brain has to process it in two different ways at the same time. It needs to see the forest and the trees."

Even so, one can push the reader a bit. Jeffrey Archer, for instance, likes to withhold information. If two lovers meet, Archer might draw away before they kiss—but that's obviously what happens next. Same for dialogue: he cuts away before the final part of a conversation, leaving the reader to figure out what is said next, only it's obvious from the context; once the reader has worked it out, he or she gets a certain pleasure from having done so.

Jeffrey Archer enjoys his craft, and so, at an entirely different level, did Thomas Mann, who used dialogue to show his characters' foibles and prejudices:

Of little Miss Weichbrodt:

In her whole insignificant figure, in her every movement, there indwelt a force that was, to be sure, somewhat comic, yet exacted respect. And her mode of speech helped to heighten the effect. She spoke with brisk, jerky motions of the lower jaw and quick, emphatic nods. She used no dialect, but enunciated clearly and with precision, stressing the consonants.

Of Herr Kesselmeyer:

[He] used this expression ["Ah, ha!"] with extraordinary frequency and a surprising variety of inflexions. He might say it with his head thrown back, his nose wrinkled up, mouth wide open, hands swishing about in the air, with a long-drawn-out, nasal, metallic sound, like a Chinese gong;

or he might, with still funnier effect, toss it out, gently, *en passant*, or with any one of a thousand different shades of tone and meaning. His *a* was very clouded and nasal. Today it was a hurried, lively "Ah ha!" accompanied with a jerk of the head, that seemed to arise from an unusually pleasant mood, and yet might not be trusted to be so.

Even in translation, every line of dialogue all these characters speak is firmly linked to their physical and spiritual being and their position in the rigid upper-middle-class society of late-nineteenth-century Germany. Here is a case of a major novelist getting things emphatically right.

The last word, though, belongs to Laurence Sterne and to *Tristram Shandy*:

Writing . . . is but a different name for conversation. As no one, who knows what he is about in good company, would venture to *talk all*; so no author, who understands the just boundaries of decorum and good-breeding, would presume to think all: the truest respect which you can pay to the reader's understanding, is to halve this matter amicably, and leave him something to imagine, in his turn, as well as yourself.

Which takes us inevitably, and not before time, to the matter of irony.

CHAPTER 6

Secret Trapdoors:
The Power of Irony

Just don't forget irony; it's the entry ticket to humanity.

**ADVICE GIVEN TO THE HISTORIAN
JOACHIM FEST BY HIS FATHER**

There are some people that if they don't know, you can't tell
them.

LOUIS ARMSTRONG

When my younger son, Guy, reached eighteen, I promised to take
him anywhere in the world. He chose Russia. Starting in St. Petersburg, with four days on the Trans-Siberian Express, the two of us
ended up in Irkutsk, 2,744 miles to the east.

About six hundred thousand people live there, making it one of
the largest cities in Siberia. It's a place to which many political exiles
were sent in the nineteenth century. In 1825, a group of army offi-

cers rose up against Czar Nicholas, but the whole project was an ig-
nominious failure. Because the fiasco took place at the end of the
year, the officers were called the Decembrists. Five plotters were
hanged, 120 banished—to Irkutsk, or yet farther east.

One of those exiled was Prince Sergei Volkonsky, who by 1838
had moved into what is now a famous house-museum. On the table
in the main room is set an imposing black metal statuette. Volkonsky
had tramped the original journey from Moscow—more than three
thousand miles—in manacles. Much later he sent back to his family
what might have passed as an act of homage—this bust of the despotic Nicholas—only it was made from the very chains he'd worn on
his forced march. This, surely, I told Guy, was irony.

When we got back to England I repeated this story to a friend of
mine. He shook his head. No, he said, it was *sarcasm*. Well, to me
Prince Sergei was being ironic.

It's a tricky word. A short, formal definition would be that irony is
a tension between what something is supposed to mean and what it
actually means—between who's in on the joke and who isn't. Julian
Barnes has a character in *A History of the World in 10½ Chapters* say,
"Irony may be defined as what people miss." Of all places, the house
magazine *Bridge Bulletin* recently ran an article that began: "Irony, in
the sense of finding unexpected truth, is frequent in literature but
rare in bridge"—a not unhelpful lead. Max Brod, Kafka's friend and
translator, says that Kafka would habitually survey himself and his
works "never quite without irony, but with friendly irony." And what
is one to make of Himmler's comment about Hermann Göring, who
had been out hunting—"That *murderer*"? Ironic, or only our reading
of it?

Maybe irony involves a disorienting approach that makes it difficult to pin down, like the blind man and the elephant—you learn
what kind of animal it is only by repeated touches. In his language
guide, *The King's English*, Henry Fowler says: "Any definition of

irony—though hundreds might be given, and very few of them would be accepted—must include this, that the surface meaning and the underlying meaning of what is said are not the same."

Take the simple proposition that opens *Pride and Prejudice:* "It is a truth universally acknowledged, that a single man in possession of a good fortune must be in want of a wife." It soon becomes clear Jane Austen means something very different: marriageable women—or their mothers—are often desperately on the lookout for a well-heeled husband. In an ironic reversal, the desire ascribed to wealthy bachelors is actually one felt by acquisitive potential spinsters. The irony deepens as the plot explores the nature of love and ends in a double wedding. That opening sentence hangs over Darcy—and our sense of him—throughout the novel.*

A galaxy of writers have their own sense of what irony may mean, each adding something to our understanding without being totally convincing. The narrator of Ali Smith's novel *Artful* gets a tattoo; it "hurts like irony." In Meg Wolitzer's novel *The Interestings,* the book's teenage heroine, Julie Jacobson, discovers irony, which "was new to her and tasted oddly good, like a previously unavailable summer fruit." However, "fairly soon after that, the snideness would soften, the irony would be mixed in with seriousness, and the years would shorten and fly." Then there is the irony that Proust describes as a form of self-protection:

---

* When concerns were expressed about over-subtlety in *Pride and Prejudice,* Jane Austen twitted: "I do not write for such dull elves/As have not a great deal of ingenuity themselves." And George Eliot produced her own ironic comment at her fellow author's expense in *Daniel Deronda:* "Some readers of this history," she writes in assumed innocence, "will doubtless regard it as incredible that people should construct matrimonial prospects on the mere report that a bachelor of good fortune and possibilities was coming within reach, and will reject the statement as a mere outflow of gall" (Collins Cleartype edition, date unknown, p. 120).

Sometimes, in spite of himself, [Swann] would let himself go so far as to utter a criticism of a work of art, or of someone's interpretation of life, but then he would cloak his words in a tone of irony, as though he did not altogether associate himself with what he was saying.

A 2012 essay in *The New York Times* cited irony as "the ethos of our age," and seems close to what Swann was doing:

Take, for example, an ad that calls itself an ad, makes fun of its own format, and attempts to lure its target market to laugh at and with it. It pre-emptively acknowledges its own failure to accomplish anything meaningful. No attack can be set against it, as it has already conquered itself. The ironic frame functions as a shield against criticism. The same goes for ironic living. Irony is the most self-defensive mode, as it allows a person to dodge responsibility for his or her choices, aesthetic and otherwise. To live ironically is to hide in public.

This helps, but we are still some way from a full definition. How does irony relate to being caustic, sarcastic, satirical, cynical, or sardonic?* *Pace* Barnes, is a passage being funny a crucial element? Does irony fall into the sphere of wit or humour—or lie where the two realms abut? Can irony take place when there's transparency? Should it always be slightly subverting, even threatening—are you able to understand what's *really* going on? The questions mount up,

---

* For a long time no one could find a source for "sardonic" in any Indo-European-based language. *Sardanios* is the original Greek word, but whence did it come? Then someone pointed out that in Sardinia there's a local plant which if you eat it you die—but with a strange, mocking look on your face.

but what is surprising is how often the meaning of the term is taken for granted.

Using Wikipedia is supposed to be a descent into hell—a vortex of plagiarism, superficiality, laziness, and idiocy—but its entry on irony is helpful and suggests that the concept is every bit as complicated as I have suggested. For instance, there is playful irony, whimsical irony, sardonic irony, quiet irony, and so on.

The word comes from the Greek, meaning—depending on the dictionary consulted—hypocrisy, deception, and feigned ignorance; or dissimulation, sarcasm, and understatement. It entered the English language at the end of the fifteenth century and in general use seeks to convey a meaning the opposite of its literal sense. In literature, it represents the technique of indicating an outcome or attitude opposite to that ostensibly implied.* In contemporary writing, it suggests a manner of organizing a work to give full expression to contradictory impulses—especially of indicating detachment from a subject, theme, or emotion. Irony differs from sarcasm in its greater subtlety.

According to Wikipedia, irony's essential feature is the indirect, often understated presentation of a contradiction between an action or expression and the context in which it occurs. Wikipedia then goes further, distinguishing four variations: verbal (I would prefer to say oral) irony—when a speaker says one thing and intends another; dramatic irony—when words and actions have a significance that the listener understands but the speaker or character does not; situa-

---

* In *The New Science* of 1725, the Italian philosopher Giambattista Vico argued that there were just four main figures of speech: metaphor, metonymy (in which a word or concept is called not by its own name but by something associated in meaning with it), synecdoche (a substitute for representation, in which a term for a part of something refers to the whole), and irony. Together these made up all "necessary modes of expression." Among the many influenced by his work were Karl Marx and Samuel Beckett.

tional irony—when the result of an action is contrary to the desired or expected effect; and finally, "cosmic irony"—the disparity between what humans desire and what the world actually serves up—the whims of the gods.

Illustrations of the first kind are not hard to find. In one of his novels, Kurt Vonnegut describes a character as "as pleasant and relaxed as a coiled rattlesnake." As soft as concrete, as clear as mud, as pleasant as a root canal: all are forms of verbal irony, though perilously close to sarcasm.

Sophocles' *Oedipus the King* is a good example of dramatic irony, as is the betrayal of Jesus by Judas—a traitor's kiss leads to Christ's crucifixion but thereby to the salvation of mankind. Then there's the Aesop fable where a king is told that his son will be killed by a lion, so he forbids him to venture into the outside world. One day the young prince, wandering around the palace, sees a tapestry in which a lion features. He strikes the featured beast with his fist, gashes his skin on a nail beneath the tapestry, and dies of gangrene.

An unusual example of situational irony came in 1981, when John W. Hinckley, Jr., attempted to assassinate Ronald Reagan, and every one of his shots missed. However, a round ricocheted off the bulletproof presidential limousine and struck Reagan in the chest. Thus a vehicle made to protect the president from gunfire was partly responsible for his being shot.

So why is irony so vital to what writers do? For me, the best answer comes from a surprising source. Søren Kierkegaard was a Danish religious philosopher in the first half of the nineteenth century (1813–55) who wrote mainly about Christian ethics. While at university, he attended a series of lectures on irony and, inspired, spent the next ten years probing into the nature of irony for his doctorate.

For him, irony was not just a literary trope but constituted a whole approach to life and, he argued, should be present in every work of art. It's not so much a matter of words, or even of character or situation, but rather a total perspective. Central to irony is "never to articulate the idea as such but only casually to suggest it, to give with one hand and take away with the other, to hold the idea as personal property."

He called his thesis *The Concept of Irony, with Continual Reference to Socrates*, and as suggested in his title he referred constantly to Socrates, who pretended to be ignorant and under the guise of being taught found a way to instruct others. With Socrates, "the outer and the inner did not form a harmonious unity, for the outer was in opposition to the inner, and only through this refracted angle is he to be apprehended."

Kierkegaard then provided a memorable image. A certain engraving portrays the grave of Napoleon, he said: "Two large trees overshadow the grave. There is nothing else to be seen in the picture, and the immediate spectator will see no more. Between these two trees, however, is an empty space, and as the eye traces out its contour, Napoleon himself suddenly appears out of the nothingness, and now it is impossible to make him disappear. The eye that has once seen him now always sees him with anxious necessity."

It recalls Socrates' replies to his inquisitors over 2,200 years before. "As one sees the trees, so one hears his discourse; as the trees are trees, so his words mean exactly what they sound like. There is not a single syllable to give any hint of another interpretation, just as there is not a single brush stroke to suggest Napoleon. Yet it is this empty space, this nothingness, that conceals what is most important."

Something of the same insight appears in many other places. Baudelaire described Rembrandt as a "sturdy idealist who makes us dream and guess at what lies beyond." Another great painter went even further: when Cézanne drew his wife in "Hortense Fiquet Sewing," he left a void at the picture's centre, as if he expected our minds to work with our eyes to fill in the gaps. Again, on the last page of *Speak, Memory*, Nabokov's memoir of his early days in Russia, his final image is of "something in a scrambled picture—Find What the Sailor Has Hidden—that the finder cannot unsee once it has been seen." As the Nabokov scholar Lila Azam Zanganeh notes, "A secret trapdoor had suddenly opened. Reading was a matter of capturing a detail in a scrambled picture, which, once perceived, unveiled a new story, often richer and stranger than the one first imagined." The trapdoor image is also used by Kierkegaard.*

This leads to two crucial understandings. First, it allows us to say things that cannot be said as matters of fact. Second, irony presupposes an understanding between author and reader (or audience). Irony allows us to leave things out. Flannery O'Connor here: "In fiction two and two is always more than four. . . . The fiction writer states as little as possible. The reader makes this connection from things he is shown. He may not even know that he makes the connection, but the connection is there nevertheless and it has its effect on him." There is a further benefit: as Dr. Johnson wrote, "We cease to wonder at what we understand."

If it is true that all novels are essentially about the passage from innocence to experience, about discovering the reality that underlies appearances, then not surprisingly, irony pervades fiction. Irony is about concealment, and the truth of what is written may grow on us—so not be obvious at a first reading. Only some way into *Animal Farm*—unless you've been tipped off beforehand—does it become clear that the book is about tyranny. And it takes until Gulliver's third voyage for us to be fully aware of Swift's purpose. A lot of High An-

---

* Freud named this effect the *unheimlich*, or uncanny, which he defined as "in reality nothing new or foreign, but something familiar and old-established in the mind that has been estranged only by the process of repression." The German word *Heim* means "home"; the uncanny is "what was once . . . homelike" but now feels strange or mystifying.

Paul Cézanne, *Hortense Fiquet Sewing,* c. 1880

glicans thought Daniel Defoe's *The Shortest Way with the Dissenters* a sympathetic description of their views, even though it's an ironic, devastating attack on them.

In *Wolf Hall,* Hilary Mantel's Man Booker Prize-winning novel, Thomas Cromwell is visiting Thomas More, Lord Chancellor of England—and his arch-enemy. They wander together through More's orchards and start—with extreme care, each circling the other—to discuss the fortunes of More's son-in-law, William Roper. How *is* young Will?

Cromwell, who is well versed in the ambiguities and ambivalences of court life and in the snares of saying anything too clearly about his religious affiliations—does a good Catholic give first loyalty to his monarch or to the Pope in Rome?—replies: "I thought that we might see him sit down a friend of Luther, as formerly he was, yet come back to the Church by the time they bring in the currants and gooseberries."

More: "Will Roper is now settled in the faith of England and of Rome."

Cromwell: "It's not really a good year for soft fruit."

Mantel then tells us: "More looks at him out of the tail of his eye; he smiles."

Cromwell is being ironic—he rounds off their talk with a casual comment about fruit, when he is actually telling his enemy that he is well aware of the character failings of his son-in-law. But Mantel, when she adds the reference to More and the "tail of his eye," is underlining the dangers in the whole conversation. Their dialogue is a game of life and death, where irony allows both men to say things that, expressed otherwise, could lead to the Tower. (That is why "slave irony" is a category all its own: a slave when he talks or writes cannot risk speaking his mind. He has to juggle power and nominal submission.)

Many of the definitions I've given suggest that irony makes play with opposites. It doesn't always. More often, what's on the page says something of value but leaves more out (irony shuns the adverb); the reader is expected to add what's missing.

In the 1980s, a *Washington Post* journalist wrote an article about North Korea using only the handouts he'd received from that benighted country's publicity offices. "Kim Jong-Il has courageously led the Democratic People's Republic into an unsurpassed period of prosperity and harmony," and so on, all meant ironically, of course. He then received a letter from the North Koreans to thank him for being the only Western correspondent who appreciated what was happening in their country, how glorious Kim Jong-Il's reign had been, along with an official invitation to visit. (Perhaps even more amazing, he accepted—a brave thing to do in 1985.)

Irony speaks to the pact between author and reader, in this case a pact that the North Korean officials refused to sign. The author expects us to be able to read between the lines. And of course he or she is paying us a compliment. Any good reader tries, in Henry James's phrase, to be "one on whom nothing is lost." We're up to it. And an author's relationship with readers is a complex one. In a *Sunday Times* interview, Martin Amis reflected:

> It's . . . a love relationship. How do you make someone love you? You present yourself at your very best, your most alive, your fullest, your most considerate. An author must be love-flushed: you must give them the most comfortable chair; you want to give the reader the seat nearest the fire, the best wine and food. It's a sort of hospitality gesture.

He goes on to criticize three writers in particular—Vladimir Nabokov, Henry James, and James Joyce—all past masters of irony— for showing "an indifference to the reader" in their later works. But then in his own fiction he writes about a central character in *The Information* (1996), "He didn't want to please the readers. He wanted to stretch them until they twanged."

So how, as a writer, do you present yourself at "your most alive, your fullest"? For years, *The New York Times Book Review* had on its inside back page short, self-standing essays. In 2001 an American novelist, Roxana Robinson, contributed one complaining of the lack of feeling in current fiction. She argued that, unduly influenced by Freud, we have become self-conscious about our emotions. So writers like Richard Ford, Cormac McCarthy—and, yes, Martin Amis—in her words, "prefer the cold end of the emotional spectrum, choosing alienation and irony." The result: "we lose . . . the whole turbulent landscape of feeling."

I profoundly disagree. The modern novel can be criticized on many grounds, but using irony to short-change emotion isn't one of them. Irony—in the sense I have been using it, and if it is used well—*heightens* the emotional stakes. If the reader can be encouraged to come halfway, responding to what the author has set down on paper, the ineffable may be understood and shared. (The same is true of dramatic performances too: as Dustin Hoffman said of his role on the HBO series *Luck*, which he played as very quiet and withdrawn, "Your audience is your co-writer, and they'll fill it in.")

This takes a leap of faith, and authors can be understandably anxious. When in 1946, the year after its first publication, George Orwell came to adapt *Animal Farm* for radio, he was concerned that readers had missed what he considered the story's turning point—when Napoleon and Snowball keep the milk and apples for themselves, a direct reference to events in Kronstadt, a naval base guarding the approach to St. Petersburg, where early in 1921 the first serious uprising against the government was put down with brutal force. Orwell added the following brief exchange:

CLOVER: Do you think that it is quite fair to appropriate the apples?

MOLLY: What, keep all the apples for themselves?

MURIEL: Aren't we to have any?

COW: I thought they were to be shared out equally.

His BBC producer, Rayner Heppenstall, cut the lines from the script as broadcast. Heppenstall's judgement was the finer: Orwell had been unduly worried that he was not being understood, but seventy years of readings have shown that his original version was quite clear enough.

By saying one thing but conveying another, one asks the reader to appreciate the larger truth. "Let each utterance gravitate towards ironic totality," to quote Kierkegaard's heavy-duty vocabulary. Coming halfway is just a metaphor, of course, suggesting a compromise, but I suggest you stretch readers even further—not until they've twanged but until they've twigged. Perhaps for the same reason, Kafka never completed many of his writings; there is no last page to *The Castle*, maybe because K., the protagonist, must never reach it, so that the reader can continue into the multi-layered text forever.* When it came to the publication of *Metamorphosis*, afraid that his publisher would put the likeness of an actual insect on the front cover, Kafka pleaded: "Not that, please not that! The insect itself cannot be depicted. It cannot even be shown from a distance."

Just what I mean comes from perhaps an unlikely source— Rudyard Kipling. His last book was a memoir, *Something of Myself*, which he started in 1935, when he was almost seventy. In the final chapter he summarizes what he has learned about his craft, the need for every word to "tell, carry, weigh, taste and, if need were, smell." He then spells out his belief that a writer should deliberately remove material from a story. One does this, he says, to increase the pressure on the reader. Such an approach isn't about avoiding emotion but about heightening it. "A tale from which pieces have been raked out is like a fire," Kipling says (using the same fireside image as Martin Amis—ironically), "that has been poked. One does not know that the operation has been performed, but every one feels the effect."

---

* Would Kafka have finished *The Castle* had he not died of tuberculosis? In a 1922 letter to Max Brod, he says that he is giving up on the story. But Kafka also told Brod on multiple occasions that the ending would involve K. living and eventually dying in the village, culminating on K.'s deathbed as he receives a notice from the castle that his "legal claim to live in the village was not valid, yet, taking certain auxiliary circumstances into account, he was permitted to live and work there." Ironically, the ending we have may be the more resonant.

This pressure of the absent is one of the cardinal marks of good fiction: William Trevor has called the short story "the art of the
glimpse," whose "strength lies in what it leaves out," and Kipling
himself uses these glimpses to masterly effect in his late short story
collections.

Another master of the short story, J. D. Salinger, regularly employed irony in the sense of nuance, indirection, and implication. In
"A Perfect Day for Bananafish" (1948), he tells of a day spent on the
beach by the main character, Seymour Glass. Meanwhile, Seymour's
wife, Muriel, spends her time in a hotel room talking to her mother
on the phone about clothing and her husband's behaviour. We see
Seymour worry about small, seemingly inconsequential things, such
as people staring at his feet, and he wears a bathrobe on the beach to
avoid people's gaze. He meets Sybil, a young girl of about four, and
is kind to her. They go off to swim together, and he tells her the legend of bananafish. The fish, Seymour says ("See-more," the little girl
calls him; in the Teutonic language the name means "mighty at
sea"), are "very ordinary-looking" when they swim into a hole, but
once in the hole. . . .

> "You know what they do, Sybil?"
> She shook her head.
> "Well, they swim into a hole where there's a lot of ba-
> nanas. They're very ordinary-looking fish when they swim
> in. But once they get in, they behave like pigs. Why, I've
> known some bananafish to swim into a banana hole and eat
> as many as seventy-eight bananas." He edged the float and
> its passenger a foot closer to the horizon. "Naturally, after
> that they're so fat they can't get out of the hole again. Can't
> fit through the door."
> "Not too far out," Sybil said. "What happens to them?"
> "What happens to who?"

"The bananafish."

"Oh, you mean after they eat so many bananas they can't get out of the banana hole?"

"Yes," said Sybil.

"Well, I hate to tell you, Sybil. They die."

"Why?" asked Sybil.

"Well, they get banana fever. It's a terrible disease."

"Here comes a wave," Sybil said nervously.

After the swim, Seymour says goodbye to Sybil, returns to his hotel room, retrieves a gun from his luggage, lies down next to his sleeping wife, and shoots himself.

It's a devastating piece, showing Salinger's signature mastery of compression and telling detail, and all the clues are there about how the story will end, why Seymour acts as he does, but so pared down that once you've recovered you go back and read the whole account again, and only then see how the impact of Seymour's death comes from so much that Salinger *leaves out*.* Here is tragic irony at its most effective, all the more so because we, the readers, have to swim so far out to get the full point; there's a big wave coming. Salinger is a perfect example of how it's not a matter of getting your readers to come halfway; get them to come—say—70 percent of the way. The text *finds* you, as Coleridge was fond of saying.

The eleventh-century Egyptian writer al-Hasan ibn al-Haytham (known in the West as Alhazen) had a fine phrase for the role of readers: it is to render visible "that which writing suggests in hints and shadows." Hemingway always tried to write on the principle of the

---

* My Kingston colleague, the novelist and poet Vesna Goldsworthy, has taken to asking her students to write the "missing episode" from "Bananafish." Incidentally, the story made Salinger's reputation—*The New Yorker* immediately gave him an extended contract; Brigitte Bardot tried to buy the film rights (he almost accepted).

iceberg: for the part that shows there are seven-eighths more under-water. And Thornton Wilder chimed in: "Art is not only the desire to tell one's secret; it is the desire to tell it and hide it at the same time."

One final illustration. In 1993, the Milan-based company Adel-phi published a first novel by a middle-aged businessman, Paolo Maurensig. It quickly became a bestseller in many countries, collect-ing admiring reviews. The book, just 140 pages long, is called *The Lüneburg Variation*, a reference to a chess strategy, and indeed at one level it is all about that game and the powerful emotions it inspires.

The novel's first sentence—"They say that chess was born in bloodshed"—bears this out. An elderly man, Dieter Frisch, is found shot dead in his garden, in a village near Vienna. In his house, a makeshift chessboard stitched together from patches of old cloth, with coloured buttons as pieces, is found on his study table. Unable to be defined as either suicide or homicide, the death is called one of "mysterious circumstances." The man had evidently been a chess fanatic, and the unnamed narrator tells us that every evening, on his train journey back from Vienna, Frisch would play a game with Herr Baum, a work colleague who took the same route home, getting out a few stops before his companion. One evening, as they play, a young man enters their compartment and tells them a story.

It is a tale about two young boys growing up in 1930s Germany; both are chess prodigies, although from very different backgrounds. One is Tabori, a Jew, the son of a wealthy art dealer. The other is the son of prosperous Aryan parents. The two become bitter rivals, and the one time that Tabori emerges as the overall winner in a competi-tion, Frisch persuades the anti-Semitic judges to rob him of victory.

World War II comes and, despite several escapes, by 1944 Tabori finds himself in Bergen-Belsen, where he is rescued from imminent death by the arrival of a new camp commandant—none other than his schoolboy rival, who has the scrawny inmate marched to his of-fice. "It has been my misfortune to find among my colleagues only lamentably inferior chess players," the SS officer explains. "You are my only hope of being able to enjoy a few decent games."

Tabori will receive extra food and a lighter work detail so long as he plays with the commandant twice a week. And there must be a wager. Should Tabori lose, then an escalating number of his fellow inmates will be put to a gruesome death, with him an enforced onlooker: the two men will be playing for human lives—only Tabori has developed a special series of moves, the Lüneburg Variation, which Frisch is unable to counter.

And so it goes. Tabori survives the last months of the war, and the camp is liberated; its commandant disappears. Resuming normal civilian life, Tabori takes on a young protégé, Hans Meyer, to whom he teaches all he knows about chess, including the Lüneburg Variation. Just before he dies, Tabori has his young charge promise to find out what has happened to his tormentor. It is Hans who enters the railway carriage where Dieter Frisch is playing chess with Herr Baum. Inside Hans's pocket is a crumpled piece of patchwork cloth. Soon Baum reaches his station, leaving Frisch alone with Meyer, who begins to recount the details of Tabori's life. "It was a story I would have to repeat to this man. That was the only way he'd be able to remember." When at last he has finished Frisch looks across and says, "And I suppose I am that man." At this point the narrative breaks off.

It is left to each reader to supply what happens next, but the clues are all there. "I thought at first that I was missing the last part of the book," wrote one reviewer on Amazon. Another complained: "The book ended rather abruptly . . . sort of left you hanging." A third weighed in: "Everything is going along swimmingly, until you get to the book's last page and wonder where the final present-day scene, the one the whole book begs for, went. It's certainly not in the book." But that is the point. As another Amazon reader put it, understanding Maurensig's intention, the novel "ends as if the author and the reader were playing a game of chess, and the author says 'Your move.'"

CHAPTER 7

Grabbing Fiction
by the Tale

Nothing matters. Everything happens.

D. H. LAWRENCE, ON ERNEST HEMINGWAY'S

FIRST COLLECTION OF SHORT STORIES,

IN OUR TIME (1925)

No, no! The adventures first . . . explanations take such a
dreadful time.

LEWIS CARROLL,

ALICE'S ADVENTURES IN WONDERLAND (1865)

What makes a successful story? Some years ago I attempted to
answer this question with about sixty students at Kingston. I followed
my talk with an hour's practical session, where I asked the class to
play "Consequences": everyone had to take a piece of paper and
write down a name (even in these days, a man's name), then pass the
paper on to the person sitting in the adjacent seat. Each student was
expected to add a further name, so that "A" would "meet" B, the

second name. The papers were passed on again. The third entry would be where A and B met. Then "he said to her," then "she said to him," "and the consequence was," "and the World said" . . . seven entries in total, after all of which sixty rough and often ridiculous stories had been created.

I asked several of the class to read out the story that they had finished up with, and can still remember one of them:

Adolf Hitler

(met)

Jane Austen

Near the roundabout at the Fair.

(He said to her): My mother warned me about girls like you.

(She said to him): Why bother with convention? You know
    I've always loved you.

(And the consequence was)

Mass emigration throughout Belgium

(And the world said)

They made a lovely couple

After a few students had read their stories out loud, I asked the class to add characterization, context, and incidental detail to whatever lines had ended up on their desks. It didn't matter that most of the concoctions were surrealist at best: when the students read their revised stories each had a different feel. Hitler now fidgeted with his moustache. Jane Austen found herself blushing uncontrollably, the fairground meeting was at night, with punk rock gangs roaming the stalls. And Hitler, hearing that he had won the love of a fine woman, was encouraged to invade Belgium, so the story suddenly had cause and effect. Of course, our attempt at Consequences was no more than a lecture-cum-parlour game; but it did illustrate how the baldest of storylines can evolve, once causality and detail are added.

Over the centuries, writers have tried to reduce the world's store of imaginative literature to an identifiable formula to which every novel or short story or epic poem must conform. Leo Tolstoy reportedly once commented, "All great literature is one of two stories; a man goes on a journey or a stranger comes to town." Would that it were so simple. We search continually for a template, some perfect recipe, for the stories we tell one another: are there only so many narratives available? And for the philosopher's stone of successful narrative we use words like "story" and "plot"—although they mean different things to different people and lead to confusion.

In his *Poetics*, Aristotle considered plot the most important element of drama, but his word for "plot" was *mythos*, which is Greek for "report" or "tale," so there was no distinction dividing plot, narrative, and drama. For Aristotle, a plot had to have a beginning, middle, and end, and its events had to relate to one another as being either necessary or probable. This definition has informed Western literature over the centuries and has led to the suspicion that maybe we could achieve a list of all the possible plots available to us—as if that would explain the creative impulse or help us to produce the perfect play or film or novel.

In the late eighteenth century, an Italian playwright, Carlo Gozzi (1720–1806), proposed that there were thirty-six "dramatic situations," no more, that could be turned into tragedy or comedy as preferred. The first four in his list, for example, were: supplication, deliverance, crime pursued by vengeance, and vengeance taken for kin upon kin. His contemporary Friedrich Schiller (1759–1805) tried to find more, as did the French writer Gerard de Nerval (1808–55), but they couldn't even reach thirty-six, settling on only twenty-four. Others tried their hand: Gustav Freytag (1816–95), a German novelist and playwright, declared that all stories could be divided into five parts: exposition (of the situation), rising action (through conflict), climax (or turning point), falling action, and resolution. At the end of the century a French writer, Georges Polti, published *Les trente-six situations dramatiques,* which he claimed was an updating of Gozzi. His categories were pretty bare, thus situation number 26 is "Crimes of Love: A Lover and the Beloved enter a Conflict"—and that's it. But this obsession with classifying and counting plots has continued, as if it could add to our understanding of storytelling in general.

When, early in 1973, I was taken on as an editor at William Collins, the company already had under contract a book about the main plots in world literature by Christopher Booker, a thirty-six-year-old jazz critic, political scriptwriter, anti-establishment newspaper columnist, and a founding editor of *Private Eye*. Twenty-two years later, when I started my own publishing company, the book had still not been completed, and for several months I worked closely with Christopher on this modern equivalent of Casaubon's *Key to All Mythologies,* before giving up in despair that it would ever be finished. But perseverance won through, and in 2004 *The Seven Basic Plots: Why We Tell Stories,* now well over seven hundred pages, was finally published, by Continuum Press. The book won warm approval from many writers, the Oxford philosopher Roger Scruton calling it a "brilliant summary of storytelling."

The manuscript, while I was working on it, was marred by Christopher's enthusiasm for Jungian theorizing, about which he was cheerfully unrepentant. But the first section, just under 240 pages, still strikes me as a wonderful exposition and helps explain what storytelling, in its widest sense, is all about. As Dr. Johnson said—quoted in the book—listening to and reading stories *helps make us whole.*

Christopher goes on to comment how we spend a phenomenal percentage of our lives with stories, "telling them; listening to them; reading them; watching them being acted out on the television screen or in films or on a stage." Stories have always been told: probably they were the first kind of literary self-expression. "They are far and away one of the most important features of our everyday existence."

Then he is off at a gallop. The original draft that I read had a heart-stopping opening two paragraphs, which for some reason have been dropped in the final version: we begin with a summary of *Beowulf,* the Anglo-Saxon epic written some time between the eighth and early eleventh centuries which tells of a small community nightly menaced by a mysterious monster, until it is slain by the young hero of the title.

The second paragraph outlines the story of a small Long Island seaside resort whose peace is shattered by the offshore arrival of a monstrous shark, which attacks victim after victim until the local police chief, Brody, along with two companions, slays the shark in a great climactic battle. This is the film and book *Jaws.* The two stories are the same. We have our first plot: Overcoming the Monster.

Booker reckons that this storyline is shared by the Sumerian *Epic of Gilgamesh;* the James Bond adventure *Dr. No;* the fairy tales Little Red Riding Hood, Jack and the Beanstalk, and Hansel and Gretel; several Greek myths, such as the Gorgon Medusa, the half-bull, half-man Minotaur, and Heracles and the many-headed Hydra; and on to *Dracula* and H. G. Wells's *The War of the Worlds.*

Next up is Plot No. 2: Rags to Riches. At its core this presents an ordinary person, dismissed by everyone as insignificant, who suddenly takes centre stage, revealed to all as exceptional. *The Ugly Duckling, Pygmalion, David Copperfield, Dick Whittington and His Cat,* and *Jane Eyre* are all examples.

Plot No. 3 is called The Quest. Far away lies a priceless goal, worth any effort to achieve. From the moment the hero learns this, the need to set out on a long, hazardous journey to reach it becomes an obsession, and the story is resolved only when the objective has at last been secured (or partly so). Into this group fall *The Lord of the Rings*, *The Odyssey*, *Treasure Island*, and *King Solomon's Mines*—even *Babar and Father Christmas*, *Around the World in Eighty Days*, and *Moby-Dick*.

Plot No. 4 is Voyage and Return. For Booker, this is different from the Quest story: the essence here is that the hero, heroine, or central group of characters travels out of their everyday surroundings into another world, only to be completely cut off from home. Eventually, usually after a series of trials and a final thrilling escape does the narrative return to the safety of home. This embraces *The Wizard of Oz*, *Peter Pan*, *Robinson Crusoe*, *Lord of the Flies*, *Gulliver's Travels*, *Journey to the Centre of the Earth*, Apuleius's *The Golden Ass*, *The Tempest*, and Waugh's *Decline and Fall*.

Over these early chapters, Booker does a good job rebutting any charge of being reductionist, and he lays out, title by title, how each story keeps to the same main structure. His next two categories are Comedy and Tragedy, both of which have not changed over two thousand years.

The essence of Comedy is always that some redeeming truth has to be brought into the light. It thus takes in the plays of Aristophanes and Plautus, *The Marriage of Figaro*, Molière and Shakespeare (including *The Winter's Tale*), *The Importance of Being Earnest*, as well as novels such as *Tom Jones*, all of Jane Austen, even *War and Peace*.

At the beginning of Plot No. 6, Tragedy, Booker tells us that, in the millions of stories created by the human imagination, two endings far outweigh all others: with a couple united in love or in a death. He concentrates on five: the Greek myth of Icarus, the German legend of Faust, *Macbeth*, *Dr. Jekyll and Mr. Hyde*, and *Lolita*. Each story has a hero tempted or compelled into actions in some way dark or forbidden. For a time he is successful, but final satisfaction is denied him, and eventually the story ends with the protagonist's violent destruction.

Just one final plot to go: Rebirth. Here a young hero or heroine falls under the shadow of a dark power. For a while, everything seems to be going well, but soon the hero/heroine is imprisoned in a state of living death, and it looks as though the dark power has triumphed, but then comes a miraculous redemption, and all is well. Booker here examines in detail *Fidelio, The Secret Garden, Peer Gynt, Crime and Punishment, A Christmas Carol,* and *The Snow Queen.*

Whether or not one agrees with Booker's analysis, it outlines the limited range of storylines available to any writer. As Ian Hislop, the editor of *Private Eye,* says, "If stories are about 'what happens next,' this book sets out to show that the answer is always 'the same things,' then to explain why." The basic stories are few in number; how then each successful story seizes our interest is up to the author's skill in creating characters, situations, and language that are original and satisfying. Alberto Manguel puts it well in his *A History of Reading,* "We read to find the end, for the story's sake. We read not to reach it, for the sake of the reading itself." It's the 'how" that is all-important.

"That's his story." "The plot thickens." "The same old story." "Losing the plot at the Oscars," a 2014 newspaper headline. The words *plot* and *story* are not interchangeable—they refer to significantly different elements in narrative—yet their exact meaning has been debated and redefined over the centuries, often leading to heated argument and unexpected partisanship.

Booker's book plumbs the seven basic *plots*—not the seven basic stories. He never defines what he means by "plot." What is a plot, and what is a story, and does clearing up the confusion help in writing fiction?

In 1927, E. M. Forster gave a series of lectures at Cambridge that many still consider the most influential attempt to define key words to do with the writing of fiction. These talks were later published as *Aspects of the Novel*, covering characters, story, plot, fantasy, prophecy, pattern, and rhythm. In the chapter entitled "Story," Forster famously makes this distinction: "'The king died, and then the queen died' is a story. 'The king died, and then the queen died of grief' is a plot." Story is one event after another; plot is controlled by causality.

If it is a story, Forster says, we ask, "And then?" A story "can only have one fault: that of making the audience not want to know what happens next." Story strips away all but the barest scene-setting, dialogue, atmosphere, symbolism, description, reflection, and characterization. Forster does not hide his contempt: for him, story is a "low atavistic form," and only good plotting can raise it to a higher plane.

A plot is "an organism of a higher type." It explains events or gives reasons for them; it should be intelligent (not simply based on curiosity), be built on memory (relating to what is happening with other parts of the story), and contain elements of surprise and mystery. Forster thus lays out his stall, and people have been buying from it ever since.

Extraordinarily, a very different point of view comes from Stephen King, who has little time for plot—scorns it, in fact—and instead glorifies story. During a long recuperation from a serious accident (a van veered onto the shoulder of the road where King was taking an afternoon stroll and threw him fourteen feet into the air), King turned his reflections on the craft of authorship into *On Writing*. It is as much memoir as guidebook, and he is eager to state what makes any novel work:

In my view, stories and novels consist of three parts: narration, which moves the story from point A to point B and finally to point Z; description, which creates a sensory reality for the reader; and dialogue, which brings characters to life through their speech.

You may wonder where plot is in all this. The answer— my answer, anyway—is nowhere. . . . I distrust plot for two reasons: first, because our *lives* are largely plotless, even when you add in all our reasonable precautions and careful planning; and second, because I believe plotting and the spontaneity of real creation aren't compatible.

King doesn't stop there. "Plot is," he says, "the good writer's last resort and the dullard's first choice." The greatest supporter of "Developing the Plot," he reckons, was Edgar Wallace, who in the 1920s wrote bestselling potboilers and invented a device called the Edgar Wallace Plot Wheel, which could be used by any writer stuck for ideas: you spun the wheel and read whatever came up in the window— an unplanned arrival, perhaps, or the heroine declaring her love. According to King, Plot Wheels "sold like hotcakes."*

Plainly, King and Forster have different definitions of the two words under examination. Is this just a semantic confusion?

The first sighting of "plot" in this sense came in 1671, courtesy of the theatre, where it described the narrative of a play that was overly intricate. By the late 1800s it was used for increasingly complex mysteries in detective stories, then evolved in the years to follow—hardly the dullard's first choice. Henry Fielding may have been criticized for

* Over in North America, circa 1906, the classic adventure writer Jack London, down on his luck, was reduced to purchasing plotlines from Sinclair Lewis at five dollars apiece (about $130, or £90, in today's currency). A few years later, Ernest Hemingway was challenged to produce, on the spot, an effective story in just six words. His reply: "For sale: baby shoes. Never worn."

letting one event fall on the heels of another, yet Coleridge thought *Tom Jones* one of the best three plots in literature. Wodehouse wrote elaborate outlines for every one of his fictions. King, however, stands his ground: "There is a huge difference between story and plot. Story is honorable and trustworthy; plot is shifty, and best kept under house arrest."*

This seems to me way off target. Plot has been reduced to annoying shifts in the narrative that bear little relation to what the characters are likely to do, the author adding details or themes or character traits that run against the story's "honesty." That wasn't what Forster meant by plot at all—but he in turn is guilty of making King's position seem ridiculous too, for the bare bones of a narrative are not what King is after either. Both Forster and King have their own idea about what "story" and "plot" are, and argue accordingly, loading the dice.

The number of writers who take sides in this debate is surprisingly large, as is the range of definitions. Edith Wharton had a poor view of plot, defining it as "an elaborate puzzle into which a given number of characters have to be arbitrarily fitted." Dorothy Sayers, summarizing Aristotle, believed that "the first essential, the life and soul, so to speak, of the detective story, is the Plot, and the Characters come second." Raymond Chandler, who was never that concerned with plot (when asked by the director of *The Big Sleep* who killed one of the characters, he famously admitted he didn't know), wrote, "I guess maybe there are two kinds of writers; writers who write stories and writers who write writing."†

---

* King famously in 1987 produced his horror story *Misery*, in which a popular novelist, one Paul Sheldon (one of King's publishers was called Paul Sheldon), wants to write a superior novel, but is kidnapped by his "number one fan" who torments him with an electric meat cutter and a propane torch until he turns out another of the Victorian-era romances that she loves. So much for "house arrest" for those who concoct plots!

† Chandler's point of view seems to differ from King's. He would take issue with

The battle over story and plot has not been confined to novelists. Two of the finest literary critics in recent times have been Harold Bloom and Frank Kermode. In one of his books, Bloom commends Kermode for observing of *King Lear* that over a hundred lines (Act 4, scene 6, 80–185), when the mad Lear meets the blinded Gloucester, the plot is not advanced at all. So is Shakespeare, to reference Chandler, "writing writing"? I don't think so. The relationship between the mad king and his blinded courtier is central to the play. Call it plot or story, in their meeting on the heath a lot "happens," it just doesn't concern who will rule Lear's kingdom, or what Albany will do next, and other secondary matters. It is like saying nothing much takes place in *Mrs. Dalloway;* yet the movement and state of a person's mind is highly dramatic and can grip us on its own merits. External events have no primacy over internal ones.

In an article about the Irish novelist John Banville, Joan Acocella contrasted his two writing modes—his literary novels, one of which, *The Sea,* won the Man Booker Prize in 2005, and his detective stories, published under the pseudonym Benjamin Black. "A murder mystery needs a strong plot," Acocella writes, "and that's Banville's weakness. If you want ambiguity, complication, doubleness—a thick texture—you can't have shot-from-guns story lines as well." But surely Chandler, a master of the genre, weaves a "thick texture" as well as murder and mayhem? Stephen King himself has commented that Donna Tartt, author of *The Goldfinch,* which won the Pulitzer Prize for Fiction in 2014, is "an amazingly good writer. She's dense, she's allusive. She's a gorgeous storyteller." It's a great offence to sell

---

editors who insisted that he cut out all descriptions on the grounds that readers disliked anything that held up the action: "My theory was that the readers just thought they cared about nothing but the action; that really, although they didn't know it, the thing they cared about, and that I cared about, was the creation of emotion through dialogue and description" (quoted in P. D. James, *Talking About Detective Fiction,* p. 86).

storytelling short—that's why we smile at the reported comment of movie mogul Sam Goldwyn selling storytelling long: "We want a story that starts out with an earthquake and works its way up to a climax."

Here we might revisit E. M. Forster's description of a story: "The king died, and then the queen died." We are already being given far more than a couple of isolated events. These two characters are royal personages, public figures, and their deaths will surely reverberate far beyond their family circle. Second, they are husband and wife. We do not know anything about their marriage, except that they are intimately connected to each other. We know all this before any element of causality is supplied. Forster, in other words, doesn't tell the whole story about story.*

This should be simple enough, but people still continue to caricature story and plot. In an essay about Anthony Burgess, Martin Amis made a distinction between the "A" novelist and the "B" novelist:

> The A novelist . . . writes in what we commonly regard as the mainstream: he is interested in character, motive and moral argument, and in how these reveal themselves through action (yes, oh dear me yes, the A novel tells a story). The spunkier and more subversive B novelist, however, is *quite* interested in these things but is at least as interested in other things too: namely, the autonomous play of wit, ideas and language (no, the B novel doesn't necessarily tell a story at all). Certainly, ambitious novelists tend to get

---

* The Forster definition somehow encourages fellow novelists to weigh in. "'The cat sat on the mat' is not a story," John le Carré has argued. "But 'the cat sat on the dog's mat' is the beginning of a story." P. D. James came up with a typical twist: "Everyone thought that the queen had died of grief until they discovered the puncture mark in her throat" (P. D. James, *Talking About Detective Fiction*, p. 4). A single line added, only now we have a murder mystery.

more B and less A as they develop. *The Portrait of a Lady* is very A, whereas *The Ambassadors* is clearly hoping to be B. *Mary* is contentedly A, *Ada* haughtily otherwise. *A Portrait of the Artist* is already fairly B, and *Finnegans Wake* is about the most B novel we have.

According to Amis, the simplest kind of novel tells a story (a word he never defines), but story can still take in character and motivation: it doesn't have to be exploding cars and morphing mutants. The more complex novel takes in ideas, wit, language.

But rather than the vexed tussle between story and plot, one wants the best of both, working in harmony, in whatever kind of fiction is being attempted. As Henry James put it in *The Art of Fiction:*

I cannot see what is meant by talking as if there were a part of a novel which is the story and part of it which for mystical reasons is not—unless indeed the distinction be made in a sense in which it is difficult to suppose that any one should attempt to convey anything. "The story," if it represents anything, represents the subject, the idea, the *donnée* of the novel. . . . The story and the novel, the idea and the form, are the needle and thread, and I never heard of a guild of tailors who recommended the use of the thread without the needle, or the needle without the thread.

It is time to tie the various strands of this argument together. For me, story and plot represent the two ends of the same spectrum. There is a slippery slope here—too much attention to story and you get a blockbuster, but of a superficial kind; too much plot, and you lose most of your audience, who want a strong and relatively uncomplicated tale. "Too much plot" can be variously interpreted, but one meaning is that the author creates a scheme for the tale to which his characters must conform, a contrivance, forcing them to do certain things that don't seem true to what we know of them or of life generally. Forster, in discussing Hardy's *Jude the Obscure,* supposes that

> the characters have been required to contribute too much to the plot . . . In the novel, all human happiness and misery does not take the form of action, it seeks means of expression other than through the plot, it must not be rigidly canalized.

This is the element of plot to which Stephen King particularly objected: if an author plans everything he wants his characters to do, the story becomes schematized. But seen at their best, story and plot intertwine and complement each other, and criticizing the one while lauding the other has little point. "Story" isn't just one event after another—it can include characterization, causality, and description—but these elements tend to be of a basic kind. "Plot" includes story, but suggests greater complexity. If a story doesn't have interesting characters it will probably have very limited appeal (Forster's point). As Ray Bradbury has a character say in *Fahrenheit 451,* "The more pores, the more truthfully recorded details of life per square inch you can get on a sheet of paper, the more 'literary' you are. That's *my* definition, anyway. *Telling detail. Fresh* detail."

An author who over-complicates the plot or makes her characters act unbelievably just to satisfy the demands of the storyline will lose our confidence (King's complaint). Such additional features as rich or symbolic language, detailed description, author asides, or fast or slow pacing do not belong to the realms of plot or story, though they exert a profound influence.

This takes us back to what characters should do. Whether it is James Bond or Leopold Bloom, Swann or Cinderella, we have to care about the people in our fictions. Bradbury added an author's note to a 2003 edition of *Fahrenheit 451*. In it he wrote:

> I sat down to another nine-day schedule to add words and scenes and turn the novella into a novel of some 50,000 words. Again, an emotional process. Again, as before, I knew that "plot" could not be imagined ahead of the event, that you had to trust your main character to live out his time, to run before you. . . . Any man who takes a sex manual to bed with him invites frigidity. Dancing, sex, writing a novel—all are a living process, quick thought, emotion making yet more quick thought, and so on, cycling round.

The urge to categorize the stories in world literature is understandable and not uninteresting, and the whole muddle over story and plot stems from good motives. But better to dance, make love, write a novel without too much regard for the textbooks.

The German equilibrists The Salambos
(named after Flaubert's historical novel) at a performance in 1901.

CHAPTER 8

Waves in the Mind:
Rhythm in Prose-Writing

There are two kinds of written language, one based on sound
and the other on sight.

EZRA POUND, *ABC OF READING*

True wit . . . gives us back the image of our mind.

ALEXANDER POPE, "AN ESSAY ON CRITICISM"

Sophia Rosoff, who lives in my apartment block, has for many
years been known as one of the best piano teachers in New York.
Those who come to her range from twenty to eighty years in age,
from wunderkinder to concert performers and leading jazz players.
In her mid-nineties now, she still teaches five days a week; when I
decided to write about prose rhythm she was one of the first people
I went to for advice.

"Ah, rhythm," she said. "All life is about rhythm."

"Thank you very much," I said, a little tartly. Could she be a bit more specific?

That was when she told me how she asks her students—not all of them, and not all the time, but often enough—to balance a raw egg vertically, either on a china plate or on her carpet. She says it's a matter of locating the yolk, getting your breathing just right, and knowing when to let go. Once they've succeeded, she'll wave them to the piano stool, now calm and ready to play. Nor is that all. Depending on the day, she may ask a pupil to walk across the room like Groucho Marx or dance a Chopin mazurka. She teaches "rhythm talk," which entails saying a word such as "little," again and again, varying the pitch. All this to get her students to coordinate their breathing with their music.

Sophia has never been one to promote herself, and I had fancied myself part of a select group who cherished her, but in the spring of 2011 a profile appeared in the Berkeley-based literary magazine *The Threepenny Review*, and her views achieved a wider airing. When the author of the piece asked Fred Hersch, a prominent jazz pianist and composer who has studied with Rosoff for over thirty years, why she attracts so much musical talent, he replied, "It's the emphasis on rhythm. . . . She always stresses that it's not a technique or a method. It's all about connection." State of mind must be in harmony with state of body.

After Sophia Rosoff had finished talking about eggs, she showed me a passage from a Virginia Woolf letter to Vita Sackville-West. It runs:

> Style is a very simple matter; it is all rhythm. Once you get that, you can't use the wrong words. But on the other hand here am I sitting after half the morning, crammed with

ideas, and visions, and so on, and can't dislodge them, for lack of the right rhythm. Now this is very profound, what rhythm is, and goes far deeper than words. A sight, an emotion, creates this wave in the mind, long before it makes words to fit it.

"A wave in the mind": can one go further than that? Fowler's *Dictionary of Modern English Usage* was first published in 1926 and quickly became a kind of Bible for writing English—so much so that it is generally spoken of simply as "Fowler."*

Woolf's letter and Fowler's first edition appeared the same year, which may explain Fowler's opening paragraph:

> Rhythmic speech or writing is like waves of the sea, moving onward with alternating rise and fall, connected yet separate, like but different, suggestive of some law, too complex for analysis or statement, controlling the relations between wave and wave, waves and sea, phrase and phrase, phrases and speech.

In a review of *Mrs. Dalloway* in 1925, the critic John W. Crawford compared the rhythm of Woolf's writing to "the development of a symphony. It is incredible that this could be done with English prose." Another of Woolf's letters, this time to Dame Ethel Smyth, the composer and musician, shows just how complex this can be:

---

* One reason for its spell was that it is actually witty. For example: "Split infinitives: The English-speaking world may be divided into (1) those who neither know nor care what a split infinitive is; (2) those who do not know, but care very much; (3) those who know and condemn; (4) those who know and approve; and (5) those who know and distinguish. . . . Those who neither know nor care are the vast majority, and are happy folk, to be envied by the minority classes."

> About HB's [Brewster's] writing . . . I should never say that
> his books were badly written because they're not literary—
> in fact, for me, like most Americans, he is much too literary
> in one sense—too finished, suave, polished and controlled;
> uses his brains not his body; and if I call him not a born
> writer, it's because he writes too well—takes no risks—
> doesn't plunge and stumble and jump at boughs beyond his
> grasp. . . . It trickles off me—his beauty—instead of raising
> the nerves in my spine.

Rhythm, I'm going to argue, is about raising the nerves in one's
spine.

The word comes from the Greek *rhythmos*, "any regular recurring
motion, symmetry . . . a movement marked by the regulated succes-
sion of strong and weak elements, or of opposite or different conditions." It refers to "the timing of musical sounds and silences," thus
"timed movements through space."

According to Fowler, a sentence or a passage is rhythmical if,
when said aloud, it falls naturally into groups of words, each well fitted by length and intonation for its place in the whole and its relation
to its neighbours. If you're writing prose, the best guide is to cultivate
an instinct for the difference between what sounds right and what
sounds wrong, a syllable-by-syllable attention to sound, a feel for
rhyme and breath. You do this—according to Fowler—by one
method only: by reading aloud.*

Some critics dislike the attention given to rhythm by prose writers.
In her 2015 book *Between You & Me*, a kind of American version of

---

* Our ancestors spelled "rhyme" as "rime," but we changed the spelling to as-
similate rhyme with rhythm.

Eats, Shoots & Leaves, the long-time *New Yorker* copy-editor Mary Norris comments, "When a writer who is not a poet invokes rhythm, copy-editors often exchange looks." Heaven forfend that some contributors to the magazine have pretensions, but attention to rhythm is a fine and necessary thing, not an affectation. Ford Madox Ford even maintained that prose "should give the effect of a long monologue spoken by a lover at a little distance from his mistress's ear," but that may say more about his infamously busy love life than his insight into prose rhythms. Anthony Trollope was more down-to-earth:

> The harmony which is required must come from the practice of the ear. There are few ears naturally so dull that they cannot, if time be allowed to them, decide whether a sentence, when read, be or be not harmonious. And the sense of such harmony grows on the ear, when the intelligence has once informed itself as to what is, and what is not harmonious.

So to settle the matter, to my satisfaction anyway: prose rhythm is an integral part of writing well, and reading prose aloud is the best way of getting rhythms right.

Laura Hillenbrand, the author of the bestsellers *Seabiscuit* (2001) and *Unbroken* (2010), told an interviewer: "Good writing has a musical quality to it, a mathematical quality, a balance and a rhythm. You can feel that much better when it's read aloud." Robert Frost, writing to a friend in 1913, took this one stage further: "I . . . have consciously set myself to make music out of what I may call the sound of sense." This wasn't about poetic diction but words generally. He later expanded on this: "*The ear does it.* The ear is the only true writer and the only true reader. I have known people who could read without hearing the sentence sounds and they were the fastest readers. Eye readers we call them. They can get the meaning by glances. But they are bad readers because they miss the best part of what a good writer puts into his work. Remember that the sentence sound often says more than the words. . . . I wouldn't be writing all this if I didn't think it the most important thing I know."

Frost was a master at making one say his lines in a certain way. The *sense* of his poems drives the sound, so that most of us recite his verses intuitively with the accents in the right place. That is harder to achieve in prose, and one has to train one's ear, but so it has been throughout human history.

Originally, all writing, whether of religious or classic texts, public pronouncements, or personal compositions, was read aloud—even if only to oneself. Books were few, oral reading the norm. With the advent of typesetting and the mass production of texts the habit of public recitation expanded to include "tacit" reading aloud—reading with the eye and not the mouth, being as fully aware of the unuttered sound as of the sense. One imagines a monastery, the centre of learning during the Dark Ages, having so many monks declaiming from the sacred texts that one day the abbot in desperation barked "Shush!" and the habit of reading silently caught on. You do not have to speak aloud to hear the rhythms of prose.

But many did so. Chaucer emended *The Canterbury Tales* after his public readings (maybe putting some of the complaints he got into the mouths of his fictional pilgrims, such as the Man of Law, who found Chaucer's rhymes pretentious). Centuries later, both Molière and Swift declaimed their work to their servants, and when they didn't understand, each author would rewrite until they did. Kafka recited to a small circle of friends "with an intoxicating fervour and a rhythmic verve beyond any actor's power," laughing uncontrollably at his own efforts, particularly over *Metamorphosis*. Edna O'Brien read her 1970 breakthrough novel *A Pagan Place* "hundreds of times out loud" and came to remember extended stretches by heart.

My favourite example is Coleridge who, while reciting a long poem to Charles Lamb, seized a button on his friend's coat so that he couldn't escape. Lamb pulled out a penknife, cut off the button, and quickly exited via the gate of the garden in which he had been trapped. Lamb would write: "Five hours afterwards, in passing the garden on my way home, I heard Coleridge's voice and on looking in, there he was, with closed eyes—the button in his fingers—his right hand gracefully waving, just as when I left him." It's as well to remember that every reader carries a metaphorical penknife.

Gustave Flaubert was another who fretted over the rhythms of his sentences and who, as he said of himself, wanted to achieve a style in prose "as rhythmical as verse and as precise as the language of science." His letters show that he wasn't one to whom flowing language came naturally: it was the result of constant hard work. The last two decades of his life were spent in the straggly village of Croisset, in a cottage next to a large forest and just thirty yards inland from the Seine. His workshop lamp was said to have burned with such regularity late at night that pilots on the water were able to take their bearings from it. Toward the end of a night of writing, Flaubert would stand at his window and, "in the absence of friends, he recited what he had written to the tulip tree, the moon, and the river."* If that weren't enough, he'd take to the forest, shouting out passages to test their rhythm.

James Wood takes up a single sentence from *Madame Bovary* to demonstrate what Flaubert did with his prose. Emma is pregnant,

---

* Starting in the winter of 2013, my wife and I viewed all 156 episodes of *The West Wing*. In one of them, President Jed Bartlet tells his wife: "Words, when spoken out loud for the sake of performance, are music. They have rhythm, and pitch, and timbre, and volume. These are the properties of music, and music has the ability to find us and move us, and lift us up in ways that literal meanings can't. Do you see?"

Abbey Bartlet replies: "You are an oratorical snob." Maybe, but he is right about the rhythm of words read aloud. "War Games," Episode 6, season 3 of *The West Wing*.

and her husband, Charles, is full of himself for having got her that way. The French reads: "*L'idée d'avoir engendré le délectait.*" Literally, this translates as: "The idea of having engendered delighted him." The Penguin Classics translation (by Geoffrey Wall) renders it as: "The thought of having impregnated her was delectable to him." As Wood argues, this is where English loses out to the original, but the point is not about what gets lost in translation but what Flaubert meant by rhythm. In the French, there are four "ay" sounds in three of the words—*l'idée, engendré, délectait.* Flaubert's novels sing with the distinctive "ay" sound of his favourite verb tense, the imperfect. Wood concludes: "The regular, repeating sound of this imperfect verb—which English translates as a verb of habit, as 'he would do something' or 'he was doing something'—is like a bell tolling the very sound of provincial boredom in *Madame Bovary.*"

The enquiry into the part rhythm plays in prose began with Aristotle: "The form of style must be neither metrical nor yet without rhythm. For if it is metrical, it becomes unconvincing, because it seems artifice. Also it distracts the hearer, by making him listen for some cadence to recur. . . . On the other hand, the unrhythmical is formless. Prose style must have form, but not meter: for the formless is both unpleasing and ungraspable."

Despite this instruction, the importance of rhythm to prose fiction is still a relatively new idea (this is true, for all the glorious rhythms of Bunyan and the King James Bible). Milan Kundera added a thought-provoking comment to an updated version of his 1967 novel *The Joke.* "In Goethe's time," he wrote, "prose could not make the aesthetic claims of poetry; perhaps not until the work of Flaubert did prose lose the stigma of aesthetic inferiority. Ever since *Madame Bovary,* the art of the novel has been considered equal to the art of poetry, and the novelist (any novelist worthy of the name) endows every word of his prose with the uniqueness of the word in a poem."

Edith Wharton, writing in the early 1920s, described the novel as "the newest, most fluid and least formulated of the arts." A few years on, Borges remarked how Flaubert "was the first to consecrate himself . . . to the creation of a purely aesthetic work *in prose*. In the history of literatures, prose is later than verse; this paradox was a goad to Flaubert's ambition. 'Prose was born yesterday,' he wrote. 'Verse is the form *par excellence* of the literature of antiquity. The combinations of metrics have been used up; not so those of prose.'"* Novels were novel.

E. M. Forster devotes an entire chapter in *Aspects of the Novel* to rhythm and the overall musicality that a long work of fiction can achieve, not just the rhythms of a sentence or a paragraph. He points to the easy rhythm in *Remembrance of Things Past* where Proust constantly returns to the theme of the "little phrase," a melody that the fictional composer Vinteuil serves up in various forms and that the characters hear at strategic moments. Forster writes of the melody, "There are times when it means nothing and is forgotten, and this seems to me the function of rhythm in fiction; not to be there all the time like a pattern, but by its lovely waxing and waning to fill us with surprise and freshness and hope." He goes on to say that rhythm is "what can stitch together a novel when the plot is not the focus." There is not much plot (in the sense of complex events) to Proust's novel, but his "rhythm, his attention to detail, and the recurring mo-

---

* Another French writer whose life overlapped with Flaubert's is Paul Fort (1872–1960), whom Paul Verlaine pronounced "Prince des Poètes," a title that was reinforced in 1912 by a national newspaper's referendum. Fort's *Ballades françaises* (which fill over thirty volumes) are printed as if they were prose, precisely to emphasize the all-importance, as he saw it, of flow, rhythm, cadence, and assonance over sheer rhyme. And the avant-garde writer and film-maker Alain Robbe-Grillet (1922–2008) often remarked how the music of the Breton waves of his childhood shaped his sentences.

tifs are what tie it together." Rhythm implies continuities and ends and organization. One of the joys in reading *Remembrance of Things Past* lies in discovering a rhythm only after reading hundreds of pages: the "waves" can be books apart.

Another well aware of the overall musical qualities of his writing was Thomas Mann. His autobiographical novella *Tonio Kröger* was published in 1903 and immediately became popular. Mann later reflected, "It may be that its musical qualities were what most endeared it to its readers. Here perhaps for the first time I learned to use music to mould my style and form. Here for the first time I grasped the idea of epic prose composition as a thought-texture woven of different themes, as a musically related complex—and later, in *The Magic Mountain,* I made use of it on a larger scale."

A more recent example is Kurt Vonnegut's phrase "So it goes," used as an ironic beat throughout *Slaughterhouse-Five* (1969), where his main character, taken prisoner by the Germans in the Second World War, is transported to Dresden to perform "contract labor" and driven into refuge in a disused slaughterhouse—Schlachthof-fünf— during the 1945 Allied bombing of the city. "So it goes" is used 106 times in the novel, whenever mortality comes up. This is what Forster calls "easy rhythm in fiction . . . repetition plus variation," the literary equivalent of a Wagnerian leitmotif. The variation here is in the circumstances, but the trope resonates through the entire novel.

Vonnegut had been captured after the Battle of the Bulge and more than once narrowly escaped being killed. After being released, in the first letter that he wrote to his family, he explained what had happened to him since his capture on December 19, 1944: the appalling conditions in which he and his fellow soldiers were kept, the bombing of Dresden, the strafing by Russian planes that followed. He set up a certain negating refrain in that letter: "Many men died . . . but I didn't. . . . the Americans came over, followed by the R.A.F. Their combined labors killed 250,000 people in twenty-four hours . . . but not me. . . . [Russian planes] strafed and bombed us, killing fourteen, but not me," an obvious if unplanned rehearsal for the coda he would use more than twenty years later. Yet even before that, he reveals in another letter that he used to listen to a favourite uncle who would use the refrain "If this isn't good, what is?" Literary motifs can be borrowed, then improved with practice.

The best book on the subject of rhythm in prose-writing is *Style*, by F. L. Lucas (1894–1967), published back in 1955. In chapter 10 he tackles rhythm head-on. He too quotes Flaubert, saying that a good style must meet the needs of respiration—no point in writing something that is difficult to speak. Although modern writing is meant for the silent reader, a sentence is unlikely to be good if anyone reading it aloud is left breathless.

I shared this insight with a friend of mine, Sam Wasson, biographer of the dancer and choreographer Bob Fosse, someone whose whole working life was given up to understanding and employing rhythm. Sam responded, "I always thought of Proust's breathlessness as a good thing, a way of evincing a dizzying passion, as heady and confusing as a flood of pure emotion." Sam is right: most rules, even about rhythm, are there to be broken. But the rules are still worth knowing.

In prose, as Aristotle indicated, a metrical rhythm will probably irritate or make the reader laugh—such as Dickens's paragraphs of blank verse, particularly in *The Old Curiosity Shop* and *Barnaby Rudge*. The trick is to avoid being obtrusive in how one uses rhythm. As Lucas puts it, "At a certain temperature a kettle begins to sing, so, when prose becomes passionate, it has a spontaneous tendency to begin to chant."

The first technique authors should master is antithesis—arranging ideas as well as syllables into some kind of symmetry. "It was the best of times, it was the worst of times," or "Four legs good, two legs bad" are made more memorable, and more effective, because of the balance between their two halves. Homer uses this device a lot, as do poets like Pope and masters of prose like Dr. Johnson. "The mind is perpetually balancing and seeking balance; perpetually truth lies between opposed extremes, and wisdom between opposite excesses," Lucas explains. But he also warns: "A style which has too many of them will seem artificial, and a style which has too few will lack point." (An antithesis in itself!)

Next comes word order, where rhythm and clarity join together. Just as the art of war largely consists of deploying the strongest forces at the most strategic points, so the art of writing depends on putting the strongest words in the most important places. In English, the crucial part of a sentence is to be found at its end, the next most emphatic at its beginning—although words or phrases that would normally appear towards the end can gain emphasis by being put at the start, from the very fact that this *is* abnormal. "Emphasis may be important: but more important still is variety. To end sentence after sentence with a thump would lead to maddening monotony."

A good example can be found in Francis Bacon's essay *On Friendship:* "A crowd is not company, and faces are but a gallery of pictures, and talk but a tinkling cymbal, where there is no love." A critic of Bacon has argued that the normal reader will mistake the first three statements for universal truths and will be disconcerted by finding the important rider, "where there is no love," at the end. That rider, says the critic, should be moved to the beginning. But such a placing would be disastrous: the stress is on the emptiness of life without love; therefore this absence has to be kept until the last moment. The reader may be jolted, but such surely is Bacon's intention.

Mark Twain believed that even in swearing one should make sure to position what he calls the "crash-words" in emphatic places. In *A Connecticut Yankee in King Arthur's Court* he has Hank Morgan criticize the King's cussing thus: "The profanity was not good, being awkwardly put together, and with the crash-word almost in the middle instead of at the end, where, of course, it ought to have been." An interesting piece of Twain advice: make your swearing rhythmical.

Another example comes not from literature but from life, when on December 7, 1941, the Japanese attacked Pearl Harbor. Franklin D. Roosevelt had little over an hour to prepare a speech to the American people that would fit the terrible occasion. In his initial draft he referred to "a date which will live in world history." In his final speech this became "a date which will live in infamy." Not only was this far stronger, it also allowed the stress to fall on the first syllable of "infamy," giving the whole phrase greater force.

Next comes onomatopoeia: using words that sound like their meanings. This can occur from the sound of words used singly or from the length of time it takes to say or read them—a device much used in poetry. Take these lines from Tennyson*:

> The moan of doves in immemorial elms,
> And murmuring of innumerable bees . . .

Or Pope's clever "And ten low words oft creep in one dull line." Examples from prose are equally thick on the ground—it just takes more meters to cover them.

Every language has words framed to exhibit the noises they seek to express—"thump," "rattle," "growl," "hiss"—but they are relatively few. Verbs like "crawl," "creep," "dawdle" have long vowels and suggest slow movement, and "skip," "run," "hop" have short vowels and suggest intense brevity. Yet "leap" and "dart" are long and rapid, while "drag," "hesitate," "dilatory," despite their short

---

* Tennyson told friends that there was a single word in English for which he could not find a rhyme—*scissors*. He might have added *orange*.

vowels, mimic slowness. So the ear is often duped; and besides—onomatopoeia tends to draw attention to itself, which may not be what one wants.

This comes close to alliteration, the next piece of technique drawing on rhythm. It is an ancient device, found in countless stock phrases and proverbs—"by might and main," "by fair means or foul," "in for a penny, in for a pound," and so on. Lucas calls this "a kind of lubricant to language, making it easier to articulate." Fair enough, but it too can be dangerous, as one can fall in love with it. Think of Shakespeare's take-off of alliteration in *A Midsummer Night's Dream*, when Bottom the Weaver, who modestly tells us that he has "a reasonable good ear in music," straining after effect, bellows forth:

> The raging rocks
> And shivering shocks
> Shall break the locks
> Of prison gates;
> And Phibbus' car
> Shall shine from far,
> And make and mar
> The foolish Fates.

Just a couple of scenes later, Shakespeare shows us how to combine onomatopoeia and alliteration in a very different speech—Puck's covert threat to Bottom:

> I'll lead you about a round,
> Through bog, through bush, through brake, through brier;
> Sometime a horse I'll be, sometime a hound,
> A hog, a headless bear, sometime a fire;
> And neigh, and bark, and grunt, and roar, and burn,
> Like horse, hound, hog, bear, fire, at every turn.

When alliteration works, as it does here, it can have great power. One final instance—two main characters from Edith Wharton's *The House of Mirth* are out walking:

> As she moved beside him, with her long light step, Selden was conscious of taking a luxurious pleasure in her nearness: in the modeling of her little ear, the crisp upward wave of her hair—was it ever so slightly brightened by art?—and the thick planting of her straight black lashes.

The incidental details are important, but what makes the passage so effective is its rhythm, one that conveys the normally hyperdetached Selden's elation at walking alongside a beautiful woman. His feelings are communicated not just in the sense of the words used but by the "L" sounds—"long light step . . . luxurious pleasure . . . her straight black lashes." As has been well said, the alliteration of the passage practically sings. Here rhythm not only accompanies sense, it makes sense.

Overall, Lucas's four central headings, antithesis, word order, onomatopoeia, and alliteration, are hard to improve on. So too are his main points of advice:

Avoid obvious patches of verse in prose. Unobvious patches often lurk in our finest pieces of impassioned prose, so they must please us—provided we don't exactly notice them.

Safety is found in variety. Disguising metrical rhythm can be achieved partly by moderate use, partly by variation in the rhythms employed, and partly by increasing the variety of their length.

Fear of verse rhythms is liable to produce leaden prose, lacking rhythm of any kind, but one can counteract a tendency to meter by deploying plenty of consecutive unstressed syllables. As with all prose effects, the more unobserved the better.

Sound and rhythm in prose can sometimes be used to echo the

sense, but such things can seem like trickery. Similarly, alliteration is valuable but perilous.

Repetition falls into something of the same category. It is generally inadvertent and the result of carelessness; in *From Here to Eternity*, James Jones unrelentingly repeats "grinned" and "grinning"; on one page alone Prewitt grins six times. Most writers worry over unintentional repetitions and also internal rhymes. Even so, repetition well handled can be remarkably effective—the words "honest" or "honesty" occur in *Othello* fifty-two times, and act as a drumbeat to Iago's and Othello's preoccupations. In *The Great Gatsby*, the word "time" or references to it appear nearly five hundred times, but they reinforce rather than annoy. Equally successful are those powerful, rumbling repetitions at the opening of *Bleak House*, particularly the descriptions of London fog. (Dickens, who had been a parliamentary reporter, argued that newspapers should present parliamentary debates with the speeches scored, as in an opera.) Mistress Quickly, announcing the death of Falstaff in *Henry V,* tells us:

So

a' bade me lay more clothes on his feet: I put my
hand into the bed and felt them, and they were as
cold as any stone; then I felt to his knees, and
they were as cold as any stone, and so upward and
upward, and all was as cold as any stone.

The speech is intensely moving, the more so for the threefold "cold as any stone." It also manages to be scurrilous, since although Mistress Quickly doesn't *mean* that she felt up a dying man, that is what comes across, all the more so as the word "stone" was sixteenth-century slang for "testicle."

Repetition in dramatic verse is one thing, but take the moment in

Henry James's *The Turn of the Screw* when the new governess addresses the reader: "I daresay I fancied myself . . . a remarkable young woman. . . . I needed to be remarkable to offer a front to the remarkable things that presently gave their first sign." The repetition works—and certainly affects the rhythm of the sentence.

When it fails, it is annoying to the reader. Michael Holroyd is one of Britain's leading literary biographers, but his recent writing can be slipshod. In *A Book of Secrets: Illegitimate Daughters, Absent Fathers* (2011), he describes the early life of an eccentric patron of the arts, Ernest Beckett, whose father was a Conservative Member of Parliament; "but [Ernest's] heart was not in politics—it was in banking. The son of a banker, he entered the family bank, Beckett's Bank, in his twenty-first year, becoming senior partner on his father's death in 1874 and eventually steering his three sons into banking." *Bank, banker, banking*—five mentions in four lines, but they do not build on one another; they simply dull our reading.

Again, Hillary Clinton's memoir *Hard Choices* (2014) frequently succumbs to wordplay that is self-absorbed rather than effective— "Will Africa's future be decided more by guns and graft or growth and good governance?" she asks. Then there is Tom Wolfe, who only does it to annoy because he knows it teases. Here he is in peacock form in his 2012 novel *Back to Blood:* "There were a couple of boring modern apartment towers glass glass glass glass sheer facade sheer facade sheer streaked facade. . . ."

Fewer words than one might think are intrinsically beautiful or indeed (with some exceptions) intrinsically ugly.* The point is that

---

* The novelist Amy Tan was once asked by Stephen King (they play together in a rock band, The Rock Bottom Remainders) if there was any one question she was *never* asked when giving talks. She told him: "No one ever talks about the *language*." And here is George Eliot in *Adam Bede*, reflecting on the words we use to describe love: "The finest language, I believe, is chiefly made up of unimposing

sentences should be easy to say (even in one's head): to quote Robert Ray Lorant, "Good prose is rhythmical because thought is; and thought is rhythmical because it is always going somewhere, sometimes strolling, sometimes marching, sometimes dancing."

A last thought on the particulars of Shakespeare's favourite rhythm—the iambic pentameter, originally imported from the French by Chaucer. This is when ten syllables appear in five pairs, making a single line of alternating stressed and unstressed syllables; or, as James Fenton puts it, "a line of five feet, each of which is a ti-tum. As opposed to a tum-ti." ("Penta" means five, "meter" measure, "iambic" an upbeat.) Thus:

If mu- / -sic be / the food / of love, / play on

The line goes: da DUM | da DUM | da DUM | da DUM | da DUM—an iambic pentameter. This can be effective well beyond Shakespeare and not just in Keats, say ("When I have fears that I may cease to be"), or Eliot (Prufrock's "I should have been a pair of ragged claws"); even modern writers can use it for special effect. In 1973 the American thriller-writer Ross Thomas published *The Porkchoppers*, a suspense novel set in the world of Big Labor. The anti-hero of the story is Donald Cubbin, the president of a powerful union up for re-election. Because he has taken to drink, it will be a close call, and the odds are stacked against him as he walks to the microphone to give a vital speech that will assure him of victory or, if mishandled, a humiliating defeat. Watching in the wings are a journalist called Guyan and Cubbin's grown-up son, Kelly.

---

words, such as *light, sound, stars, music*—words really not worth looking at, or hearing, in themselves, any more than *chips* or *sawdust*: it is only that they happen to be the signs of something unspeakably great and beautiful" (Collins popular edition, p. 579).

"They say that I should quit my job and run."

He paused and then repeated the line stronger, louder, and with even more scorn:

"They say that I should quit my job and run."

Another dramatic beat, and then the blast:

"Quit, hell! I've just begun to fight!"

It brought some of them to their feet cheering and whistling, and those who didn't rise pounded their hands together as much in anticipation of a good show as in appreciation for Cubbin's declaration.

"I'll be damned," Guyan said. "What is it? Does he do it every time?"

"You tell him, Kelly," Imber said.

"It's a combination," Kelly said. "I don't think he knows he's doing it really. He just knows that it works. Did you get those first two lines?"

Guyan glanced down at some notes he'd made. "Yeah. It's really not much of a line when you read it: 'They say that I should quit my job and run.'"

"Till Birnam Wood remove to Dunsinane," Kelly said. . . . "Five feet to the line, iambic pentameter. But he doesn't only steal the beat from Shakespeare, he also borrows from the blues. The first line of all real blues songs is usually repeated and if you think about it, they're also iambic pentameter, or try to be. . . . He's been doing it as long as I can remember. . . . He said he just kept thinking up lines until he got one that felt right."

"He just kept thinking up lines until he got one that felt right": an echo of Virginia Woolf's—and Fowler's—"waves in the mind." For all those tropes that help make up rhythm in prose, it can still boil down to what *feels right*.

Early in 2014 I went to a talk given by the novelist Allan Gurganus (*Oldest Living Confederate Widow Tells All,* among others). One particular remark struck home: "Rhythmically, the King James Bible is what we all aspire to." Later I came across a pamphlet by Dr. Lane Cooper, *Certain Rhythms in the English Bible,* published in 1952. The language is sometimes a little technical—*dactyl:* a long syllable followed by two short syllables; *iambus:* a prosodic foot of two syllables, a short followed by a long; *anapest:* two short syllables followed by a long one; *cretic:* two longs surrounding a short—but Cooper helps explain why the Bible's rhythms have been so powerful through the centuries. "If," he says,

> preachers, orators and writers would spend a little time noting the rhythms of [the KJV] they would grow discontented with the sentences that please them now. Consider, for instance, the effect of the long row of dactyls in this sentence: "who hath believed our report, and to whom is the arm of the law revealed?" or the change from iambus to dactyl in the sentence "the sun to rule by day, for his mercy ruleth for ever."

Cooper goes on to cite, as an example of the use of anapests, "My doctrine shall drop as the rain, my speech shall distil as the dew," and then the use of cretic feet in the translation of James, I, 19: "swift to hear, slow to speak, slow to wrath." One likes to think of the forty-seven translators of the King James Version reading their work aloud to one another and nodding in appreciation.

Inextricably connected to rhythm is style (F. L. Lucas called his book by that very word, after all). In Bernard Tavernier's 1986 film *Round Midnight,* the saxophonist played by the real-life sax master Dexter

Gordon gives advice to an aspiring musician, sharing with him the essence of style: "You just don't go out and pick a style off a tree one day," he says. "The tree's inside you, growing naturally."

One can help the tree to grow. Stendhal, often praised for the clarity of his writing style, said simply, "I copy the Code Napoléon," the French civil code established by Bonaparte in 1804, which stressed clearly written and accessible law. (After Stendhal's death, friends discovered his drawers packed with handwritten copies of the Code.) Martin Luther emulated the style of the Thuringian chancelleries, thus helping shape the modern German language in a way to rival the effect on English of the King James Bible.

Not surprisingly, Norman Mailer has firm views on the matter. "Style," he says, "of course, is what every good young author looks to acquire. In lovemaking, its equivalent is grace. Everybody wants it, but who can find it by working directly toward the goal?" The trick, he confides—*one* trick—is to find a tone that fits the essential material. "There may be too much of a tendency among young intellectuals," he writes, "to think if one can develop a consciousness . . . one will be able to write when the time comes. That assumption, however, may not recognize sufficiently that the ability to put words on a page also comes through years of experience and can become a skill nearly separate from consciousness and bear more resemblance to the sophisticated instinct of fingers that have been playing scales for a decade."

Once more, the linking of writing and music. In actual speech, tone of voice, too, is a vital element, as it so often indicates the meaning of what is being said. For instance, the words "All right" may imply enthusiastic agreement or indicate a surly compliance.* In the

---

* Agatha Christie's 1950 mystery *A Murder Is Announced* has a piece of dialogue where what is said—where the stress falls—provides a vital clue to the murderer: whether muddled Miss Murgatroyd said, "*She* wasn't there" or "She wasn't

same way, the "tone" of a piece of writing can show the writer's attitude and may heavily qualify or tilt the literal meanings of the
words themselves. On the page, the eye can gather up the sounds of
a paragraph or dialogue, can take in melody or cadence. The eye is
not so quick in catching a voice.

Writers have known this down the centuries. "It is the mind that
makes for good style," wrote Michel de Montaigne in 1580. The
long-time theatre reviewer for *The New Yorker*, John Lahr, asked what
attracted him to a particular book, replied: "I'm often drawn by tone
and by the slant of the language. The way the sentences pop. A few
well-angled sentences announce to me if this is a voice whose command I can trust or whose quirkiness intrigues. Style, after all, is me-
tabolism."

In November 2011 I attended a talk given by Ernest Hemingway's latest biographer, Paul Hendrickson. Many people have written pastiches of the Hemingway style, he told his audience, "and
indeed when he writes badly that style is easy to parody. But in the
end only Hemingway could write a *good* Hemingway sentence—and
that music is inside his head."

This is surely where we came in, sitting beside Sophia Rosoff and
the vertical egg, waiting to take our turn at the piano, riding the
waves in our mind.

------

there." And part of British police training is to take a simple six-word sentence, "I
didn't sleep with your wife," and repeat it, each time putting the stress on a different word, so getting six quite different meanings.

A commuter reads *Lady Chatterley's Lover* on the London Underground on November 3, 1960—the day the book went on sale to the general public.

CHAPTER 9

"Just Like Zorro":
Writing About Sex

Sex is our most intense form of communication in a language no one can decipher or interpret.

EDMUND WHITE, 2013

All this fuss about sleeping together. For physical pleasure I'd sooner go to my dentist any day.

NINA IN *VILE BODIES*, EVELYN WAUGH, 1930

"Sex," my school headmaster would boom out at the beginning of his sermons (for he was an ordained priest), "is the Latin for six, and there are six commandments of the Church." After that opening, he could pretty well roam where he liked, possibly leaving us to wonder which six commandments he had in mind but certain that he had our attention. Because nearly everyone is interested in sex (the brain, after all, is the body's largest sexual organ), most are happy to read about it, and—as I know from perusing fiction sub-missions over the years—eager to write about it too. "Sex"—no clerical headmaster here, but Iris Murdoch speaking—"is a compli-cated, subtle, omnipresent, mysterious, multifarious business; sex is everywhere."

This chapter is not about pornography (from the Greek, "the writing of harlots"), nor erotica, although many good books contain pornographic passages and much good writing about sex is erotic, whatever else it may be. It is about how sex has been conveyed in fic-tion from Samuel Richardson on to no-holds-barred modern novels and about how to write about sex today—if it is wise to attempt to do so at all.

That scenes depicting sexual relations should be important in il-luminating a story's themes and developing plot is obvious enough: the novel can be the most intimate of art forms, the one that puts the reader's mind and heart most closely in touch with its characters. Yet how scenes of physical intimacy have been written has depended on censorship and the fashions and obsessions of the time. As the critic George Steiner, who speaks English, German, French, and Italian fluently, has said: "Each language draws taboo lines in quite different places. Things which in one language are the bedroom's final wild privilege are in another language almost public, and vice versa. The pacing of the words one uses is completely different in different lan-guages. Even breath control is different in different languages, and it's very important in sexual intercourse and in foreplay." And in the literary depiction of sex. A "sex scene" may be to one person the sensitive probing of a character's feelings, to another an acute em-barrassment, while to a third simply a turn-on. (Monica Lewinsky famously gave Bill Clinton a copy of Nicholson Baker's sexually ex-plicit novel *Vox*, for motives one can only guess at.)

So how should a writer approach sex scenes? Sex engages all five of our senses, so one shouldn't ignore the more subtle cues. But it's nearly always best to avoid detailed descriptions or elaborate imagery. The 2012 Nobel laureate in literature, Mo Yan, in one of his novels, likens a woman's breasts to "ripe mangoes"; in *Brazil* (1994) John Updike compares a penis to a yam; both unfortunate similes. One thinks of Miss Prism in *The Importance of Being Earnest:* "Ripeness can be trusted. Young women are green. [Dr. Chasuble starts.] I spoke horticulturally. My metaphor was drawn from the fruits." I recall being approached by a boy at my junior school (so I would have been about twelve) who showed me a well-thumbed novel called *Angélique and the King*, by Sergeanne Golon, set in the court of Louis XIV. Angélique's breasts were described as "like fresh round apples."* Perhaps there is something in common between a woman's breasts and apples, or melons, or pears, or lemons, or mangoes. But far more is *not* shared. One can often sense what has made a writer choose a particular metaphor, but more often than not the "other side" of the metaphor—what is *not* in common between the things compared—makes the analogy ridiculous.

Some twenty-two years ago, *Literary Review* founded a Bad Sex in Fiction Award. The annual prize, announced then-editor Auberon Waugh, would go to whoever had perpetrated the worst sex scene in a novel, the aim being "to draw attention to the crude, tasteless, often perfunctory use of redundant passages of sexual description in the

---

* From the same novel: "He took Angélique into his arms again. 'How lovely you are! How sweet to all the senses!'

"Anticipation had driven them crazy. Angélique groaned and bit the silken epaulette of his blue coat. Péguilin laughed softly.

"'Easy, my little vixen. You'll get what you want.'

"She yielded to him. The golden veil of voluptuous oblivion descended over them. She was merely an ardent body, greedy with desire, unconscious of where she was or even of the partner whose practiced touch made her whole being quiver. . . ." Sergeanne Golon, *Angélique and the King* (New York: Lippincott, 1960), p. 111.

Oh, for those far-off days of innocence!

modern novel, and to discourage it." The first winner was the famous broadcaster and author Melvyn Bragg, for *A Time to Dance*. He was not pleased.

Since then, an array of famous names has graced the shortlists: Thomas Pynchon, Julian Barnes, Alice Walker, Carlos Fuentes, Isabel Allende, Vikram Seth, Jeanette Winterson, Ian McEwan ("Had she pulled on the wrong thing . . . ? He gave out a wail. . . ."), Salman Rushdie, Paul Theroux, Tom Wolfe, Joyce Carol Oates, Stephen King, Gabriel Garcia Márquez, Mario Vargas Llosa, Norman Mailer, Doris Lessing, J. G. Ballard, Iain Banks, David Mitchell, Ben Okri, and Ali Smith (her protagonist, amid orgasm, "We were a bird that could sing Mozart")—hardly a major contemporary novelist has not had their turn in the stocks.

So is it true that, as stated by Alexander Waugh, Auberon's son and current chair of the prize committee, "sex in fiction simply doesn't work"? Each December, the magazine surveys that year's crop of novels, a task often given to the witty in-house reviewer Tom Fleming. As he says, "The difficult task of conveying the power of the orgasm on the printed page leads many a novel to be scuppered by metaphor-drenched, stream-of-consciousness accounts." But beyond the metaphors, novelists so engaged can fall into many kinds of overwriting—sentimentality combined with vulgarity, pretentious philosophizing, an abundance of abstract nouns, torrents of water imagery, overwhelming clinical detail, absurd similes, and glaringly purple prose. Some authors write as if bearing news about sex that no one had experienced before, rather than the opposite.

Surveying the entries for 2011, Sarah Lyall wrote in *The New York Times* how "the books' sexually active protagonists are compared, among other things, to wakening beasts, lightning rods, outrageous sea creatures and 'the midnight train.' They are panting fast and hard, and long and slow; they are sniffing, heaving, kneading, rubbing, pinching, flicking, biting, burrowing, darting, plunging, thrusting, bucking, shuddering, shivering, trembling, swelling and convulsing." Given this long litany of failure, one cannot help wondering why we are so determined to write about sex, to try and describe it when our attempts so often end in ridicule.

In March 2012 I spent an afternoon at the *Literary Review* going through their files. It was certainly an education. A penis is described as "a springy, mustard-pot surprise" (David Huggins), on other occasions as a "rosy, perky gherkin" (Isabel Allende), and "the cylinder rod of his plunger" (Catalan author Quim Monzo). Paul Theroux's is "a demon eel thrashing," while another finds itself "splashing about . . . as in a bottomless swamp of dead fish and yellow lilies in bloom" (the Hungarian Péter Nádas). In Kathy Lette's *To Love, Honour and Betray*, a lover's "erect member was so big I mistook it for some sort of monument in the centre of a town. I almost started directing traffic round it."*

An alarming number of novelists seem to have jettisoned any capacity for self-criticism. Here is Tama Janowitz, the much-vaunted author of *Peyton Amberg:* "When she and Victoria had done it, it had been like trying out some strange Japanese cuisine, something that

---

* One extract I particularly liked—for the magazine's comment about it—is from *The Final Testament of the Holy Bible*, by James Frey: "And he kept moving, real slow, and moving real deep inside, and it built until I saw it and felt it. It was love, and joy, and pleasure, and every part of my body sang some song I had never heard but was the prettiest, most beautiful song ever, and it was blinding and pure and my brain went the whitest white ever, and I saw infinity, forever and ever, I saw infinity, and even understood it, and understood everything else in the world, all the hate and rage and death and passion and jealousy and murder, and none of them even mattered, I felt one hundred per cent secure. I felt nothing bad. I saw the past and future."

Literary Review commented: "I think this is a description of an orgasm—but it could equally be severe concussion."

wriggled, still alive, in a dish. Or having to swallow the contents of a bearded mussel attached to a rock, while all the while one knew the tide was rapidly coming in." And the 2005 prizewinner, Giles Coren's novel *Winkler:* as the energetic heroine tried to grab her lover's member, "which was leaping around like a shower dropped in an empty bath, she scratched his back deeply with the nails of both hands and he shot three more times, in thick stripes on her chest. Like Zorro." Sex is often funny, but comic sex scenes can be ruined by such self-consciousness. Both Janowitz and Coren are successful and have been lauded for their sophisticated insights, but the need to write about sexual intimacy and the feeling that they have to do so in ever more novel ways seem to have left them blind to how their descriptions will appear to others.

As Julian Barnes noted in a 2013 talk, writers of sex scenes may suffer the anxiety that they may be giving themselves away—that readers may conclude that a particular sex act has happened to the author close to the manner described and believe that such fear may best be hidden in treating the subject humorously.

At the *Literary Review* award's annual event, celebrities grace a large party at the long-established In & Out Club in the centre of London. Double entendres flourish, and some novelists have deliberately included extravagant scenes, hoping to get shortlisted. Recent nominations include congress with a dog, a lobster, and a robot, and it can sometimes be unclear whether an author is being humorous or serious. This encounter from Tom Wolfe's 2012 novel *Back to Blood* is far from erotic, nor is it funny:

> BEAT thung BEAT thung BEAT thung THRUST hump THRUST hump THRUST hump hump humping BEHIND her HUMP thung THRUST the turgid crotch of his trunks in her buttocks RUT rut rut rut. . . .

Too many novelists write about sex in ways that would seem on the one hand unconvincing and doomed to failure and on the other off-puttingly cynical. William F. Buckley liked to recall a dinner with Vladimir Nabokov, who told him that he was smiling because he had polished off his "O.S.S." in that afternoon's writing session.

"What's an O.S.S.?" Buckley asked.

"The obligatory sex scene," explained the author of *Lolita.*

It's a depressing scenario: writers either put in a sex scene, however badly written, because they hope it will boost sales, or they write such scenes to the best of their abilities—and fall short. Small wonder that the Bibliothèque Nationale in Paris has a section reserved for erotic literature called "L'Enfer"—Hell.*

For her bestseller *Lace* (1982), which has sold more than three million copies in thirty-five countries, Shirley Conran, who felt herself not capable of writing well about sex, hired fellow-novelist Celia Brayfield to contribute twelve erotic scenes, two of which featured a goldfish and a diamond in unusual settings, paying her £500 for her work. Yet the book was originally conceived as a non-fiction sex manual, offering advice to teenage girls who wrote to Conran in her role as a newspaper columnist. Brayfield later published a number of bestselling novels of her own (*Pearls, White Ice, The Prince*), and also an excellent guide for fellow-novelists, *Bestseller,* in which there is a helpful section on writing about sex. On one issue, I disagree with her. "Most of what we have learned—consciously or unconsciously—about sex-

---

* When in the 1990s the biographer Richard Holmes was there researching some erotic letters that Théophile Gautier had written to his wife, the missives were delivered to him by clerks wearing protective red aprons and red rubber gloves. I wonder: do they still?

ual writing is of no use to us," she says. "In direct descriptive writing about sex, our inheritance from the past is only pornography and a tiny collection of erotic literature." In fact, past literature, looked at carefully, gives us plenty of insights on how to tackle the subject.

In the eighteenth century in Britain, its cities growing, its print culture spreading, and its explorers' encountering far-flung peoples with very different sexual mores, pornographic pamphlets and libertine clubs proliferated. Some 40 percent of British women were pregnant when they married. Attitudes were changing, not least due to a motley crew of journalists, courtesans, rakes, and philosophers who focused on sex and how people might read about it. By the 1750s, three great innovators, Samuel Richardson (1689–1761), Henry Fielding (1707–54), and Laurence Sterne (1713–68), were engaging the subject. And censorship, or the reticence of the times, proved to be both blight and opportunity.

Richardson's *Pamela; or, Virtue Rewarded* (1740) was the first to see publication, but despite a plot that focuses on the "near-rape" of its heroine, sexual feelings are never examined in any depth—so much so that a disgusted Fielding spoofed it in *Shamela*, a bawdy series of letters in which the supposedly chaste and innocent heroine exhibits her more spirited side.

Laurence Sterne was quick to follow. His *A Sentimental Journey* is full of female characters directly contrasting with the ultra-chaste Pamela. Neither novelist could afford to be specific,* but each had his

---

* An exception is *Memoirs of a Woman of Pleasure* (popularly known as *Fanny Hill*, the hill of the fanny being the *mons veneris*), an erotic novel by John Cleland published in 1748. Considered "the first original English prose pornography, and the first pornography to use the form of the novel," it is one of the most prosecuted and banned books in history, and Cleland spent the rest of his career trying to live it down, but it shows how at ease the eighteenth century was with describing sex, as opposed to the entanglements of later ages; and also that erotic writing should be about things that make people happy, not embarrassed or awkward. It also displayed a welcome humour about things sexual; when late on in the novel

own code words. Blushing, for example, is one of the most prominent sexually charged physical responses in Sterne. It had been seen
as a desirable trait in ladies of fashion, but here were women forth-
rightly linking their visible responses to sexual arousal. In *A Sentimental Journey*, for instance, when the novel's hero, Yorick, feels the pulse
of the lady from Brussels, he suggests that "if it is the same blood
which comes from the heart, which descends to the extremes . . . I
am sure you must have one of the best pulses of any woman in the
world." Sterne was an early teacher that there is more than one way
of being explicit.

Already, the novel—as its name proclaimed, the great new literary form—was producing its own vocabularies, its own stock of metaphors, about sex. Sterne's major work, *The Life and Opinions of
Tristram Shandy* (1759–67), is almost obsessed with "matters copula-
tive." Whiskers, noses, buttonholes, cocked hats, hobbyhorses, crev-
ices in the wall, slits in petticoats, green petticoats—all take on a
second role. There is no direct description or naming of parts: everything is double-meaning, innuendo, never more so than the moment
Tristram is actually conceived:

> "Pray, my Dear," quoth my mother, "have you not forgot to
> wind up the clock?" . . . "Good God!" cried my father. . . .
> "Did ever woman, since the creation of the world, interrupt
> a man with such a silly question?" Pray, what was your fa-
> ther saying? . . . Nothing.

From this exchange between Tristram and his imagined reader
we can conclude that his father may have been saying nothing but
was *doing* a great deal—specifically, begetting Tristram.

Fanny protests as a sailor/customer sodomizes her, he exclaims, "Pooh! My dear,
any port in a storm."

In terms of sexual symbolism, even Jane Austen would chance her arm. In *Mansfield Park*, a day trip to Sotherton Court predicts the ruin of Maria Bertram, Sir Thomas's eldest daughter, who is betrothed to the weak-chinned idiot James Rushworth. The young people stroll through the grounds of his big house, until they come to phallic iron railings and the wild countryside beyond. Maria and Henry Crawford, both flirting, want to climb over. Fanny Price cries out to Maria: "You will certainly hurt yourself against those spikes, you will tear your gown." She was rarely so suggestive. As Edith Wharton says: "Jane Austen's delicate genius flourished on the very edge of a tidal wave of prudery. Already Scott was averting his eyes from facts on which the maiden novelist in her rectory parlour had looked unperturbed; when Thackeray and Dickens rose in their might the chains were forged and the statues draped."* From 1750 till 1850 prudery and well-coded sexual suggestiveness ran parallel; by early Victorian times, novelists were increasingly restricted in what they could say.

These were the days when eroticism was transferred to objects and a contemporary book of etiquette advised that a lady should not sit on a seat still warm from a gentleman's "person." (It is a myth, though, that the legs of pianofortes had to be covered, lest they prove too suggestive.) Novelists had to find their own way to address sexual relations—even one so outwardly reserved as Charlotte Brontë. In *Jane Eyre* (1847) she relied on symbolism, so when Rochester and Jane are caught in a heavy storm, not only the weather mirrors Rochester's feelings: "I could scarcely see my master's face, near as I was. And what ailed the chestnut tree? It writhed and groaned; while wind roared in the laurel walk, and came sweeping over us." Later

---

* For several years in her teens Edith Wharton thought that "adultery" meant having to pay a higher rate for travel, having as a child seen a notice that read: ADULTS 50C; CHILDREN 25C.

Rochester covers Jane in kisses and three times visits her room, although they spend the night in separate apartments. "Before I left my bed in the morning, little Adèle came running in to tell me that the great horse-chestnut at the bottom of the orchard had been struck by lightning in the night, and half of it split away."

Brontë could hardly have suggested arousal and frustration more clearly, so it is little wonder that contemporaries denounced her novels as immoral. Conversely, her sister Emily's *Wuthering Heights* overflows with sexual imagery, but there is no suggestion that its star-crossed lovers ever get to grips with each other. An exasperated Charlotte called Heathcliff's feelings for Catherine Earnshaw "perverted passion and passionate perversity."

Attitudes were similarly conflicted across the Channel. When *Madame Bovary* was serialized in the *Revue de Paris* in 1856, the government brought an action against Flaubert and his publisher on the charge of immorality, but both were acquitted. Six years later, *Les Misérables* was published, but when hero and heroine head for the bedroom we read: "Here we pause. At the doorway of wedding nights stands an angel with her finger on her lips." We are allowed no further—although Victor Hugo was probably well aware of the "lips" double entendre.*

George Eliot was hardly a writer of bawdy farce or sexual frolicking, but she was determined to show the sexual lives of her characters. At a crucial moment in *Middlemarch* (1870), Will Ladislaw, in love with Dorothea, rises from his chair, his face and neck flushed with frustrated anger, a moment that one literary critic has judged "the closest the Victorian novel ever came to describing an erection."

---

* Many modern authors who dread dead spaces elsewhere in their novels likewise have stopped short at the bedroom door, as if that were somehow more considerate. As Anne Tyler admitted, "I would never be in bed with my characters; I try to show them respect." See Julian Barnes, "The Essay: Explaining the Explicit," BBC Radio 3, March 11, 2013.

If that seems a little subtle, in *The Mill on the Floss* (1860) Eliot included a passage that has an almost brazen openness:

> As Mrs. Tulliver uttered the last sentence, she drew a bright bunch of keys from her pocket, and singled out one, rubbing her thumb and finger up and down it with a placid smile while she looked at the clear fire. If Mr. Tulliver had been a susceptible man in his conjugal relation, he might have supposed that she drew out the key to aid her imagination in anticipating the moment when he would be in a state to justify the production of the best Holland sheets. . . .

Others followed in her tread. Throughout his writing life, Thomas Hardy was at odds with the guardians of propriety, and his first works, published anonymously, were thought to have been by George Eliot. His 1874 novel *Far from the Madding Crowd* had passages suppressed or changed by its editor Leslie Stephen, who wrote to his bewildered author that the seduction of a serving girl had to be treated in "a gingerly fashion," admitting that his cuts had been made through "an excessive prudery of which I am ashamed."

As a realist, Hardy felt deeply that art should describe and comment upon actual situations, yet he continued to suffer from bowdlerizing editors, and went on fighting until *Tess of the d'Urbervilles*. As with his other fictions—"novels of character and environment," he termed them—he offered the story first for serialization, fully expecting it to be rejected. *Murray's Magazine* and *Macmillan's* both turned it down for its "improper explicitness" and "rather too much succulence." Hardy promptly cut out or abridged some chapters, and the novel was accepted by *The Graphic*—a mock marriage being substituted for Tess's seduction. *The Graphic*, however, belying its name, refused to print the chapter describing the baptism of Tess's baby and also objected to the description of Angel Clare carrying in his

arms, across a flooded lane, Tess and her three dairymaid companions. The magazine's editor suggested that it would be more deco-
rous if the women were taken across in a wheelbarrow, and so it
came to pass—a possibly far more erotic description. Only one
reader complained of the serialized story—a gentleman with a family of daughters who thought mention of a bloodstained ceiling was
indecent; Hardy could never understand why. Meanwhile the two
major excisions were published in other magazines, anonymously.

When Tess's story appeared in volume form, complete and un-
abridged, it quickly swept through Europe in translation—German,
French, Dutch, Italian, and Russian. During its year-long serialization in a Moscow monthly, one of its keenest readers was Tolstoy.
Tess marked "a distinct epoch in English fiction," wrote one reviewer.
But the revolution in sexual descriptions had to wait a decade or two
yet.[*]

At last came the earthquake. Just as World War I broke out, James
Joyce began writing *Ulysses*. Dirty work, said the world: a tale filled
with masturbation, defecation, and sexual fantasy. The book was
outlawed in the United States. The final chapter's forty-five-page or-
gasmic monologue by Molly Bloom may seem tame now but remains
erotic, funny, and entirely in character. George Orwell leaped to its
defence in his essay "Inside the Whale":

---

[*] Tess complains to her parents that they failed to warn her of the dangers an
unchaperoned young girl might meet: "Why didn't you tell me there was danger?
Why didn't you warn me? Ladies know what to guard against, because they read
novels that tell them of these tricks. . . ." These are the very words that Christian
Grey, the anti-hero of *Fifty Shades of Grey*, inscribes in a first edition of *Tess* that he
gives to the slave-object of his affections, Anastasia—whose undergraduate thesis
is a critique of Hardy's novel. As Tim Parks has noted, *Fifty Shades of Grey* (90
million copies sold worldwide in the first two and a half years) "is resolutely conservative: transgression is explored and enjoyed not to call moral or social codes
into question but to reinforce them." Tim Parks, "Why So Popular," *The New York
Review of Books*, February 7, 2013, p. 12.

Here is a whole world of stuff which you supposed to be of
its nature incommunicable, and somebody has managed to
communicate it. . . . When you read certain passages in
Ulysses you feel that Joyce's mind and your mind are one,
that he knows all about you though he has never heard your
name.*

At the same time that Joyce was producing his masterpiece, D. H.
Lawrence (1885–1930) was fomenting his own revolution. Many
thought his work obscene too—immoral, depraved, "the dirty handkerchief side of life." What was original about his writing was his
obsession with the importance of sex, of one person touching another, of physical intimacy: he aimed to restore emphasis on the
body, offsetting it against what he saw as Western civilization's over-
emphasis on the mind.

Sons and Lovers appeared in 1913 without troubling the censors.
Had it been printed as its author originally intended, the manuscript
would have been about five hundred pages, a commercial non-
starter. His original publisher, Heinemann, rejected it as unstruc-
tured and too outspoken, so Lawrence rewrote it and sent it off to his
friend Edward Garnett, a reader for the rival firm of Duckworth,

---

* Joyce is often coupled with Henry Miller (1891–1980), in that both were prosecuted for obscenity. But Miller himself described his writing as straight autobiography, and as Orwell says of Miller's *Tropic of Cancer* in "Inside the Whale,"
"*Ulysses* is not only a vastly better book, but also quite different in intention."
Miller is a reporter who mixes observation with fantasy and shares with Joyce—to
quote Orwell again—"a willingness to mention the inane, squalid facts of everyday life. Joyce is an artist in a sense in which Miller is not and probably would not
wish to be. . . . Miller is simply a hard-boiled person talking about life." He was a
literary innovator who helped free the discussion of sex from legal and social re-
strictions; otherwise he is not much help to us—not least because, as Terry Eagleton tellingly notes, "Pornography finds it hard to tell a story. Sex is too repetitive
a business for that." Terry Eagleton, "Grub Street Snob," *London Review of Books*,
September 13, 2012, p. 28.

who censored some passages and cut others until the manuscript was almost a hundred pages shorter. Lawrence was miserable but penniless and in no position to resist.

What is interesting is what was cut, and why. In the original, when Paul Morel, the book's protagonist, and his girlfriend Clara frolic on the Lincolnshire seashore he kisses "the two white, glistening globes she cradled." After Garnett had edited the passage, Paul is simply kissing "her." Garnett also trimmed a later reference, where Paul holds one of Clara's breasts in each hand "like big fruits in their cups." When Paul starts his second affair, with Miriam, and sees her naked for the first time, he reflects: "She had the most beautiful hips he had ever imagined." Garnett, possibly thinking that hips were an odd item for Paul to focus on and a likely euphemism, changed "hips" to "body." He was doing his author good service, and Lawrence was even grateful in the end—the book is dedicated to Garnett.

The trouble is that, for all Lawrence's moral earnestness, his sexual descriptions can come across as didactic, over-emphatic, emotionally raw, and sometimes unintentionally comic. He was uneven. Cutting away at such passages isn't always the answer—editors can be wrong. Even so, one wishes other novelists of Lawrence's time had been half as courageous—echoing perhaps Lytton Strachey's comment about Virginia Woolf: "It is really most unfortunate that she rules out copulation."

Lawrence was to become more explicit in future novels, with predictable results. In 1915 *The Rainbow* was banned in the U.K. and remained so for eleven years. Five years later, its sequel *Women in Love* caused even greater outrage. A typical review read: "I do not claim to be a literary critic, but I know dirt when I smell it, and here is dirt in heaps—festering, putrid heaps which smell to high Heaven." But it was Lawrence's last major novel, *Lady Chatterley's Lover*, which brought him the notoriety that still clings to his name—his story of how an aristocratic woman of twenty-seven, Constance, Lady Chatterley, finds sexual happiness in the arms of her husband's gamekeeper.

First published privately in Florence and Paris in 1928, the book was reprinted in 1960 in Britain by Penguin, which was immediately prosecuted under the Obscene Publications Act 1959. The trial became a major public event. Under the act, publishers could escape conviction if they could show that a work was of literary merit. The jury came down on Lawrence's side, and Penguin immediately published an unexpurgated edition—and found they had a bestseller on their hands.

One objection to the novel was the frequent use of the words *fuck* and *cunt*. At the front of the first unexpurgated American edition, Grove Press had printed an encomium from the well-known establishment figure Archibald MacLeish. What had been excluded in the censored copies of the novel, he wrote, "is any passage which contains one of the old, familiar, four-letter Anglo-Saxon words which we all know but which the hypocrisy of censorship pretends we do not, or any passage which describes the common-place facts of sexual intercourse, or any passage which attempts to penetrate the mystery of human love which, as Yeats unanswerably puts it, has 'raised its mansion in/The place of excrement.'"

In an essay, "A Propos of Lady Chatterley's Lover," Lawrence had written that his aim was "to make the sex relation valid and precious, not shameful," and sex, he said, "means the whole of the relationship between man and woman." It's an important theme for a novel whose original title was "Tenderness," and much of the writing is highly effective:

> With a queer obedience, she lay down on the blanket. Then
> she felt the soft, groping, helplessly desirous hand touching
> her body, feeling for her face. The hand stroked her face

softly, softly, with infinite soothing and assurance, and at last there was the soft touch of a kiss on her cheek.

She lay quite still, in a sort of sleep, in a sort of dream. Then she quivered as she felt his hand groping softly, yet with a queer thwarted clumsiness among her clothing. Yet the hand knew, too, how to unclothe her where it wanted. He drew down the thin silk sheath, slowly, carefully, right down and over her feet. Then with a quiver of exquisite pleasure he touched the warm soft body, and touched her navel for a moment in a kiss. And he had to come in to her at once, to enter the peace on earth of her soft, quiescent body. It was the moment of pure peace for him, the entry into the body of a woman.

Lawrence was didactic, sure, and one has to be patient reading him, but his writing can take one's breath away.

In a charming memoir of a lifetime collecting books, the French bibliophile Jacques Bonnet suggests why we should still bother to write or read about sex. Libido is what moves literature, and for many people their first sexual experience is from the pages of a book. "It is very rare," Bonnet writes, "for a novel to contain no love story at all. . . . They [the characters] also have sex lives. The narrative approach of an author to this subject will vary with style and temperament . . . from complete silence to precise indeed anatomical detail, the variations are infinite."

And yet . . . how far do you go with the naming of parts, which parts do you name, what words do you give them? Where between the Latinate and the Anglo-Saxon does one settle? Elizabeth Benedict, an American novelist on the faculty of Princeton University's creative writing programme, has written an entire handbook, *The Joy* *of Writing Sex.* "A sex scene," she says, "is not a sexual manual for beginners," adding that the writer must "make it essential to the story or understanding of the characters." Elsewhere she points out, "You can't do that if you lapse into an all-purpose, porn-inspired vocabulary."* Certainly one should avoid words that better suit a hospital or doctor's examination room—*penis, testicles, vagina.* But a self-conscious "grand" vocabulary is also a turn-off.

One important truth is that desire is much sexier than the actual climactic moment—what Lawrence called, in his 1920s way, the "crisis." Take this scene from Marcel Proust's *Remembrance of Things Past,* whose narrator is full of longing for his lost lover, Albertine, who used to go bathing in the Loire early each morning, accompanied by a young laundress and her friends. Another of the party is relating what happens:

> Seeing Mlle. Albertine was always wiggling against her in her wrapper she made her take it off and used to caress her with her tongue along the throat and arms, even on the soles of her feet which Mlle. Albertine stretched out to her. The laundress undressed too, and they played at pushing each other into the water; after that she told me nothing more, but being entirely at your orders and ready to do anything in the world to please you, I took the young laundress to bed with me. She asked me if I would like her to do

---

* The Internet has a twelve-point checklist by the novelist Steve Almond. "Step 9: It takes a long time to make a woman come. . . . Please don't try to sell us on the notion that a man can enter a woman, elicit a shuddering moan or two, and bring her off. . . . Rarely . . . do men and women announce their orgasms. They simply have them. Their bodies are taken up by sensation and heaved about in various ways. Describe the heaving." Another point runs: Real people do not talk in pornographic clichés. Most of the time, they say all kinds of weird things during sex, such as, "I think I'm losing circulation" or "I've got a cramp in my foot" or "Did you come already?"

to me what she used to do to Mlle. Albertine when she took off her bathing-dress. And she said to me: "If you could have seen how she used to quiver, that young lady, she said to me (oh, it's just heavenly) and she got so excited that she could not keep from biting me." I could still see the marks on the girl's arms.

In *Pale Fire*, Nabokov would deride the creation of Albertine as an "improbable *jeune fille*" with a "pasted-on bosom," but the characterization is unfair: this is erotic, very moving in the context of the novel, and far removed from the detailed explicitness of most sex writing.*

More recently, here is Philip Roth in his early novella *Goodbye, Columbus*. His hero has spent chapters dreaming about his girlfriend, then they go out swimming: "She caught the bottom of her [bathing] suit between thumb and index finger and flicked what flesh had been showing back where it belonged. My blood jumped." As does ours. Back in the 1970s, Roth taught creative writing at the University of Pennsylvania, and one of his seminars was on "The Literature of Desire." The students packed in, hoping to hear him discuss sex scenes in detail. What they got was an analysis of the novels of Kafka, Flaubert, Musil, Kundera, Mishima, Bellow, and Malamud, and Roth delighting in the subtle eroticism of such passages as this,

---

* I am aware that nearly all my examples have been of heterosexual sex. There are excellent examples of homosexual and lesbian sex scenes, from Colette, who wrote about both lesbian and heterosexual love, through James Baldwin's *Giovanni's Room* and Alan Hollinghurst's five novels to the early trilogy and latest novel by Edmund White, *Jack Holmes and His Friend,* and Sarah Waters's *Fingersmith* (2002; shortlisted for the Booker and Orange prizes) or *Tipping the Velvet* (1998), both set in 1890s London: the latter title is Victorian slang for cunnilingus. Other contemporary women novelists who have written powerfully about sex (heterosexual, mainly) are Nell Zink (*The Wallcreeper*), Eimear McBride (*A Girl Is a Half-Formed Thing*), and, spectacularly well, Elena Ferrante.

from *Madame Bovary:* "She was just eating a maraschino ice that she held with her left hand in a silver-gilt cup, her eyes half closed, and the spoon between her teeth." The more his students studied the sentence, recalled one of them in the pages of *The New York Times,* the sexier it got.

In 2010, in a talk at the Cheltenham Literary Festival, Martin Amis declared that writing well about sex was "impossible" and that "very few writers have got anywhere" with the subject. He went on: "My father used to say that you can refer to it but you can't describe it. It's inherent in the subject. It's not that someone's going to hit upon the right way. It's that there *is* no right way. I have said that there are no 'No Entry' signs in fiction . . . but there sort of is around sex."

One can sympathize with Amis (despite his attempt to solve the

Sidonie-Gabrielle Colette (1873–1954), the French writer and performer (Picture Post/Felix Mann and Kurt Hutton).

vocabulary problem by once having a character speak of having "Mailered" a woman) but not surrender the argument. In October 2013, *The New York Times Book Review* posted a special feature titled "The Naughty Bits" in which various authors were asked why writing about sex was so difficult, and what they thought made a good sex scene. Nicholson Baker contributed the idiosyncratic phrase "thwartedness, surprise, innocence and hair." Another author, Sheila Heti, made the perhaps obvious but important point that "an interesting sex scene is about the character in that situation, so it's impossible to think of a compelling sex scene appearing in a book in which sex or sexuality doesn't somehow operate throughout. You can't write sex well if you don't think sex is a significant part of life."

There were interesting suggestions for successful attempts, such as Chekhov's story "The Kiss" and even Mrs. Dalloway's love for Sally Seton, but the best overall contribution was from Edmund White. He liked to write sex scenes, he said, "because they strike me as among life's peak experiences, along with dying and death, one's first 'Ring' cycle and a first gondola ride through Venice." But, he warned,

> Don't confine the sexiness to sex scenes. Tolstoy's Anna has her wide hips and gliding step; Vronsky has his thick neck. We can never forget their bodies, nor what an exciting couple they must make. Colette is the great poet of the body and the erotic gesture, and she never screens out all the mixed signals lovers send each other. Sex is the brightest thread in the thick, strangely cut fabric of our lives; we can never know what it means, but we're always sure we're certain.

If one looks for a novelist to emulate, my choice falls on someone who writes as well about sex as he often writes badly about it: John Updike.

In 2008, after his fourth consecutive nomination for the *Literary Review* bad sex prize, he won a Lifetime Achievement Award (he chose not to be there to receive it), then the next year, with a memorable scene of oral sex in *The Widows of Eastwick*, was shortlisted yet again. By this time Updike had acquired an unenviable reputation. Philip Roth (a friend before they fell out over a review Updike wrote about a memoir by Roth's former wife Claire Bloom) later scorned *Couples* as "another genitalic novel." Allan Gurganus had complained of his "herniating conscientiousness . . . [and] excess zeal at detailing each wet texture, every scent. . . . Here is a fellow in his study, exercising a satyr's drives through an angel's vocabulary." In a legendary takedown of Updike in 1997, David Foster Wallace cited a friend of his, likely a female one, who called the author "just a penis with a thesaurus."

One can see why. In *Gertrude and Claudius* (2000), the woman of the title "would have lain down in warm mud for him, even the mud of the pigsty, to enter the exaltation she found in his brute love." In *Villages* (2004), an adulterer appraises his lover's vagina: "[It] did not feel like Phyllis's. Smoother, somehow simpler, its wetness less thick, less of a sauce, more of a glaze." And, following a bout of oral sex, the heroine of *Seek My Face* (2002) displays the result "on her arched tongue like a little Tachiste masterpiece"—tachist being a method of action painting in which the pigment is splashed or dribbled upon the canvas in apparently random pattern (Updike had studied art for a year, at Oxford). His defence? "Description is a form of love." Biographer Adam Begley sums up: "Updike's literary reputation had been permanently skewed. The luscious prurience of the sex scenes made the author's name a byword for 'cerebral raunch.'"

Yet when he is good, the effect is completely different. *Kirkus Reviews*, the trade magazine of pre-publication reviews, judged that, for all its own criticisms of Updike, he composed sex scenes "better than almost anybody else now writing." Roth called him the only American writer who ever approached the guiltless sensuality of Colette, and "a great writer of the erotic." In his early (1960) novel *Rabbit, Run*, Updike takes great care over his vocabulary: the word *orgasm* never appears, while *climax* figures once, and references to body parts are minimal. Updike's biographer Adam Begley comments:

> My guess is that Updike avoids more clinical terms not for propriety's sake, or even for aesthetic reasons, but because a vague "it" does more to suggest transcendence. . . . When, for example, Rabbit insists that Ruth be entirely naked before they make love, Updike concentrates on the effect of Ruth's bare skin on Rabbit's aroused sensibility without naming any more of the exposed body parts than strictly necessary.

"Desire is sad," wrote Somerset Maugham in his story "Rain," and that is something too that Updike understands. I quote the following short extract from *Couples* for its psychological insight, descriptive power, and, indeed, erotic content—without any of the over-ripe metaphors of his post-2000 writing. Here is sex in all its complexity, depth, and pain:

> Though he had skated patiently waiting for her skin to quicken from beneath she had finally despaired of having a climax and asked him simply to take her and be done. Released, she had turned away, and in looping his arm around her chest his fingers brushed an unexpected sad solidity.
> *Angel, your nipples are hard.*
> *So?*
> *You're excited and could have come too.*
> *I don't think so. It just means I'm chilly.*
> *Let me make you come. With my mouth.*

No. I'm all wet down there.

But it's me, it's my wetness.

I want to go to sleep.

But it's so sad, that you liked my making love to you after all.

I don't see that it's that sad.

Just because one can write sex well doesn't mean the characters involved are likeable or sympathetic: I hope I have quoted enough to show how effectively this scene works on the page. *Couples* was published in 1968, a mid-career novel that went on to sell several million copies in hardback. Updike always protested that the book was "not about sex as such: it's about sex as the emergent religion." It was "the only thing left," and in such circumstances adultery becomes the modern equivalent of romantic adventure and spiritual aspiration. He protests too much; but the twenty-three novels he wrote range from the worst sex writing to some of the best.

To my mind, writing well about sex is a fine ambition but difficult to carry off successfully. Try, but be ready to junk the pages. As further inspiration, read *The Song of Songs*, the long erotic poem in the Old Testament that has been described as the single most instructive example of how to write effectively about physical love. And after that, perhaps, John Donne's elegy "To His Mistress Going to Bed":

> Now off with those shoes: and then safely tread
> In this love's hallow'd temple, this soft bed. . . .
> By this these Angels from an evil sprite,
> Those set our hairs, but these our flesh upright.
> Licence my roving hands, and let them go
> Before, behind, between, above, below.
> O, my America! my new-found-land,

My kingdom, safeliest when with one man mann'd. . . .
To enter in these bonds, is to be free;
Then where my hand is set, my seal shall be.
Full nakedness! All joys are due to thee.

The poem was refused a publication licence in 1633 (two years after Donne's death) but was included in an anthology twenty-one years later. Just think what a Donne novel might have been like.

With all this knowledge of Mr. E.
& ... authority to ... it,
more ... Lead'd late. Build ... — her
mind deeply busy in revolving what she
had heard, feeling, thinking, recalling
& foreseeing everything, shocked ...
... Elliot, sighing over future, ... long
... pained for Lady Russell. ...
...
...
...
...
... Lady Russell ... confidence
had been entire. — ... The Embarrass
ment which must be felt from their
... in his presence! — How to be:
have to him. — how to get rid of him —
what to do by any of the party at
home? — where to be blind? where
to be active? — It was altogether a
confusion of images & doubts — a
perplexity, an agitating ... which
she could not see the end of. ...
And she was in Gay St. & still so
far engrossed, ... that she started ...
addressed by Adml. Croft, as if a
person unlikely to be met there

Jane Austen's draft of the first page of Chapter 10 of *Persuasion*.

Vision and Re-vision
(Part 1)

If it sounds like writing, I rewrite it.

ELMORE LEONARD

The wastepaper basket is the author's best friend.

ISAAC BASHEVIS SINGER

In my hands is a slim volume with faded grey covers, which I spotted by chance on the shelves of the New York Society Library. Published by the Oxford University Press in 1926, the book consists of the final two chapters of the original version of *Persuasion*, some forty pages, together with sixteen leaves of notes that gloss the differences between these early versions and the edition published in 1818, a year after Jane Austen had died. It is the only surviving draft for any of her work, and expands eleven pages to thirty-five, virtually all the extra lines extending the period of suspense between Anne's leaving Mrs. Smith, where she learns of Mr. Elliot's past, and her renewing her vows with Captain Wentworth.

Myriad smaller variants occur in every paragraph. It looks as if the 1926 book once included several facsimiles of Austen's handwritten pages, the only pieces of manuscript from her finished novels to survive (they lie in state in the British Library), but most have been torn out, and just one remains. The script is neat, tilting to the right, but words and lines that displeased her have been scored through, almost violently, with her black pen.

Writing of Mr. Elliot and Mrs. Clay, Austen conjectures, "It is now a doubtful point whether his cunning or hers may finally carry the day," where originally she had *finesse* instead of *cunning*. When Anne finds herself alone with Admiral Croft and learns that Captain Wentworth is about to appear, Austen's first draft had her walk out of the room "not with determined spirit." This she altered to "did not with a more passive determination walk quietly out of the room"—a small change, but effective.

When the moment arrives where Anne and Wentworth are alone, he talks—in the draft—in "the voice of a Man who would speak whether he could or no"; in the revised version, he speaks "in a voice of effort and constraint." (One of the remarkable aspects of the novel is that the primary obstacle to any happy ending is Wentworth's obstinate refusal to give any indication that he is in love with Anne.) The long explanation for his conduct that Wentworth offers Anne in their crucial meeting is, in the drafted chapter, all in indirect speech— far less forceful than the direct speech of the final version.

This is an important revision in itself, but the book shows that in their overall conception these chapters were radically different from what finally appeared in print. Here, Anne is invited by Admiral Croft to stop off at his cottage, where he has with compassion aforethought also asked Wentworth. The two estranged lovers then set about explaining themselves in splendid isolation. After so much misunderstanding, their words are moving but presented in a straightforward way, lacking much drama.

In just three weeks of intense composition, Austen undertook a major rewrite. In the revised chapters 22 and 23, Anne and Wentworth find themselves in a room so crowded with people that they have no privacy. Wentworth seats himself at a desk to compose a letter while Anne talks to Captain Harville about how differently men and women show their love. As Claire Tomalin notes in her sympathetic biography of Austen, "The last two chapters, as she revised them, are so dramatically crafted that they remain, even after many readings, almost unbearably tense and moving, as the lovers, unable to speak directly to one another, communicate by other means. Wentworth drops his pen, and pretends to be writing another letter when really he is writing to Anne. Every word she says to Harville is intended for Wentworth."

In her own short biography of Austen, fellow novelist Carol Shields added her appreciation: "The scene becomes a ballet of glances given and received, of understandings reached not directly but through a look, a gesture, and the unspoken subtext of all that has been said aloud. These two lovers are not shown in an unreal isolation as in the original ending, but are clearly part of the moving, bustling world, two people sending their connecting glances across a crowded drawing room."

In all, it is one of the most effective revisions in literature.

Most writers know that first drafts need further work, but the way they make their revisions varies enormously. Flaubert, a fanatical reviser, proclaimed that a would-be author should read fifteen hundred books in order to write one. "Prose is like hair," he would say, "it

improves with combing." Edith Wharton told a friend enthusiasti-
cally, "I am engaged in the wholesale slaughter of adjectives." "I revise every minute of every day," wrote Virginia Woolf. Raymond
Chandler advised, "Throw up into your typewriter every morning.
Clean up every noon." Arundhati Roy, winner of the Booker Prize,
has called the process "sandpapering," Graham Greene "doing the
fingernails." "I like writing after breakfast," Greene explained, "and
revising after a good dinner, when I have Dutch courage." Jane Austen's novels nearly all began as broad farces before she refined them,
and there are hundreds of examples of how a lumpen first attempt
was turned to burnished gold.

Sometimes the effort taken sounds obsessive. Gray's *Elegy* is 128
lines long: he spent seven years writing it. Horace dictated that a
writer should set aside a finished poem for nine years and only then
decide whether it was worth publishing. Virgil worked on the *Aeneid*
for ten years (a rate of *at most* three or four lines a day) and nearing
death declared that his epic account was not as he truly wanted it
and should be destroyed. Kafka burned 90 percent of his work, but
the day before he died he could not stop doing a last round of edits
on "The Hunger Artist." When Mann came to revise *The Magic
Mountain,* he rewrote the entire manuscript on higher-quality paper,
believing that the sheer act of copying—during which he would
make his revisions—was the best way to control his material.

Tolstoy went through nine versions of *The Kreutzer Sonata.* At least
that is only a novella—his wife copied out *War and Peace* seven times,
from beginning to end, while the great man himself would write
draft after draft (more than a dozen for one section of the book).*

---

* Much time and effort went into paring down his text to eliminate the intrusion
of his authorial voice. He would redefine and reclassify his cast, combine the
characteristics of two or more character-types into one, rewrite their speeches,
and add full-bodied characterizations, then often discard it all. Ultimately, the
protagonists developed enough literary substance of their own. Just how he re-

Balzac liked to begin at midnight and work for eighteen hours at a stretch, with results that led to the despair of his printers:

> Lines were drawn from the beginning, the middle, and the end of each sentence towards the margins of the paper; each line leading to an interpolation, a development, an added epithet or an adverb. At the end of several hours the sheet of paper looked like a plan of fireworks, and later on the confusion was further complicated by signs of all sorts crossing the lines, while scraps of paper were pinned or stuck with sealing-wax to the margin.

There is no one way to set about either writing or rewriting: Disraeli dressed in evening clothes when composing his novels, John Cheever in just boxer shorts. Thomas De Quincey wrote in a room until it was so full of papers and books that there was no room for him, at which point he locked it up and got another. Friedrich Schiller kept a drawer full of rotting apples in his desk, saying that he needed their decaying smell to help him write. Henrik Ibsen had one of the strangest working habits of all, placing a picture of August Strindberg over his desk as inspiration. "He is my mortal enemy," Ibsen explained, "and shall hang there and watch while I write." Philip Roth, who like Hemingway and the young Nabokov composed standing up, would send finished manuscripts to friends, then record their reactions on tape, a remarkable show of self-confidence.

The great humorist and founding member of the Goons Spike Milligan had his own distinctive methods:

---

vised the book is examined in Kathryn B. Feuer, *Tolstoy and the Genesis of "War and Peace"* (Ithaca, N.Y.: Cornell University Press, 1996).

Once he had started work on a script he disliked ever having to stop; he wrote as he thought, and if he came to a place where the right line failed to emerge, he would just jab a finger at one of the keys, type "FUCK IT" or "BOLLOCKS," then carry on regardless. The first draft would feature plenty of such expletives, but then, with each successive version, the expletives grew fewer and fewer, until by about the tenth draft, he had a complete, expletive-free script.

Mark Twain had a variation on this routine: "Substitute 'damn' every time you're inclined to write 'very;' your editor will delete it and the writing will be just as it should be." Frequent expletives may have come naturally to Milligan, whose formative days were spent in the British army in the Second World War. (He was used to filling in and making do: as part of a gun crew, he would join the others shouting "bang!" in unison during training, as they had no shells with which to practice.)

Henry James was a reviser of a different order and a decidedly different style. He wrote his masterpiece *Portrait of a Lady* when he was thirty-seven, in 1881, composing extremely quickly. In 1906, he rewrote it, and the revisions all go one skin deeper. For instance, in an attempt to make the patois of Henrietta Stackpole more convincing, he changes the wording of a declaration she makes to Isabel, "I am going to marry Mr. Bantling and I am going to reside in London," to the more awkwardly un-English-sounding, "and locate right here in London." The revised version sounds not only estranged from British English but also more defiant. *Bang!*

Some authors revise with a ferocious enthusiasm. Diana Athill, for years John Updike's editor, has recalled how, in his early days, he allowed himself to be "carried away by his own virtuosity":

A glass was broken, I think by a wife in her kitchen, and this was heard by her husband in the next room, and the description of the sound went on for several lines. Examined carefully, that description was an amazingly accurate analysis of the sounds produced by a breaking glass, but it made you stop and think, "What a clever piece of writing," not "Ouch! She has dropped a glass": a useful object lesson about overdoing it for fellow perfectionists.

In French, this is described as too *voulu*, meaning "willed," a too calculated or self-conscious effect, something that has the air of being overcrafted. Writing well is a matter of getting the balance right— between getting the ideal word or phrase and working the text too hard so that it appears self-conscious or laboured; between saying enough for the reader to understand and saying not too much; making sure the reader attends to the song, not the singer.

So much of revision is small changes and knowing when and what to omit. Hemingway once wryly observed that half of what he wrote he left out. Anton Chekhov, besieged by writers wanting his opinion on their work, would advise them all, "Cut, cut, cut!" "Writing a book is like building a coral reef," P. G. Wodehouse considered. "One goes on adding tiny bits. I must say the result is much better. With my stuff it is largely a matter of adding colour and seeing that I don't let anything through that's at all flat."

Norman Mailer was so delighted by one small edit he made that he recorded it in *The Spooky Art* as an example of good revision. The book was *The Deer Park* (1955), and originally he had written:

"They make Sugar sound so good in the newspapers," she declared one night to some people in a bar, "that I'll really try him. I really will, Sugar." And she gave me a sisterly kiss.

Mailer changed "declared" to "said" and later added "older sister," so that the passage now read: "And she gave me a sisterly kiss. Older sister." He felt very pleased with himself:

> Just two words, but I felt as if I had revealed some divine
> law of nature, had laid down an invaluable clue—the kiss
> of an older sister was a worldly universe away from the kiss
> of a younger sister—and I thought to give myself the Nobel
> Prize for having brought such illumination and *division* to
> the cliché of the sisterly kiss.

Yet Mailer's attention to detail varied. He told Diana Athill (his editor too) what a release it had been when suddenly, having worked himself into a lather over the choice between two words, it occurred to him that no one would notice, so he could just speed on. But people *do* notice, or at least the best readers.

According to neuropsychiatry, writing and editing employ different brain functions, and many writers are unable to switch easily from one to the other, so it is well to find out early whether one is good at editing one's own work. Chekhov wrote: "Dissatisfaction with oneself is one of the cornerstones of every real talent." Maybe, but it can also be destructive. Cyril Connolly ruined his creative output because he was so critical of his own writing (on his death, four unpublished novels were found in his apartment); Balzac over-revised himself into an early grave. When William Carlos Williams was preparing his last book for the press, he grew so anguished by his perceived shortcomings that, according to his biographer, he "tore the manuscript to pieces and dumped them in the trash." His wife fished out the fragments and posted them off to his publisher, "who put them together like a jigsaw puzzle."

It is one thing to see for yourself (or not see) what is wrong and another to accept the views of someone else. Nabokov called editors "pompous avuncular brutes." Asked to shorten his first novel, *Buddenbrooks*, Thomas Mann protested that its length was "its essential characteristic, not to be laid hands on lightly." In 1856, Trollope, after receiving an advance of £100 (worth two hundred times that in today's currency) for *Barchester Towers*, a "most welcome increase in my income," was appalled when he was asked to shorten the book: "how two words out of six are to be withdrawn from a written novel, I cannot conceive." George Bernard Shaw was even fiercer. In a letter to *The Times*, he wrote:

> There is a busybody on your staff who devotes a lot of his time to chasing split infinitives. Every good literary craftsman splits his infinitives when the sense demands it. I call for the immediate dismissal of this pedant. It is of no consequence whether he decides to go quickly or quickly to go or to quickly go. The important thing is that he should go at once.

Shaw was one of a number of authors who abhorred being edited by other people. It is not necessarily arrogance or even self-belief, but the wish to be, like Shakespeare and his sonnets, the "onlie begetter," who can get things right without help from outside. In my experience, few writers *like* to be edited. I recall working with the Scottish writer William McIlvanney on his novel *The Papers of Tony Veitch* and tentatively suggesting that certain passages be toned down (to my eye, some metaphors were not just purple but the deepest mulberry). McIlvanney was furious and insisted that I be removed as his editor. I was sad about this, as he was otherwise a charming man and a good writer. Come publication, in 1983, while reviews made the same points I had, the book went on to win the Crime Writers' Silver Dagger Award. One-all, perhaps.

Tact can be a great lubricant. Kurt Vonnegut, asked to work on a friend's book, sent him ten suggestions but told him to do only those things that "rang a bell," and not take any action just because he had suggested it. That is the perfect advice, although it doesn't always succeed. Vonnegut made his views plain, but while not exactly coating them in honey he allowed room for his friend to make up his own mind and, importantly, stay in charge of his own creation.

If one judges that the author can take it, telling the truth is always best. Such an approach was taken by Evelyn Waugh with his great letter-writing pal Nancy Mitford, who had complained to him about the revision process: "There are corrections on every page of the typescript & I have done the original MS over & over again—I rewrote the whole thing twice." Waugh replied tersely: "Now none of this. . . . Revision is just as important as any other part of writing and must be done con amore." I do like that "con amore." But many writers revise with a heavy heart.

Some authors pretend never to revise but then one learns that an outside voice has been crucial. When Joyce Johnson told her lover Jack Kerouac that she had embarked on a novel, he grimaced. "He asked me if I rewrote a lot and said you should never revise, never change anything, not even a word." This duly gave rise to the myth that Kerouac wrote *On the Road* by feeding a single 120-foot-long roll of thin drawing paper into his typewriter until three weeks later he had finished, not changing a word. According to the legend, he wanted a non-stop, unpaginated flow appropriate to his convictions about spontaneous composition and to the narrative itself. But far from never revising, Kerouac spent years on improvements and new drafts. He just thought it uncool to own up to it.

The critic Thomas Powers has described what really happened:

It took him five years to find a publisher, who then insisted on some basic editorial work: on breaking up the river of words into sentences, paragraphs and chapters, without which the book is easy to put down; and then, more important, told him that the tangle of back-and-forth road trips made no sense. Kerouac might have refused but did not. He listened to his editor, compressed the many journeys into a few, each with its own purpose and consequence, and thereby gave the book its structure of quest.

Even *that* was after Kerouac had received, in 1950, a sixteen-thousand-word letter from his great friend and muse Neal Cassady (model for the character Dean Moriarty). As a result, he tossed his earlier efforts and rewrote the entire novel in the stream-of-consciousness, "creative non-fiction" style that he then sent off to publishers. (It was on the next draft that he hand-wrote two crucial further changes: "On the Road" instead of "The Beat Generation" and "Jack" Kerouac instead of "John.") Kerouac had begun writing on April 2, 1951; on September 5, 1957, *The New York Times* at last hailed the work as "an historic occasion."

Kerouac loved to pontificate. Powers notes that Kerouac "divided American writers between the taker-outers and the putter-inners." In the first group he placed Scott Fitzgerald and Henry James, "who wrote and rewrote to render a book down to a polished gem." The second group included Whitman and Wolfe, who "reached out to embrace the whole impossible landscape of American experience to make a mighty book like the Mississippi river in flood." Kerouac believed himself to be firmly in the second category.

Again, as to Wolfe, the truth is different. Maxwell Perkins, the editor who oversaw the works of Hemingway, Fitzgerald, and Wolfe and who was famous for leaving more on the editing-room floor than ever saw print, wrote in strenuous defence of his profession to another of his authors who had said that Wolfe was complaining that his work was being sabotaged by heavy-handed editing:

Nothing was ever taken from Tom's writings without his full consent. When he could go no further with *Of Time and the River* [finally published in 1935], he brought it to me and asked me to help him, and I did it with very great reluctance and anxiety. Tom *demanded* help. He *had* to have it.

Wolfe was obviously something of a nightmare when it came to revising. He himself admitted that, "my efforts to cut out 50,000 words may sometimes result in my adding 75,000." But Perkins was self-knowing enough to recognize that he was the plain man addressing the unplain man, the carpenter advising the architect. Early in their relationship, Wolfe had told Perkins: "The business of selection and revision is simply hell for me." Perkins replied, "You must struggle too, and perhaps even more than in the writing, in the shaping and revising." At first, Wolfe was grateful for such advice, but over time grew resentful and switched publishers. He never wrote so well again.

Revision can often be the servant of publishing needs, but sometimes their victim. In December 1937, in response to his publishers telling him that the public wanted "more about hobbits," J.R.R. Tolkien began work on what would become *The Lord of the Rings*. He soon realized that the new book would not only change the context of the original Hobbit story, but lead to substantial changes to the character of Gollum. In the first edition of *The Hobbit*, Gollum had willingly bet his magic ring on the outcome of the riddle-game, and he and Bilbo part amicably. In the second edition, to reflect the new concept of the ring and its corrupting abilities, Tolkien made Gollum more aggressive towards Bilbo and distraught at losing the ring. He sent this revised version to his publisher as an example of the kind of changes he needed to make, but heard nothing back. When he was sent proofs of a new edition, he found the sample text incorporated. The revised text was published in 1951 in both the U.K. and the United States.*

The most celebrated of recent editing tales concerns the American short-story writer Raymond Carver. It is primarily about authors and their editors, but it also raises the question of who has the final say. In 2007 Carver's widow announced that she planned to publish seventeen of his stories as originally written, before being worked on by his long-time editor at Knopf. This was Gordon Lish, a man who held a high opinion of his own talents, was an aggressive editor, and who gave himself the nickname "Captain Fiction."

According to Charles McGrath, who was Carver's editor at *The New Yorker*, Lish transposed, retitled and rewrote (endings especially), and frequently cut Carver's stories by 50 percent or more to get at what he felt to be their essence. It was Lish's doing that Carver won a reputation as a minimalist, particularly for his 1981 breakout book *What We Talk About When We Talk About Love.*

The most famous instance of Lish's editing is "A Small, Good Thing," in which a couple waits to see if their child will emerge from a coma. According to McGrath, Lish changed the title to "The Bath," cut the story by two-thirds, and eliminated a key passage, "a moment of redemptive hopefulness at the end." Instead of the original positive conclusion, the couple is left frozen in despair. In a letter dated July 8, 1980, Carver acknowledges that Lish had "made so many of the stories in this collection better, far better than they were before," but as years went by he became so upset about "A Small, Good Thing" that he wrote to Lish begging him to restore the stories

---

* Yet accident can be the author's friend. W. H. Auden was checking his proofs when he saw that a misprint had produced a better line than his original; thus "The poets know the name of the seas" became "The ports know the name of the seas." It took Auden, though, to recognize it as an improvement.

to how he had written them, and ultimately he restored the original version for *Where I'm Calling From,* a 1987 collection of stories not edited by Lish.

Who should have the final say? As Sylvia Beach, owner of the Paris-based bookstore and publishing enterprise Shakespeare and Company, remarked after James Joyce had broken his contract with her over *Ulysses*—she had published the novel in France—and taken the book to Random House, "A baby belongs to its mother, not to the midwife, doesn't it?"

A more collaborative case of an editor working with an author and involving not authorial surrender but rather a creative partnership is that of William Golding and *Lord of the Flies.* Golding began his breakthrough novel in 1951 (the same time as Kerouac) and finished it in October the following year. The original title was *Strangers from Within,* although there would be several more—*Beast in the Jungle, An Island of Their Own, This Island's Mine, Fun and Games, The Isle Is Full of Noises, To End an Island*—before an editor at Faber came up with *Lord of the Flies.**

---

* One area of revision obviously is whether one has the right title, and the history of publishing is full of stories of lucky escapes—*Gone with the Wind* might have been *Bugles Sang True, Not in Our Stars,* or *Tote the Weary Load. Pride and Prejudice* was originally *First Impressions. Nineteen Eighty-Four* was *The Last Man in Europe; Lolita* was *The Kingdom by the Sea; The Sun Also Rises* was *Fiesta;* and *War and Peace* was *All's Well That Ends Well. Brideshead Revisited* was originally *The House of Faith,* and *Portnoy's Complaint* wavered between *The Jewboy, Whacking Off,* and *A Jewish Patient Begins His Analysis. The Great Gatsby* had a rash of early incarnations, including *Among Ash-Heaps and Millionaires, Trimalchio in West Egg, On the Road to West Egg, Under the Red, White and Blue, Gold-Hatted Gatsby,* and *The High-Bouncing Lover.* My favourite, however, is Ian Fleming's *Moonraker,* which was first titled *Mondays Are Hell.* Raymond Chandler, whose ear has been described as the sharpest of the twentieth century, said that the titles of books (and indeed films) should conjure "a particular magic which impresses itself on the memory." *The Maltese Falcon,* he added, "makes the mind ask questions." "Lord of the Flies" is a literal translation of "Baal-Zebub," the old Canaanite god of evil. Golding thus accepted a title that has echoes and parallels from the Bible that he would have known well.

The typescript went first to Jonathan Cape, then Putnam's London office, Chapman and Hall, Hutchinson, Curtis Brown (it occurred to Golding he might after all need an agent), and The Bodley Head until, on September 14, 1953, he sent his "by now rather tattered typescript" to Faber. The firm's professional reader, one Polly Perkins, recorded her verdict on the top left-hand corner of Golding's submission letter: "Time: the Future. Absurd & uninteresting fantasy about the explosion of an atom bomb on the Colonies. A group of children who land in jungle-country near New Guinea. Rubbish & dull. Pointless."

Fortunately, Faber had just taken on a young editor, a promising ex-Oxford scholar named Charles Monteith. One Tuesday afternoon, he picked up *Strangers from Within* from the reject pile on a whim. During that week, after office work had ended for the day, he would return to the script and find it gripping. It had certain minor flaws—commas littered the pages "as thickly as currants in a fruit loaf"—and Piggy's "common" speech, conveyed by misspellings such as "ass-mar" for "asthma," was a trifle excessive, but a couple were more serious.

Monteith had been in publishing for less than a month, but he could see that there was a major structural problem: as well as the description of atomic war at the novel's opening, there were two other unnecessary digressions—an air battle, after which the dead pilot floats down by parachute onto the island and, toward the end, a naval engagement between some enemy ships and the fleet to which the "trim cruiser" that rescues all the boys belongs. Second, Monteith found Simon, the Christ figure, unbelievable and felt that any strictly miraculous events in the story had to be "made ambivalent, eliminated, or 'toned down' in such a way as to make Simon explicable in purely rational terms."

Despite doubts about the novel voiced by senior members at Faber, Monteith was allowed to contact its author. At their first meeting, both men were nervous, but as they talked "a cautious trust, and even liking" was established. Monteith stated his editorial points; Golding went away to make revisions, and within three days sent back new versions of the beginning, middle, and end, with the previously separate prologue, interlude, and epilogue merged into the main text. The portrayal of Simon still had to be dealt with, as Golding admitted in an accompanying letter. He concluded: "Rereading the novel as a stranger to it, I'm bound to agree with all your criticism and am full of enthusiasm and energy for the cleaning up process." The changes exceeded Monteith's hopes—at their meeting all he had suggested was a shortening of the nuclear war passages, not their elimination. He now sent Golding the emended portions with penciled suggestions. "You are perhaps still tending to over-emphasize," he cautioned, "to make points rather too directly." In a letter four days later, Golding accepted every one of Monteith's criticisms and corrections. "I recognize my own anxious tendency to overstate and propose to guard against it," he wrote.

Monteith's next letter warned against the danger of turning Simon into a prig, "a self-righteous infant who insists on saying his prayers in the dorm while the naughty boys throw pillows at him." All that was needed was to show, early on, that Simon was "in some ways odd, different, withdrawn, and therefore capable of the lonely, rarified courage of facing the pig's head and climbing the mountain top."

Here editor and author were at odds: Golding wanted Simon to have direct communication with God, for the novel to "convey a theophany." Nevertheless, when a new draft arrived at Faber in January, Monteith's latest suggestions were incorporated (together with a new title, *Nightmare Island*), with the added injunction, "If you want to throw away any more Simon go ahead." Monteith replied immediately, apologizing for having "badgered you so much." Even so, he continued to work on the script, toning down Simon still further and redrafting several sentences. At one point he crossed out more than a page in which Ralph thinks Simon has an "aura" and is "charged with a particular significance" and also deleted a passage where Ralph thinks "Simon had a not-light around him"—meaning, in all probability, a light that was not natural. Once again, he was able to see what Golding was aiming for and suggest the best way to achieve it. The final piece of the jigsaw puzzle was that Golding, even when unsure, was willing to put his trust in another's hands.

The following month Monteith wrote offering a contract and an advance—Faber's "Book Committee" had authorized £50, but Geoffrey Faber, in view of the author's patience, threw in an extra £10. Soon another editor at the firm, Alan Pringle, came up with "Lord of the Flies," which the author liked; although Golding demurred somewhat on the chapter headings—"my instinct is slightly against them"—he accepted the list that Monteith drew up, and lo, the weeks of revision were over. Or almost. The process of demystifying Simon continued even at the proof stage.

Lord of the Flies was published on September 17, 1954, a year and three days after Golding had sent it to Faber. It received outstanding reviews (and several offers for film rights), with scarcely a dissenting voice. The only damp spot was the reaction from American publishers, who, although they were reading the finished book, were generally unimpressed—at least twelve companies turned it down, including Knopf, twice. Eventually Coward-McCann made an offer, for $1,000, which Faber happily accepted. The British company would remain Golding's agent as well as his publisher for the rest of his life, and Monteith his editor. In his fine biography of Golding, John Carey writes of the editorial to-and-fro: "What emerges from the correspondence is the good faith of both men, and also Monteith's skill at personal relations." It's a pity, I feel, that novels rarely carry an acknowledgements page.

CHAPTER 11

Vision and Re-vision
(Part 2)

I have rewritten—often several times—every word I have
ever published. My pencils outlast their erasers.

VLADIMIR NABOKOV

I'm all for the scissors. I believe more in the scissors than I do
in the pencil.

TRUMAN CAPOTE

M id-August in 2013, I was at a friend's wedding in Aspen, Colorado.
He is a literary agent, and at some point during the weekend I was talking with two of his authors. The conversation turned to revision.

WRITER 1: My problem is repetition.

WRITER 2: Mine is overwriting. That's better—it's bigger.

WRITER 1 (RISING TO THE CHALLENGE, AND WITH AN EDGE):
Yes, but is yours fixable?

Most drafts, like Golding's, have two or three major problems: any more than that, the manuscript is probably not viable. First-time authors especially have some things they do extremely well, some they manage effectively, and others that they are relatively poor at or are not able to do at all. Even the most experienced authors can have aspects to their writing that they cannot improve—in the years that I edited Fay Weldon she would always send in drafts with weak male characters, then cheerfully agree to their being made more rounded, if not actually sympathetic. With one of her best novels, *The Life and Loves of a She-Devil* (1983), she said she would happily go on revising for several more rounds, but there comes a time to stop: the *New Yorker* editor and essayist Roger Angell would say that sometimes if you pull out all the weeds you end up with a crisp green lawn— utterly inert.

Fay was a delight to edit, and there were rarely disagreements. Generally, if authors accept more than, say, 90 percent of what I suggest, I am unhappy—no editor should expect to get it all right—as I am if they accept less than about 80 percent. Hemingway's oft-quoted advice was "Write drunk; edit sober,"* and certainly authors should keep a clear head when they weigh up what their editors advise. Frequently, a writer will say, "I have the core of a story in me, but I am not sure I have told it to the best effect." Jeffrey Archer

---

* This remark has also been credited to W. H. Auden, while in 1964 Peter De Vries published *Reuben, Reuben*, a novel based on the life of Dylan Thomas, in which a character says: "Sometimes I write drunk and revise sober, and sometimes I write sober and revise drunk. But you have to have both elements in creation—the Apollonian and the Dionysian, or spontaneity and restraint, emotion and discipline." *Reuben, Reuben* (New York: Bantam, 1965), p. 242.

asked the editor of his first two novels, Corlies "Cork" Smith, "You do so much for my writing, what's really the difference between us?" In his characteristic Philadelphia drawl, Cork replied: "The first draaaft, Jeffrey."

Early on, as a young editor at William Collins and Sons, I worked on the first novel by Gerald Seymour, then a noted Independent Television News reporter who had sent in a suspense story that was published as *Harry's Game*. On the Tuesday before Gerry Seymour and I were to discuss the script I attended the weekly editorial meeting presided over by Sir Billy Collins, then a semi-benevolent dictator in his mid-seventies. He loved good storytelling (the Collins list at that time boasted such authors as Alistair MacLean, Hammond Innes, Jack Higgins, Winston Graham, Herman Wouk, Agatha Christie, and Ngaio Marsh) and out of the office would always be reading the latest Collins novels. That day he strode into the large conference room where twenty staff awaited him and said with some satisfaction that over the weekend he had read three manuscripts, in each of which a central character had been killed off. Before the meeting, he had telephoned all three authors, who under his insistence had agreed that the character concerned would be allowed to live.

At the end of Gerry Seymour's novel the protagonist, an undercover army officer named Harry, is brutally shot dead in a showdown with the IRA terrorist he has been tracking. I vowed to myself that I should try to follow Billy Collins's example. When Seymour and I met, I suggested that Harry should survive. My author shook his head. "I can't do that," he said. "It would be against the whole spirit of the book." Billy Collins's six-foot-four figure rose up before my eyes. "Well," I forged on, "couldn't he just be badly injured?" Gerry shook his head. "Maybe brain-damaged?" I persisted. Again, he shook his head mournfully. By this time I was desperate. "OK, then—what about *permanent* brain-damage?" Years later Gerry would remind me of this exchange. I deserved it.*

Reviving central characters is hardly the mainstay of the revising process. Jonathan Franzen in one of his essays compiled a useful list of what to look out for when revising: "sentimentality, weak narrative, overly lyrical prose, solipsism, self-indulgence, misogyny and other parochialisms, sterile game playing, overt didacticism, moral simplicity, unnecessary difficulty, informational fetishes. . . ." It is a good list (actually compiled in a manifesto-like way as a declaration of everything to which his own work stood in opposition), to which one might add having too many characters, setting the wrong tone or pace (too slow *or* too fast), and muddled exposition.

Simple, clear prose is not the only way to write, but it is the best. As William Strunk wrote in his classic *The Elements of Style* back in 1918, "A sentence should contain no unnecessary words, a paragraph no unnecessary sentences, for the same reason that a drawing should have no unnecessary lines and a machine no unnecessary parts." Gabriel Garcia Márquez would often say that "ultimately, literature is nothing but carpentry."

---

* This is not an attempt to dilute my foolishness, but recently I read an article in which Nick Hornby records his revulsion at reading Pete Dexter's shocker *Train*: "What happens is that in the process of being raped, the central female character gets her nipple sliced off, and it really upset me. I mean, I know I was supposed to get upset. But I was bothered way beyond function. I was bothered to the extent that I struck up a conversation with the author at periodic intervals thereafter. 'Did the nipple really have to go, Pete? Explain to me why. Couldn't it have just . . . nearly gone? Or maybe you could have left it alone altogether? I mean, come on, man. Her husband has just been brutally murdered. She's been raped. We get the picture. Leave the nipple alone'" (Nick Hornby, *Ten Years in the Tub* [London: Believer Books, 2013], p. 82). Editors and readers alike can get "bothered way beyond function."

So first: metaphors. It is difficult to do better than Herodotus, describing a snowy day, coming up with "the air is full of feathers," but writers love to coin new likenesses. Asked why he didn't leave dangerous Buenos Aires under the Peronistas to take up a comfortable position at Harvard, Borges replied, "Censorship is the mother of metaphor."* Yet, in his lecture "The Metaphor," he also noted the futility of any attempt to come up with brand-new metaphors. This latter argument is not finally persuasive, but it includes a lovely list of metaphors used in Icelandic poetry at the beginning of the thirteenth century, from "seagull of hatred," "the roof of a whale's mouth" (an allusion to the sea), to—meaning the mouth—"house of teeth."

Nietzsche wrote that the desire to create metaphors was the desire to be different, the desire to be elsewhere. Perhaps. Whatever the motive, bad or inappropriate metaphors can creep into most writing, as can bathetic or lame sentences. When revising, one needs to test each metaphor to make sure it rings true.

A cousin to this is hackneyed phrasing. Nabokov regarded cliché as the key to bad art (not just writing), while Martin Amis, who titled his 2001 collection of essays *The War Against Cliché*, argued: "All writing is a campaign against cliché. Not just clichés of the pen but clichés of the mind and clichés of the heart."

Most clichés betray themselves easily enough, but some of the less obvious can be deadly. It is humbling how often one falls into hackneyed expressions without realizing it. One can have fun with the result: around 1946 (the date is important for the examples he uses), the Irish writer Flann O'Brien composed this "catechism of cliché":

---

* Of all recent major writers of serious fiction, Borges perhaps had the wickedest sense of humour. An example: in an essay on his fellow Argentine novelist Julio Cortázar, he writes: "When Dante Gabriel Rossetti read the novel *Wuthering Heights*, he wrote to a friend: 'The action takes place in Hell, but the places, I don't know why, have English names.'" Jorge Luis Borges, *Selected Nonfictions* (New York: Viking, 1999), p. 111.

When things are few, what also are they?

Far between.

What are stocks of fuel doing when they are low?

Running.

How low are they running?

Dangerously.

What does one do with a suggestion?

One throws it out.

For what does one throw a suggestion out?

For what it may be worth.

The writer and critic Geoff Dyer wondered what was the minimum number of words necessary for something to be positively identified as a cliché: "Two? With 'bitter cold' and 'searing heat' we are dealing with the deadest of wood, but no one would—if you'll forgive this old triple-worder—bat an eyelid over 'bitter' or 'cold' in isolation. . . ."

In English alone, a new word is said to be coined every ninety-eight minutes. Writers, who love words, are often tempted to make them up—Shakespeare, for instance, introduced more than 1,700 (including *assassination, bump, critic,* and *road*). John Milton coined *Pandemonium* and *self-esteem,* Lewis Carroll invented *chortle, slithy* (meaning smooth and active) and *squawk,* while *diplomacy, electioneering,* and *municipality* were the brainchildren of Edmund Burke—but it is dangerous ground. Will Self's novels introduce several Joyce-like neologisms, such as *shivergreen, saltsplash, splutterance, fitszackerly,* and *schlockenspiel,* which come off as distracting showmanship. While I like the Samuel Beckett line "Dance first. Think later," when you dance with language watch your step.

Whole books have been written on punctuation (which should not be confined just to the physical aspect of aspiration and stress), and Balzac warned budding writers "not to habitually prop your sentences on crutches, such as italics and exclamation points, but make them stand without aid; if they cannot emphasize themselves, these devices are commonly but a confession of helplessness."

In 1943 the poet Robert Graves and co-author Alan Hodge published a handbook for writers called *The Reader over Your Shoulder*, and among much useful advice it includes: "Punctuation should be consistent and should denote quality of connection, rather than length of pause, between sentences or parts of sentences."

Martin Amis, often at his best as a literary critic, is good on commas. They were a High Renaissance invention, attributed to a Venetian printer named Aldo Manuzio, who around 1490 was working on the Greek classics and, wanting to avoid confusion, began separating words and clauses: *komma* is the Greek for "something cut off." The smallest adjustment can reap dividends, Amis argues, taking a single sentence from Saul Bellow's story, *A Theft*. Of a character called Clara Velde, Bellow writes: "The mouth was very good but stretched extremely wide when she grinned, when she wept." Amis glosses, "Students of literary economy should examine its comma."

Semicolons can also be addictive. Stephen King wrote that his fellow writer Joyce Carol Oates "will employ enough semicolons to qualify for a place in the Guinness Book of Punctuation," while Kurt Vonnegut told his students at Iowa never to use semicolons at all, employing a single semicolon in his autobiography *A Man Without a Country* "to make a point. . . . The point is: rules only take us so far, even good rules." (In my attempts to stem the flow of Jeffrey Archer's prose, I found that Archer had nicknamed me "Semi-Cohen.")

John Updike called paragraphs and chapters "those pit stops for the mind." Some writers ignore them entirely—Will Self's *Umbrella* has no chapters and few paragraph breaks, and *Shark* (2014) dispenses with them entirely. Others, like Proust, have paragraphs that go on till the end of time. In an essay on William Gaddis entitled "Mr. Difficult" (Gaddis, besides "tree-trunk-wide" paragraphs, employs inventive punctuation and dense, tiny typography), Jonathan Franzen admitted, "One night I gave up in the middle of a four-page paragraph."

Francine Prose's *Reading Like a Writer* includes an account of a Rex Stout mystery, *Plot It Yourself,* in which his detective Nero Wolfe is called upon to determine in a case of plagiarism whether three manuscripts could have been written by the same person. His conclusion is based on "the most telling feature"—paragraphs:

> A clever man might successfully disguise every element of his style but one—the paragraphing. Diction and syntax may be determined and controlled by rational processes in full consciousness, but paragraphing—the decision whether to take short hops or long ones, and whether to hop in the middle of a thought or action or finish it first—that comes from instinct, from the depths of personality.

I don't know whether this is true, but it sounds convincing.

In *Lessons from a Lifetime of Writing,* the action/adventure author David Morrell (who created the character of Rambo, among others) says he based his style on two essays by Edgar Allan Poe, "The Philosophy of Composition" and "The Poetic Principle," both of which advocate short chapters, such that a reader can complete one chapter (or structural unit) in a sitting. Morrell scrupulously follows this advice to accommodate the reader's bladder, TV interruptions, phone calls, a neighbour who drops in, the arrival at a station.

Then there is the question of asking for advice. "Talent is developed in privacy." So said Marilyn Monroe, quoting Goethe! Mark Slouka, who contributes a series on writing to *The New York Times* ("If writers agree on anything—which is unlikely—it's that nothing can damage a novel in embryo as quickly and effectively as trying to describe it before it's ready"), has listed the following pointers about when and whom one should consult (if anyone at all): (a) Trust a few, necessary voices; (b) Try, as much as possible, to avoid torturing these brave souls with your insecurities; and (c) Shut up and write. This advice also unveils an important truth: revision starts before you have even finished that first draft.*

Despite all the above, most writing rules are there to be broken. "Good Master Schoolmaster, do not English this," wrote the American novelist David Markson, quoting Burton's *Anatomy of Melancholy* as a plea for editors not to improve his prose. In a further *cri du coeur*, the wonderful Turkish-American essayist Elif Batuman declared:

> I would greatly prefer to think of literature as a profession, an art, a science, or pretty much anything else, rather than a craft. What did craft ever try to say about the world, the human condition, or the search for meaning? All it had were its negative dictates: "Show, don't tell"; "Murder your darlings"; "Omit needless words." As if writing were a matter of overcoming bad habits—of omitting needless words.

It isn't, of course. I also laughed heartily at this piece of advice from Nick Hornby, whose glorious collection of essays *Ten Years in the Tub: A Decade Soaking in Great Books* I have been reading as I revised this chapter. "Anyone and everyone taking a writing class knows that

---

* How writers react to criticism after publication is another matter. Chekhov called professional critics horseflies that keep the horse from ploughing, Flaubert "the leprosy of letters," while Sainte-Beuve commented that "No one will ever create a statue for a critic." For Tennyson they were lice in the locks of literature. "Pigs at the pastry cart," said Updike; asking a writer what he thinks about critics is like asking a lamp post what it feels about dogs, said John Osborne. Thomas Carlyle's *Sartor Resartus* was damningly abused by reviewers. Once he became famous, he had it reissued—with the reviews as an appendix.

the secret of good writing is to cut it back, pare it down, winnow, chop, hack, prune, and trim, remove every superfluous word, compress, compress, compress," he begins.

> The truth is, there's nothing very utilitarian about fiction or its creation, and I suspect that people are desperate to make it sound manly, backbreaking labor because it's such a wussy thing to do in the first place. The obsession with austerity is an attempt to compensate, to make writing resemble a real job, like farming, or logging. (It's also why people who work in advertising put in twenty-hour days.) Go on, young writers—treat yourself to a joke, or an adverb! Spoil yourself! Readers won't mind!

Over the years, I have learned that authors' abilities to revise vary widely. Some are barely able to improve a first version and some refuse to try. Others transform an unconvincing effort into a revitalized second—third—sixth draft. Here is the story of a marvellous piece of revision I was lucky enough to have witnessed at first hand.

In 1974 Richard Holmes wrote a much-admired life of Shelley. There was no immediate follow-up, and by the early 1980s he was still unsure what he should turn to next. We had been at school and university together (although he was a year or two ahead of me), and reconnecting in the early 1980s we talked about what he might write, settling on a book of perhaps a dozen essays on nineteenth-century British writers who had "gone abroad" at some key moment in their lives, with the notion that Richard would make the same journeys. Early candidates included Coleridge in Gottingen, Hazlitt in Paris, Shelley in Lerici (on the Italian Riviera), Stevenson in the Cevennes, and Oscar Wilde in Dieppe. Also in the frame were Keats in Rome,

Byron in Venice, and Browning in Florence. This "Ur-version" was to be called *Romantic Travellers*.

Our joint worry was that such a book might not come together in a coherent way, so I suggested that Richard narrow down his list. He tried a draft of an opening section about Stevenson's *Travels with a Donkey*, but an overall scheme still eluded him.

Some weeks later, he went to the Royal Festival Hall on London's South Bank to listen to *Symphonie Fantastique*, written in 1830. Its subtitle is "An Episode in the Life of an Artist, in Five Parts," and the music tells the story (as Berlioz explains in his programme notes) of an artist gifted with a lively imagination who has poisoned himself with opium in the "depths of despair" because of a "hopeless love." After the concert, as Richard walked alongside the Thames, it came to him that "what I had been writing was indeed 'episodes in the life of an artist'—mine." He went back and re-wrote the Stevenson section, beginning with the first paragraph. "All that night I heard footsteps. . . . I was eighteen." He recalls now:

> I had used the word "I." In fact without realizing it I had used the word "I" in two ways in the same paragraph—the young experiencing self, and the older remembering self. Suddenly the whole drive of the book became autobiographical; or at least *allowed in the autobiographical voice* for the first time in my writing life, alongside the biographical one. So the book became about the places *I had been to*, in the company of my subjects, or "in their footsteps." And thus about my time in their company; and therefore the whole process of researching and writing a biography.

Section 2, which was to cover Mary Wollstonecraft marooned in Revolutionary Paris, was still in gestation; but Section 3, on Shelley in Italy, on the Gulf of Spezia, followed immediately; and thus the rambling descriptive *Travellers* began to evolve into an intense, intimate, and personal journey. This change brought in Section 4 (Nerval rather than Hazlitt in Paris, because Richard had researched him and Gautier there for two emotionally fraught years in the mid-1970s). Finally, Section 2 took shape, partly as an analogue to Richard's own chronology (the student riots of the 1960s), partly to turn the book into a balanced quartet (music again). And partly because—inspired by Berlioz—"I wanted to write about a woman and a love affair . . . mine!"

Several months later Richard came back with a draft of what would become his classic work on biography, *Footsteps*. The result was an exceptional piece of non-fiction (a category Richard scorns, as if one were to refer to men as "non-females"). Not only had he found his voice, he had done what Jane Austen had done in her revisions to *Persuasion*: he had re-envisioned what he was trying to do.

My Concise Oxford (1964) defines *revision* as "to read or look over or re-examine or reconsider and amend faults in," but that dilutes the force of the word. *Begin afresh, afresh, afresh.* "Revision" is most powerfully and precisely a fresh vision, a new way of seeing what you have done and what you intend: *re-vision*. At the very start of *Anna Karenina*, Tolstoy has the reprobate Stepan Arkadyevitch Oblonsky declare confidently *"Vsyo obrazvetsia"*—everything will form itself into the ideal. He was the optimist; but so in one part of his or her being is every imaginative writer, as they set about getting it right.

Dina Goldstein, *And They Lived Happily Ever After (Do they?)*

CHAPTER 12

The Sense of an Ending

The end of a novel, like the end of a children's dinner party, must be made up of sweetmeats and sugar-plums.

ANTHONY TROLLOPE, *BARCHESTER TOWERS*

The good ended happily, and the bad unhappily. That is what Fiction means.

MISS PRISM (WHO ONCE WROTE A THREE-VOLUME NOVEL)
IN *THE IMPORTANCE OF BEING EARNEST*

In their signature ways, Anthony Trollope and Oscar Wilde both recognized the longing we have for novels to conclude happily—indeed, for any story to do so. The Victorians were particularly keen: the last chapter was known as the "wind-up," which Henry James caustically described as "a distribution at the last of prizes, pensions, husbands, wives, babies, millions, appended paragraphs and cheerful remarks." James pioneered the "open" ending, often cutting off a story or novel mid-conversation. "'Then there we are,' said Strether" are the final words of *The Ambassadors*. David Foster Wallace went one better with his first novel, *The Broom of the System*, which also ends mid-sentence, with Rick Vigorous trying to seduce the gorgeous Mindy Metalman, saying, "I'm a man of my." Maybe Wallace was reacting to the demands of his editor, who had asked instead for "a brilliantly theatrical close."*

Nietzsche said that it took genius to "make an end"—to give a touch of inevitability to the conclusion of any work of art. Saul Bellow remarked on his lack of "the will or the capacity to continue to a definite conclusion" and added that, "I sometimes think the comedy in my books is a satire on this inconclusiveness." Endings are notoriously problematic, and writers can struggle to bring their tales to a satisfying finale. Should the concluding pages be especially pregnant with significance? What are the ramifications of the hero or heroine being killed off? How to tie up loose ends? The U.S. film industry has a special term referring to a fictional character whose job it is to explain parts of the plot to other characters and to the audience. An old Hollywood hand and friend of mine, Steve Brown, told me it was

---

* A small but distinguished group of writers who ended novels mid-sentence would also include Nikolai Gogol (*Dead Souls*, 1842; possibly he intended the ending as a cliffhanger, as the novel was intended to be the first of a trilogy); Laurence Sterne (*A Sentimental Journey Through France and Italy*, 1768; the sentence has a typical innuendo to it: "So that when I stretch'd out my hand, I caught hold of the Fille de Chambre's—"); Samuel Beckett (*Malone Dies*, 1951, in which the text, and Malone's consciousness/existence, vanish in a series of dwindling fragments); James Joyce (*Finnegans Wake*, 1939), Vladimir Nabokov's short story "The Circle" (1934), Thomas Pynchon (*Gravity's Rainbow*, 1973), and Bret Easton Ellis (*The Rules of Attraction*, 1987), all four meant to parallel their respective openings; and most recently Jonathan Safran Foer (*Everything Is Illuminated*, 2002, where the final half-sentence may, according to one's interpretation, double as a suicide note).

"Irving the Explainer," but the names Morris, Jake, and Sam are also used to indicate this storytelling cliché, so often used in mystery tales, where the end has the police or a private investigator confronting a room full of suspects and explaining who committed the crime and why and how it was done. The origin of the phrase is probably in Yiddish theatre.

In his classic work *The Sense of an Ending* (1967) Frank Kermode looks at the way novels are concluded as part of a general survey of the apocalyptic mode of thinking in human history. "We cannot, of course," he writes, "be denied an end; it is one of the great charms of books that they have to end." But often for the reader, novels do not end well. Clichés, repetitious language, lack of resolution, cop-outs—bad endings can take various forms. On a blog called "Landless" there is an entry headed "The 10 Worst Ways to End a Novel," with contributions such as "They all lived happily ever after," "Thank God it was all just a dream. . . . or was it?" and "From that day onward, the mystery of the mysterious mist remained unexplained." Endings so often seem arbitrary, an accommodation, not something found in real life. But as Kermode concedes: "The novel will end; a full close may be avoided, but there will be a close; a fake full stop, an 'exhaustion of aspects.'" He then adds, crucially, "Ends are ends only when they are not negative but frankly transfigure the events in which they were immanent."

That can be a tall order. George Eliot was almost incapable of resolving difficult situations and admitted that the conclusion to *The Mill on the Floss* didn't really work: she had painted herself into a corner. "Conclusions are the weak points of most authors," she said, adding, "Some of the fault lies in the very nature of a conclusion, which is at best a negation."

When in 1872 *Middlemarch* was published, it was a four-volume novel in an age when three volumes was the norm. Eliot felt "something like a shudder" when asked to assess its finished length while she was still in the throes of composition. She noted that it would end up no longer than some of Thackeray's works, "and I don't see how the sort of thing I want to do could have been done briefly." Her anxiety persisted, however, and a month before the final part of the novel was published (it appeared first in serial form) she wrote to a friend, "Expect to be immensely disappointed with the close of *Middlemarch*." She then chose to add a "Finale" similar to the list detailing the fates of its leading characters that nowadays appears on screen at the end of a film.[*]

"Every limit is a beginning as well as an ending," she starts the chapter. "Who can quit young lives after being long in company with them, and not desire to know what befell them in their after-years?" There follow nine pages detailing the future lives of Fred Vincy and Mary Garth, Ben and Letty Garth, Lydgate and Rosamond, Dorothea and Will Ladislaw. The one missing figure is Camden Farebrother, vicar of Lowick, who has failed to win Mary's love and loses the election to be chaplain at the new hospital. One feels George Eliot had a real sympathy for this character but knew that he would have been bound for a life of further disappointment and sadness. Her sentiment for him would not allow her to write that future down.

Yet the paragraph that concludes the whole novel is one of the

---

[*] Jane Austen's nephew would write of her: "She would, if asked, tell us many little particulars about the subsequent career of some of her people. In this traditionary way we learned that Miss Steele never succeeded in catching the Doctor; that Kitty Bennet was satisfactorily married to a clergyman near Pemberley, while Mary obtained nothing higher than one of her uncle Philip's clerks, and was content to be considered a star in the society of Meriton; that the 'considerable sum' given by Mrs. Norris to William Price was one pound; that Mr. Woodhouse survived his daughter's marriage, and kept her and Mr. Knightley from settling at Donwell, about two years; and that the letters placed by Frank Churchill before Jane Fairfax, which she swept away unread, contained the word 'pardon.'" James Edward Austen-Leigh, *Memoir*, 1870.

finest that George Eliot ever wrote. In particular, in her recent book about *Middlemarch*, the *New Yorker* writer Rebecca Mead describes its final sentence as "one of the most admired in literature, and with good reason." Yet when Mead found Eliot's raw draft it "was like discovering that Leonardo had first tried painting a snub nose on the Mona Lisa, such was the difference." The original runs:

> The effect of her being [Dorothea's] on those around her was incalculably diffusive; for the growing life of the world is after all chiefly dependent on unhistoric acts, and that things are not so ill with you and me as they might have been is owing to many of those who sleep in unvisited tombs, having lived a life nobly.

The revised version is similar yet vitally different:

> The effect of her being on those around her was incalculably diffusive: for the growing good of the world is partly dependent on unhistoric acts; and that things are not so ill with you and me as they might have been, is half owing to the number who lived faithfully a hidden life, and rest in unvisited tombs.

As Mead notes, the music of the line, as well as its import, are significantly changed. Instead of the "growing good of the world," the draft has the "growing life of the world," at once less specific and less moving. The added phrase "after all" provides a gesture of persuasion that undermines the solemn authority of the passage, while "chiefly dependent" instead of "partly dependent" and "owing" rather than "half owing" give the sentence a much more optimistic tone than the version that appeared in print, with what, in her analysis, Mead terms "its irresistible melancholic grandeur." The revisions to the word order, after the final comma, also create something altogether more resonant. Those hidden lives are, in draft, lived "nobly," a word suggesting moral qualities that are outwardly recognized by others. The final version's "faithfully" shifts the emphasis away from the implied judgement of an external observer and places the emphasis upon a validation that comes from inner conviction. The hidden lives of which Eliot writes have become more humble, but richer too. "What do I think of *Middlemarch?*" Emily Dickinson wrote to her cousins in 1873. "What do I think of glory?"

Eliot was writing for a serial, so she could not spend too long in revising. Without such pressure, one can go on tinkering forever. In an interview in 1958, Hemingway declared that he rewrote the final words of *A Farewell to Arms* "39 times before I was satisfied." Literary historians have concluded that he actually set down forty-seven endings, sometimes more blunt, sometimes more optimistic, ranging from a short sentence to several paragraphs.

In what critics now call "The Nada Ending," Hemingway's final lines read: "That is all there is to the story. Catherine died and you will die and I will die and that is all I can promise you." In the "Live-Baby ending," the story rounds off: "There is no end except death and birth is the only beginning." Ending no. 34, suggested by Scott Fitzgerald, has him conclude the world "breaks everyone, and those it does not break it kills. . . . It kills the very good and very gentle and the very brave impartially. If you are none of these you can be sure it will kill you too but there will be no special hurry."

None of these musings survives in the final version, the last paragraph of which reads: "But after I had got them out and shut the door and turned off the light it wasn't any good. It was like saying good-bye to a statue. After a while I went out and left the hospital and walked back to the hotel in the rain." *Finis.* It is hard to imagine leaving the dead body of the woman you love as being like saying goodbye to a statue. Maybe Hemingway should have taken Fitzgerald's advice, or settled for one of his own earlier versions. But his choice underlines a general temptation: to seek out some grand statement or Humpty-Dumptyish knock-down argument or sentences intended to wrench your heart, and the result is overwriting (to my ear, at least). Of course, such endings are possible—just extremely difficult to pull off.

The advice of friends can be a mixed blessing. Charles Dickens thought he had the right ending to *Great Expectations* when in June 1861 he sent its last chapters to the printer, and to relax after his efforts went to stay with his friend Edward Bulwer-Lytton, a popular crime and historical novelist to whom he decided to show the final instalment in proof.

In it, Pip hears that the oafish Bentley Drummle has died and his great love Estella has quietly remarried a country doctor. Then, in the concluding three paragraphs to the novel, two years after Pip's return from travelling out east,

> I was in England again—in London, and walking along Piccadilly with little Pip—when a servant came running after me to ask would I step back to a lady in a carriage who wished to speak to me. It was a little pony carriage, which the lady was driving; and the lady and I looked sadly enough on one another.
>
> "I am greatly changed, I know, but I thought you would like to shake hands with Estella too, Pip. Lift up that pretty child and let me kiss it!" (She supposed the child, I think, to be my child.)
>
> I was very glad afterwards to have had the interview; for, in her face and in her voice, and in her touch, she gave me the assurance, that suffering had been stronger than Miss

Havisham's teaching, and had given her a heart to understand what my heart used to be.

What appealed to Dickens in this version was its originality: "[the]
winding up will be away from all such things as they conventionally
go." But Bulwer-Lytton advised against such a downbeat ending.
Uncertain, Dickens consulted Wilkie Collins, his regular confidant:
"Bulwer was so very anxious that I should alter the end . . . and
stated his reasons so well, that I have resumed the wheel, and taken
another turn at it. Upon the whole I think it is for the better." In the
new ending Pip meets Estella in the ruins of Satis House (Miss Havisham's cobweb-beswept old home), the last sentence changing from
"I could see the shadow of no parting from her" to "I saw no shadow
of another parting from her."

He then wrote to his friend (and eventual biographer) John Forster: "You will be surprised to hear that I have changed the end of
Great Expectations from after Pip's return to Joe's. . . . I have put in as
pretty a little piece of writing as I could, and I have no doubt the
story will be more acceptable through the alteration." The substitu-
tion, almost always selected in modern editions, has Pip and Estella
meeting in the grounds of Satis House:

> "I little thought," said Estella, "that I should take leave of
> you in taking leave of this spot. I am very glad to do so."
>
> "Glad to part again, Estella? To me, parting is a painful
> thing. To me, the remembrance of our last parting has been
> ever mournful and painful."
>
> "But you said to me," returned Estella, very earnestly.
> "'God bless you, God forgive you!' And if you could say
> that to me then, you will not hesitate to say that to me
> now—now, when suffering has been stronger than all other
> teaching, and has taught me to understand what your heart

used to be. I have been bent and broken, but—I hope—into a better shape. Be as considerate and good to me as you were, and tell me we are friends."

"We are friends," said I, rising and bending over her, as she rose from the bench.

"And will continue friends apart," said Estella.

I took her hand in mine, and we went out of the ruined place; and, as the morning mists had risen long ago when I first left the forge, so the evening mists were rising now, and in all the broad expanse of tranquil light they showed to me, I saw no shadow of another parting from her.

This, "the Satis House ending," has usually been thought to imply that Estella and Pip (who tends to express affirmatives by negating their contrary) walk off into the sunset together, but there is considerable ambiguity in that last line. Although they leave hand in hand, Estella has just stated that she wishes to remain alone ("and will continue friends apart"), while a couple of pages earlier Pip has told Biddy that he intends to remain a bachelor. The joining of hands could be amicable rather than romantic, and perhaps what we should take Pip to mean in the final line is that their parting in the ruins of the past had been final, because any bitterness or misunderstanding had been emotionally resolved and they do not need to meet again. "Had Dickens wanted Pip and Estella to live together happily ever after," notes the critic Rupert Christiansen, "he could easily have done what he does at the ends of *David Copperfield*, *Little Dorrit* and *Bleak House* and told us as much."

While that ending has been the standard one since 1862, the first editions read "I saw the shadow of no parting from her," while the manuscript has "I saw the shadow of no parting from her, but one." The first edition's awkward phrasing certainly suggests marriage, and the manuscript's version is even more emphatic, implying Pip

and Estella's union until death. Yet Dickens scratched out each of
these versions, and revised the ending to have it both ways.* His final
choice brings to mind the last words to Hilary Mantel's *Bring Up the
Bodies,* the second instalment of her fictionalized life of Thomas
Cromwell: "There are no endings. If you think so you are deceived
as to their nature. They are all beginnings."

Modern novelists, particularly the ones we rate most highly, tend
to eschew such sentimental leanings: No "wind-up" for them but
rather a wind-down. Samuel Beckett's great trilogy, *Molloy, Malone
Dies,* and *The Unnamable,* ends: "You must go on. I can't go on. I'll go
on," a comment about both writing and living. His last prose work,
the short (two-thousand-word) *Stirrings Still,* concludes:

> Such and much more, such the hubbub in his mind so-
> called till nothing left from deep within but only ever fainter
> oh to end. No matter how no matter where. Time and grief
> and self so-called. Oh all to end.

These concluding words seem an existential cry, a longing for an
ending to the business of living, let alone to his chosen fiction. In
every sense, it is unbearable. *Stirrings Still* was published in March
1989. Beckett died that December.

Perhaps we are dealing in metaphysical and religious fashions. All
novelists have to tilt at the "dull windmills of a time-bound reality,"

---

* Forster felt the original ending "more consistent" and "more natural" and published the unused ending as a footnote in his 1872 biography, but he accepted the
new version's popularity. George Orwell wrote, "Psychologically the latter part of
Great Expectations is about the best thing Dickens ever did," but, like several early
twentieth-century writers, including George Bernard Shaw (who published the
novel in 1937 for the Limited Editions Club with the first ending), felt that the
original version was more consistent with the natural working out of the tale and
the book's underlying mood. I agree: Dickens sold out.

but how to decide, as the Second Witch in *Macbeth* has it, "When the hurly-burly's done / When the battle's lost and won"? Even the final scenes in a number of Shakespeare dramas, while required for the restoration of order, can seem anticlimactic. Do we really need Fortinbras holding forth as he stands over Hamlet's body, or the Prince of Verona telling us that Romeo and Juliet's deaths were a sad business, or Malcolm's words at the end of *Macbeth*? How a story ends can be fashioned by the culture of the times, or by the art form involved, as well as by the readers' or audience's expectations. I am reminded of an old cartoon of an author sitting disconsolately at his typewriter with the caption: "Oh hell. . . . suddenly a fusillade of shots rang out, and they all fell down dead. The end." Many of Shakespeare's plays had to end with a high body count, because that's what the groundlings were waiting for. Had Darcy told Elizabeth that he couldn't marry her as he needed to go away and find himself, or worse, had he realized immediately that he loved her, and announced his love in the opening pages, *Pride and Prejudice* would never have lasted through the ages.

In an aside in *Northanger Abbey*, Jane Austen acknowledges that a novelist cannot conceal the timing of the end of the story because of the telltale compression of the pages. When John Fowles provides a mock-Victorian "wind-up" to *The French Lieutenant's Woman* (in which Charles settles down happily with Ernestina) we are not deceived, for a quarter of the book remains. Going on with the story of Charles's quest for Sarah, Fowles offers us two further alternative endings— one that ends happily for the hero, the other unhappily. He invites us to choose between them but tacitly promotes the second as more authentic, because it is more open, with the sense of life going on into an uncertain future; greater expectations.

Luckily, many works of fiction end in a satisfying way. Among leading examples one might cite are *The Great Gatsby*, *The Adventures of Huckleberry Finn*, *Middlemarch*, and *Wuthering Heights* (which my worldly-wise monk-headmaster always said contained the finest last paragraph in world literature). All four are considered classic conclusions, and rightly so.

Twain ends his story with Huck Finn as untamed as ever, still longing for love, his optimism presented with typical Twain irony:

> But I reckon I got to light out for the Territory ahead of the rest, because Aunt Sally she's going to adopt me and sivilize me and I can't stand it. I been there before.

All of Huck's moral crises, the lies he has told, the conventions of society he has broken, have been revealed as part of a great game. The knowledge of Jim's emancipation colours, even erases, everything that has come before: life is presented as ultimately a matter of imperfect information and ambiguous situations, and the best one can do is to follow one's head and heart, which is what Huck now intends to do.

Getting the tone right is vital, setting up the reader for the last hurrah. *Gatsby* concludes on an elegiac note of pessimism and a reminder of Carraway's refrain, "What I had almost remembered was incommunicable forever":

> Gatsby believed in the green light, the orgastic future that year by year recedes before us. It eluded us then, but that's no matter—to-morrow we will run faster, stretch out our arms farther. . . . And one fine morning—
>   So we beat on, boats against the current, borne back ceaselessly into the past.

The voice is melancholic, nostalgic. So perhaps is the end to *Wuthering Heights,* but there is also a serenity, even a tenderness, as at long last Heathcliff is laid to rest by Catherine's side under the long grass on the edge of the churchyard:

> I lingered round them, under that benign sky: watched the moths fluttering among the heath and harcbells, listened to the soft wind breathing through the grass, and wondered how any one could ever imagine unquiet slumbers for the sleepers in that quiet earth.

None of the three endings—nor that of *Middlemarch*, quoted earlier—provides prizes, pensions, or cheerful remarks, and with each one might interject, "But what happens *next?*" Perhaps Catherine and Heathcliff will roam the heath as ghosts evermore. Yet there is a note of resolution, of a journey completed that leaves us saddened, perhaps, but satisfied.

The endings to stories of all kinds have been called "cathartic discharges," the final eruption, in the reader, of powerful emotions, and so they may be. But why end a story at all? Where both Dickens and Fowles are ambiguous, Tolstoy is certain what will happen to his leading players. *War and Peace*, famously, has a final hundred pages in the form of two epilogues, the first of which details the married life of Pierre and Natasha seven years later, and many are the readers who wish those extra pages had never been penned; they add little.

It is natural that we should anticipate, in literature at least, that marriage should signify not only an intimate union stamped with society's approval but also something more. Francine Prose says:

> We want to believe in enduring love partly because we know that we will always be subject to, and at the mercy of, the pendulum swing between chaos and cohesion, happi-

ness and heartbreak. And so we continue to root for the enchanted couple. . . .*

Much modern fiction has been the *opposite* of rooting for the enchanted couple, but that still requires that our emotions be brought to the right boiling point. People can disagree about the best way to wind up a tale to get that full "cathartic discharge." Yet the chances are that one will intuitively know how one's story should end when one gets there.

During my schooldays at Downside Abbey outside Bath, in Somerset, I was taught by a Benedictine monk named Illtyd Trethowan. At Oxford, a brilliant student, he contracted polio, leaving him with a withered left arm, which he would play with during classes, as if (to our teenage eyes) it were a pet cat. He had special hatreds (such as the novels of George Meredith) and other mannerisms too, including a drawn-out "arummm" that would punctuate most sentences. Dom Illtyd was the author of several books on the philosophy of religion and, in his retirement, a visiting professor at Brown University. He taught me English and also a special course that was compulsory for those who wanted to get into Oxford or Cambridge, "The General Paper," which could cover just about anything.

The classes for this oddly conceived subject were held in a small library devoted to history. It had but a single table, long enough to

---

* Annie Proulx has recently admitted that she wishes she had never written her story "Brokeback Mountain," which went on to become a highly successful film, because so many people wrote in to her to complain about its unhappy ending. "They rewrite the story, including all kinds of boyfriends and new lovers and so forth after Jack is killed. And it just drives me wild." *The New York Times,* January 2, 2015, p. C2.

hold about twelve boys and the master. Illtyd would sit at one end of the table, and the more challenged of his pupils would crowd into the seats at the other. As I recall a particular class from the mid-1960s, one of these boys was a teenager knowing beyond his years named Jules Concannon, who decided to hold a sweepstake over whether Dom Illtyd would get to a hundred "arummms" before the end of the forty-minute class. IOUs and other forms of barter were exchanged, and the lesson got under way.

The Concept of Mind by Gilbert Ryle, an Oxford philosopher who was a particular bête noire of Illtyd's for his belligerent humanism, was the book under discussion, and soon the table settled down to Illtyd talking in his fashion, with plenty of arummms and excursions, his grizzled head nodding gently as he spoke, the class unusually rapt as Concannon silently made his count. The minutes ticked by. Dom Illtyd talked on and on. ". . . which is why one asks, where in this account of Ryle's is there any discussion of where his values come from . . . ?" Here he paused, his right hand manipulating his left. Concannon shifted uneasily in his seat. The library clock showed one minute to the hour. On the worksheet in front of Concannon the tally had reached 99. Over the length of the table the suspense was mounting, and our teacher's moment of reflection seemed unusually prolonged. At last Dom Illtyd spoke again: "Well, I suppose I had better go 'arummm' once more or you'll never reach your hundred."

The bell for the end of class rang out.

The acuity of schoolmasters.

The perfect ending.

Cathartic discharge.

After I left the school I would sometimes visit Illtyd in his small room up in the monastery, and we became good friends. I reminded him once of a piece of advice he had given us about how we wrote our essays. Don't think that at the end of what you have written, he would tell us, you have to sum up with some great statement or wearisome recapitulation of arguments already made. When you have said what you want to say,

Stop.

Acknowledgements

For those who have never written a book, or been heavily involved in one, the extended community of friends and professionals who help nearly all such efforts to a finished state would surprise them. This is a relatively short work, but the list of those to thank is still a long one.

How to Write Like Tolstoy began with lectures at the University of Kingston on Thames, and quickly expanded after that. I was invited to be a visiting professor there by a friend and author of mine, Brian Brivati. I was soon working with the head of the creative writing team at Kingston, Meg Jensen, and not long after that she and Brian got married: Kingston proved to be a friendly place.

Another teacher there, Vesna Goldsworthy, read the manuscript in its early stages and made vital suggestions. The head of the faculty, David Rogers, was a continual support, and for more than seven years my students too were an excellent sounding board.

Among others who read the entire manuscript and made valuable comments were Valerie Grove, a stickler for good (and unboring) English, and three novelists: my Italian fencing friend Andrea Bocconi (who told me to keep my long stories short), Betsy Carter, and Dave King (who also teaches writers at NYU). John and Nina Darnton (also novelists) and their ex-Penguin Press editor daughter, Liza, were invaluable readers, while my son Toby and daughter Mary made useful comments on several chapters, although my younger son Guy's command that I should go off and write a novel did not accelerate matters.

Others I would like to thank are Bill Albers, Nicola Bennett, Lucinda Blumenfeld, David Bodanis, Catrine Clay, Julian Cotton, Sebastian Faulks, Victoria Glendenning, Joel Glucksman, Richard Holmes, Virginia Ironside, Annette Kobak, Rebecca Mead, Nicholas Partridge, Zina Rohan, Mary Sandys, Elisabeth Sifton, Linden Stafford, Anne Marie Stoddard, Catherine Talese, Rose Tremain, Ilya Wachs, Sam Wesson, and Melissa Ximena.

As with previous books, Tim Dickinson in Washington, D.C., helped the original manuscript become infinitely better: I have become used to his inspiring me with long-forgotten poems or passages from novels which he recites from memory, with (and I have checked) barely a slip. But he will also pick up an erring comma as well as an errant judgement, and is ever a pleasure to work with.

At Random House I delighted in my editorial skirmishes with the ebullient Will Murphy (the best fencer of his generation), who slowly but surely steered my ship into port. His assistant, Mika Kasuga, kept me from drifting off-course, while cheering from the headland were Susan Kamil, Tom Perry, and Gina Centrello, early supporters all. Evan Camfield presided with his usual calm authority over the book's production, Dana Leigh Blanchette was its imaginative designer, Archie Ferguson did the excellent jacket design for the American edition, and in Martin Schneider I had the most conscientious and knowledgeable of copyeditors: I consider myself very lucky.

My British publishers, Oneworld, have been a pleasure to work with from start to finish, and in particular I would like to thank Sam Carter, whose enthusiasm and eagle eye (particularly over wayward references to Italian suspense novels) are treasured, Jonathan Bentley-

Smith, for his all-round help and his taste in shoes, James Jones, for designing the cover, and Kate Bland, who I feel could get me a spot on *The Muppets* or *Match of the Day* if I asked her.

The Robbins Office was, simply, life-enhancing. David Halpern has always been there for me, while I have forgotten how many times Rachelle Bergstein read and commented on various drafts, only that each reading led to new insights. Janet Oshiro in particular made my task that much easier. Then there is the agency's presiding spirit, Kathy Robbins. Besides her onerous spousely duties, she has read and re-read numerous drafts (almost on the Sophia Tolstoy scale); exhorted, cajoled, bullied, charmed, and inspired everyone involved in the book's production; and has energized my dallying and galvanized my dillying. If I may say so, she and Tolstoy would have made a formidable team.

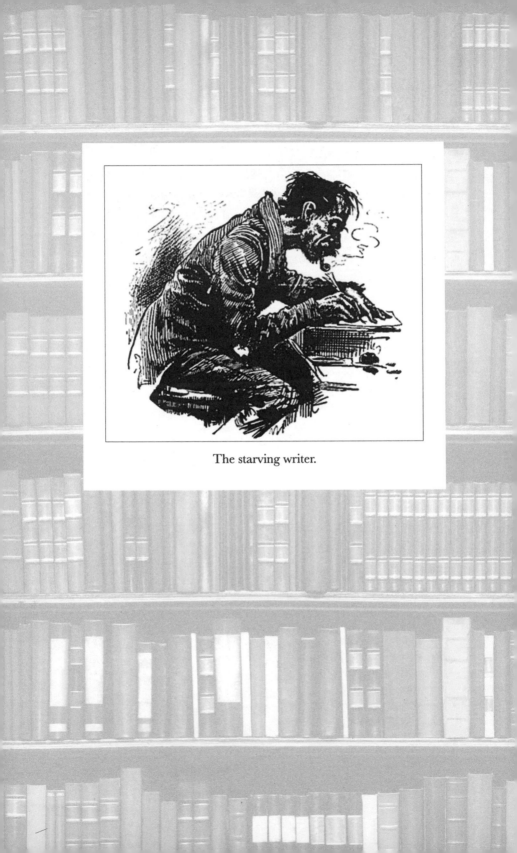

The starving writer.

There ain't nothing more to write about and I'm rotten glad of it, because if I'd a knowd what a trouble it was to make a book, I wouldn't a tackled it.

MARK TWAIN, *HUCKLEBERRY FINN*

Notes

PREFACE

xi **"I was finally a writer"**: *The Paris Review,* Summer 2006, p. 127.

xi **"There are three rules for writing a novel"**: William Somerset Maugham, quoted in *The Week,* December 14, 2013.

xi **At a New Year's Eve dinner party:** See Mark Singer, "Secrets of the Magus," *The New Yorker,* April 5, 1993, p. 54. Singer quotes David Mamet about his friend and frequent collaborator: "He knows the difference between doing things and not doing things. The magician performs a task and the illusion is created in the mind of the audience. And that's what acting is about." Not, of course, just acting or magicianship. Cf. Joseph Conrad, in "Henry James, An Appreciation, 1905": "All creative art is magic." Joseph Conrad, *Notes on Life and Letters* (London: Dent, 1921).

xiii **"These letters were the initials of the words"**: Leo Tolstoy, *Anna Karenina,* Part IV, Ch. 13. There are some fourteen translations of the novel (two in 2014 alone), each with their own strengths. I have made use of several of them for the version that appears here.

xvi **"a drinker with a writing problem"**: Behan died of complications from alcoholism in 1964.

xvi **"Now, hands up all of you"**: I was told this story by Behan's editor at Hutchinson, but cannot vouch for its truth. The novelist Paul Scott has recorded a more chaste version: "There is a story—isn't there?—of a man of letters who was invited to address an audience on the subject of creative writing. Reaching the rostrum after the usual gratifying preliminaries with members of the faculty, he enquired how many of the people gathered there intended to become writers. Nearly every hand rose. 'Then why are you sitting here?' he asked. 'Go home and get on with it.'" Paul Scott, *On Writing and the Novel* (New York: Morrow, 1987), p. 171. I prefer my version.

xvi **"Does anybody ever say, 'Here's X'":** Interview with Steven R. Centola, *Conversations with Ann Beattie*, ed. Dawn Trouard (Jackson: University Press of Mississippi, 2006), p. 75.

xvi **Teachers, she suggested, can't put:** Cf. a similar argument in Flannery O'Connor, *Mystery and Manners* (New York: Farrar, Straus and Giroux, 1985), p. 83.

xvi **"writing ability is mainly a product of good teaching":** John Gardner, *The Art of Fiction: Notes on Craft for Young Writers* (New York: Vintage, 1985), p. ix.

xvii **"Isn't writing a hard job though?":** *The Letters of Ernest Hemingway: 1923–1925,* ed. Sandra Spanier, Albert J. DeFazio III, and Robert W. Trogdon (Cambridge: Cambridge University Press, 2014).

xvii **"like a cow with a musket":** D. J. Taylor, *Orwell* (London: Chatto, 2003), pp. 91–92. See also Peter Stansky and William Abrahams, *The Unknown Orwell* (New York: Knopf, 1972), pp. 222–23, and Michael Shelden, *Orwell: The Authorized Biography* (New York: Harper, 1991), p. 119.

xx **"Abridge, abridge! Begin on the second page":** Chekhov, quoted in Janet Malcolm, *Reading Chekhov: A Critical Journey* (New York: Random House, 2002), p. 172.

xx **"they cannot read while working":** Francine Prose, *Reading Like a Writer: A Guide for People Who Love Books and for Those Who Want to Write Them* (New York: Harper, 2006), p. 9.

1. GRAB, INVITE, BEGUILE

3 **"So what were we talking about?":** Theresa Rebeck, *Seminar* (London: French, 2012).

3 **Into the face of the young man:** P. G. Wodehouse, *The Luck of the Bodkins* (London: Herbert Jenkins, 1925), p. 7.

4 **"I love deadlines":** M. J. Simpson, *Hitchhiker: A Biography of Douglas Adams* (London: Justin, Charles, 2003), p. 236.

4 **Gertrude Stein liked to look at cows:** For this, and the information on Allen, see Mason Currey, *Daily Rituals: How Great Minds Make Time, Find Inspiration, and Get to Work* (New York: Knopf, 2013), pp. 250, 120, and 9.

4 **"A novel is a long job":** Iris Murdoch, interviewed by Jeffrey Meyers, "The Art of Fiction," *The Paris Review*, no. 117, Summer 1990.

4 **"But it will have nothing":** George Steiner, "The Art of Criticism No. 2," *The Paris Review*, no. 137, Winter 1995.

4 **"the perfect absence note":** http://www.theparisreview.org /interviews/2718/the-art-of-fiction-no-94-e-l-doctorow.

5 **"And so the old gardener blew his nose":** Robert Graves, *Goodbye to All That* (London: Cape, 1929), p. 18.

5 **"Many books open with an author's assurance":** Michael Ondaatje, *The English Patient* (New York: Vintage, 1983), p. 93.

6 **Another biblical scholar:** Frank D. McConnell, *The Bible and the Narrative Tradition* (New York: Oxford University Press, 1986), p. 4.

7 **"The first rule in telling a story":** P. G. Wodehouse, *Laughing Gas* (London: Herbert Jenkins, 1936), pp. 7–9.

7 **"I believe that a well-known":** Agatha Christie, *The Murder on the Links* (London: Bodley Head, 1923), p. 5. Christie possibly bowdlerized a Robert Benchley opening: "'Dammit,' said the Duchess to the King. 'Take your hand off my leg.'" In *The Writing of Fiction*, however, Edith Wharton has it: "The '"Hell," said the Duchess as she lit her cigar,' with which an Eton boy is said to have begun a tale for his school magazine, in days when duchesses less commonly smoked and swore, would undoubtedly have carried his narrative to posterity if what followed had been at the same level." Wharton's and Christie's use of the phrase appeared the same year, 1923, as did Dorothy Sayers's first novel, *Whose Body?*, where Lord Peter Wimsey's very first words are "Oh, Damn." Coincidence?

8 **"almost knocked me off the bed":** Gabriel Garcia Márquez, *The Paris Review*, no. 82, Winter 1981.

8 **"Hale knew they meant to murder him":** Graham Greene,

Brighton Rock (Harmondsworth: Penguin, 1938, reprinted 1963).

10 **Thomas Mann begins *Buddenbrooks*:** Thomas Mann, *Buddenbrooks*, trans. H. T. Lowe-Porter (Harmondsworth: Penguin, 1957), pp. 67, 159. Other translations phrase this opening quite differently.

11 **"When someone gets in your face":** "Up Front," *The New York Times Book Review,* January 29, 2006, p. 4.

11 **"the narrative hook":** Robert Heinlein, Introduction, *Double Star* (New York: Del Rey, 1970), p. x.

12 **"a kind of authority":** Francine Prose, *Reading Like a Writer,* p. 17.

13 **"Except for the Marabar Caves":** The opening to *A Passage to India* is discussed in detail in Terry Eagleton, *How to Read Literature* (New Haven: Yale University Press, 2013), pp. 8–15.

15 **"Certainly, to envisage too clearly":** Thomas Mann, *A Sketch of My Life* (Paris: Harrison, 1930), p. 48.

15 **"as images always do":** Paul Scott, *On Writing and the Novel,* pp. 82–83.

16 **"starts with the locale":** *The New York Times,* August 4, 2010, p. B18.

17 **The nineteenth-century German philosopher:** Friedrich Schlegel, fragment no. 206 from *Athenaeum Fragments* (1798), trans. Peter Firchow: "A fragment, like a miniature work of art, has to be entirely isolated from the surrounding world and be complete in itself like a porcupine."

22 **"But that voice":** Mohsin Hamid, *The New York Times Book Review,* September 29, 2013, p. 35. Nabokov wrote the first draft of *Lolita* during a road trip across America, composing at night in the backseat of his car—the only place, he said, with no noise and no drafts.

22 **"in the midst of all that flighty exhibitionism":** Francine Prose, *Reading Like a Writer,* p. 100.

23 **"One of the most difficult things":** Gabriel Garcia Márquez, *The Paris Review,* Winter 1981.

23 **"What's so hard about that first sentence":** Joan Didion, *The Paris Review,* no. 74, Fall–Winter 1978. In an Internet essay (www.dailywritingtips.com/20-great-opening-lines-to-inspire-the-start-of-your-story/), the critic Mark Nichol lists twenty possible openings: the absurd; the acerbic; the bleak; the confiding; the cynical; the disorienting; the enigmatic; the epigrammatic; the expository; the

foreboding; the gritty; the inviting; the picaresque; the pithy; the poetic; the prefatory; the romantic; the sarcastic; the sour; and the unexpected. But these categories describe a tone of voice—sarcastic, confiding, acerbic—rather than a general approach.

23 **authorship "is like a love affair"**: "Mavis Gallant," Talk of the Town, *The New Yorker*, March 3, 2014, p. 27.

2. CIRCULAR RUINS

25 **"The color of Fanny Price's eyes"**: Vladimir Nabokov, "Good Readers and Good Writers" (1948), in *Lectures on Literature: British, French, and German Writers*, ed. Fredson Bowers (New York: Harcourt Brace Jovanovich, 1980).

25 **"I feel sorry for novelists"**: Julian Barnes, *Flaubert's Parrot* (London: Cape, 1984).

26 **"It was intolerable!"**: *Turgenev's Letters*, ed. A. V. Knowles (New York: Scribner, 1983).

26 **The novel rises in late antiquity**: See Michael Wood, "Report from the Interior," *The London Review of Books*, January 9, 2014, p. 29.

28 **"Her shape was not only exact"**: Henry Fielding, *Tom Jones* (New York: Barnes and Noble, 2004), p. 137.

28 **"quite an extraordinarily handsome"**: Fyodor Dostoyevsky, *Crime and Punishment*, trans. David Magarshack (London: Penguin, 1967), p. 20.

28 **"The novel," argues David Lodge**: David Lodge, *The Art of Fiction*, pp. 182–83. In his novel *Nice Work* (1988) Lodge creates an academic called Robyn Penrose who holds that "character" is a bourgeois myth, an illusion created to reinforce the ideology of capitalism.

28 **"in whom most of us can recognize"**: David Lodge, *The Independent*, March 3, 2005. Odd to think that *Ulysses* was initially conceived as an extra story in *Dubliners*; but then *Finnegans Wake* was originally conceived as the nineteenth episode in *Ulysses*.

28 **"A real person, profoundly as we may"**: Marcel Proust, *Remembrance of Things Past: Swann's Way*, Part 1, trans. C. K. Scott Moncrief (London: Chatto, 1966), pp. 112–13.

29 **But once again, even in such specific**: This list comes from

Jacques Bonnet, *Phantoms of the Bookshelves* (London: MacLehose Press, 2010), p. 84.

29 **"The novel, properly handled"**: D. H. Lawrence, *Lady Chatterley's Lover* (London: Penguin, 2010), p. 146.

29 **In two further letters to friends:** *Turgenev's Letters,* ed. A. V. Knowles. See also Isaiah Berlin, "The Gentle Genius," *The New York Review of Books,* October 27, 1983.

30 **"At Petersburg, so soon as the train stopped":** For this perception I am grateful to Peter Mendelsund, *What We See When We Read* (New York: Vintage, 2014), p. 36.

31 **"Do you remember":** See Tatyana Tolstoy, *Tolstoy Remembered,* trans. Derek Coltman (New York: McGraw-Hill, 1977), p. 276.

31 **"one of literature's greatest masters of manipulative tech-**

*"O.K.—let's get our stories straight, and our
characters sympathetic and well drawn."*

niques": Janet Malcolm, "Dreams and Anna Karenina," *The New York Review of Books,* June 25, 2015.

31 **Nabokov claimed that all great novels:** See Azar Nafisi, *Reading Lolita in Tehran* (New York: Random House, 2003), p. 241.

32 **"There is no psychology":** Philip Pullman, *Fairy Tales from the Brothers Grimm: A New English Version* (New York: Viking, 2012).

32 **"Kafka's characters tend to be":** Franz Kafka, *The Castle,* introduction by Max Brod, p. xiii.

32 **"handsome" or "pleasing":** Martin Amis is discerning about this in one of his essays. "She deals in auras, in presences, her creations fill a certain space with a certain personal style." Martin Amis, *The War Against Cliché: Essays and Reviews, 1971–2000* (New York: Vintage, 2002), pp. 436–37.

33 **V. S. Pritchett used bodies as emotional pointers:** See Martin Amis, "In Praise of Pritchett," *The London Review of Books,* May 22, 1980, from which I have taken my two examples. Towards the end of his life I commissioned Pritchett to write a biography of Chekhov. At lunch, I asked him if Chekhov had any lessons for him. For a moment, modesty battled with truthfulness; then he said, "No, I don't think so."

33 **"For my nymphet I needed a diminutive":** Vladimir Nabokov, *The Playboy Interview,* ed. G. B. Golson (New York: Playboy Press, 1981), p. 66.

34 **"did not give life to imaginary beings":** See Mary F. Sandars, *Honoré de Balzac: His Life and Writings* (New York: Dodd, Mead, 1905), p. 21.

34 **"excellent fictitious names":** Allan Gurganus, "The Man Who Loved Cemeteries," *The New York Times,* October 31, 2013, p. A29.

34 **The American writer Hilma Wolitzer:** From a lecture Wolitzer gave to the Society Library, New York, December 2011.

35 **"You must consider how the name":** See also various websites about the naming of characters, especially an essay, "What's in a Name?" by Jan Fields, and an article by Brian A. Klems, "The 7 Rules of Picking Names for Fictional Characters."

37 **Thus Devushin:** See Robert Payne, *Dostoyevsky: A Human Portrait* (New York: Knopf, 1958), p. 197.

38 **"He didn't make any description":** *Editor to Author: The Letters of Maxwell E. Perkins,* ed. John Hall Wheelock (New York: Scribner, 1987), pp. 205–6. In a letter to Scott Fitzgerald, after having just read the first draft of *The Great Gatsby,* Perkins wrote: "I would know Tom Buchanan if I met him in the street and would avoid him," p. 39.

39 **"There is a sense in which":** Robert Payne, *Dostoyevsky: A Human Portrait,* p. 196.

39 **"She always stood sideways":** See Sol Stein, *Stein on Writing: A Master Editor of Some of the Most Successful Writers of Our Century Shares His Craft Techniques and Strategies* (New York: St. Martin's Press, 1995).

39 **a sharp comparison:** See Daniel Mendelsohn, "Do Critics Make Good Novelists?" *The New York Times Book Review,* May 11, 2014, p. 39. Mendelsohn is quoting a comparison made by the British sociologist John Thompson.

39 **"capable of surprising":** E. M. Forster, *Aspects of the Novel* (London: Penguin Classics, 2005), p. 78.

40 **"What I find heartbreakingly difficult":** Quoted in Richard Poirier, "How Far Shall I Take This Character?" *London Review of Books,* November 2, 2000, p. 5, in a review of James Atlas's *Bellow: A Biography.*

40 **"You think about a certain situation":** Iris Murdoch, *The Paris Review,* no. 115, Summer 1990.

40 **"The big question for me":** Peter Carey, *The Paris Review,* no. 177, Summer 2006, pp. 129–30.

41 **"You may only know your characters' externals":** Anne Lamott, *Bird by Bird: Some Instructions on Writing and Life* (New York: Anchor, 1995), pp. 45–46.

41 **"the twists and turns":** Joe Wright, director of a recent film version of *Anna Karenina;* see also Terrence Rafferty, "Degrees of Fidelity to Tolstoy's Heroine," *The New York Times,* Arts and Leisure section, p. 23.

41 **"dressed and painted to represent":** See Alberto Manguel, *A History of Reading* (London: Flamingo, 1997), p. 17.

41 **Impossible precision:** Ibid.

43 **"Hemmed them in with her knowing essayism":** See James

Wood, "Perfuming the Money Issue," *London Review of Books,* October 11, 2012, p. 3.

44 **"A character I thought was"**: See the contribution by "Pepper," June 23, 2009, at absolutewrite.com/forums/showthread.php?146007 -the-major-ness-of-minor-characters.

44 **"My characters tell me so much"**: Harold Pinter, *The Sunday Times,* 1962.

44 **"*Falling in Place* seems to me"**: Interview with Larry McCaffery and Sinda Gregory, 1982, *Conversations with Ann Beattie,* ed. Dawn Trouard, p. 48.

45 **"Woke up and realized"**: P. D. James in conversation with Peter Kemp at the 2012 Cheltenham Festival of Literature.

46 **"lay upon my conscience"**: *Autobiography of Mark Twain,* ed. Harriet Elinor Smith, vol. 1 (Berkeley: University of California Press, 2011), pp. 157–58.

46 **"there is no creeping"**: "The Overcoat," *The Complete Tales of Nikolai Gogol,* vol. 2, ed. Leonard J. Kent, trans. Constance Garnett (Chicago: University of Chicago Press, 1985), p. 320.

46 **"In all that she considered"**: See John Walter Cross, *George Eliot's Life as Related in Her Letters and Journals* (New York: Biblio Bazaar, 2008).

46 **"Things," he wrote**: Thomas Mann, *A Sketch of My Life,* pp. 44, 46.

47 **"description of the state"**: Frederick R. Karl, *William Faulkner: American Writer* (New York: Weidenfeld, 1988), p. 318.

47 **"where there is a creative mind"**: See Janet Malcolm, *Psychoanalysis: The Impossible Profession* (London: Vintage, 1982), p. 17.

47 **"write down, without any falsification"**: See Wikipedia entry for "free association."

48 **"It is not improbabilities of incident"**: Entry for January 2, 1886.

48 **"to anyone on the receiving end"**: New York Public Library seminar on George Eliot, November 2014.

48 **"put their thumb in the pan"**: D. H. Lawrence, *Study of Thomas Hardy and Other Essays,* ed. Bruce Steele (Cambridge: Cambridge University Press, 1985), quoted in Terry Eagleton, *How to Read Literature,* p. 100.

48 **"E. M. Forster speaks of his major characters"**: Vladimir Nabokov, *The Paris Review*, no. 41, Summer–Fall 1967.

50 **"A character dies on the page"**: Jonathan Franzen, *Farther Away* (New York: Farrar, Straus and Giroux, 2012), pp. 125–27. I remember hearing Geoff Dyer speak at Cheltenham Literary Festival in October 2009, and noting down his comment: "If the story is pulling just fractionally ahead of what the characters are creating, then I don't like it. . . ."

50 **"It's the nearest we'll ever get"**: See Sarah Lyall, "Three Beginnings, Reverse Chronology and a Novel That Starts Over in Every Chapter: What Will Kate Atkinson Think of Next?" *The New York Times Magazine*, March 24, 2013, p. 25.

50 **"Writers always say characters surprise their authors"**: *The New York Times Style Magazine*, November 16, 2014, p. 138.

51 **"is a process and an unfolding"**: See Rebecca Mead, *My Life in Middlemarch* (New York: Crown, 2014), p. 139.

52 **"transcribed conversations, real emails"**: From the publishers' publicity material for Sheila Heti's 2012 novel *How Should a Person Be?*

52 **"Increasingly I'm less interested"**: See James Wood, "True Lives," *The New Yorker*, June 25, 2012, p. 66.

52 **For most writers, it takes considerable hard work:** This point is well made by Zoë Heller, "Write What You Know," *The New York Times Book Review*, March 30, 2014, p. 31.

52 **"People tend to underestimate the power"**: Vladimir Nabokov, *The Playboy Interview*, p. 65.

52 **"Fiction is not crypto-autobiography"**: *Conversations with John Cheever* (Jackson: University Press of Mississippi, 1988), p. ix.

53 **"Fact and fiction, fiction and fact"**: Gail Godwin and Rob Neufeld, *The Making of a Writer: Journals 1961–1963* (New York: Random House, 2007), p. 236.

53 **"had mistaken impersonation for confession"**: Philip Roth, *The Counterlife* (New York: Vintage, 1996); see also Philip Roth, *Reading Myself and Others*, and Martin Amis, *The War Against Cliché*, p. 288.

53 **Whoever reckons that the words:** Philip Roth, "My Life as a Writer," *The New York Times Book Review*, March 16, 2014, p. 16.

3. STOLEN WORDS

55 **"Plagiarize, plagiarize, plagiarize!":** Tom Lehrer, "Lobachevsky," from *Songs by Tom Lehrer,* 1953. Lehrer, himself a university mathematician, sings of how the Russian mathematician influenced him: the song is "not intended as a slur on [Lobachevsky's] character," the name being chosen "solely for prosodic reasons."

55 **"Not every imitation ought to be stigmatized":** Samuel Johnson, "The Criterions of Plagiarism," *The Rambler,* vol. 3, 1751, pp. 24–31.

56 **"relying just on memory":** See *The Library of Alexandria,* p. 38.

56 **Despite Aristophanes the Librarian:** See John Burrow, *A History of Histories* (New York: Knopf, 2008), p. 158.

56 **"Shakespeare was a wonderful teller of stories":** Bill Bryson, *Shakespeare: The World as Stage* (New York: Harper, 2007).

"You know that thing where you stand like a statue, then move real fast, then stand like a statue again? You totally stole that from me."

56 **whole passages of text were lifted:** See Haydn-Williams, "Illicit Shortcuts," *The Author,* Spring 2009, p. 11.

57 **"Sterne's Writings":** Oliver Goldsmith, *The Vicar of Wakefield: A Tale,* vol. 5, p. xviii.

58 **"All my novels are written":** Letter to Auguste Dumont, March 16, 1877, in *Émile Zola: Correspondence,* ed. B. H. Bakker, (Montreal: Montreal University Press, 1980), ii, pp. 548–49. See also Mario Vargas Llosa, *Aunt Julia and the Scriptwriter* (New York: Farrar, Straus and Giroux, 1982), p. 3, where the main character's actual job is to plagiarize.

58 **"That's something that poets":** See http://dash.hardvard.edu/handle/1/4000221.

59 **"Oh, dear me, how unspeakably funny":** Mark Twain, letter to Helen Keller, March 17, 1903, *Mark Twain's Letters,* vol. 1 (1917), ed. Albert Bigelow Paine (New York), p. 731.

59 **"One of the surest of tests":** T. S. Eliot, *The Sacred Wood* (New York: Knopf, 1921). The footnotes that Eliot appended to *The Waste Land* were designed, he admitted, to "spik[e] the guns of critics of my earlier poems who had accused me of plagiarism." "The Frontiers of Criticism," in *On Poetry and Poets* (London: Faber, 1957), p. 109.

61 **"To put one's name to language":** Letter to the Editor from Richard C. Doenges, *The New York Times,* August 10, 2010.

61 **"a table-manners violation":** The words of a copyright expert at Columbia University, quoted in Lizzie Widdicombe, "The Plagiarist's Tale," *The New Yorker,* February 13, 2012.

62 **In Britain, there are more:** See Charles McGrath, "Plagiarism: Everybody in the Pool," *The New York Times Book Review,* January 7, 2007, p. 33; and Gary Slapper, "Cheating? No, It's All Our Own Work . . . ," *The Times,* October 15, 2009, p. 9.

62 **As Judge Richard Posner comments:** Richard Posner, *The Little Book of Plagiarism* (New York: Pantheon, 2007), p. 36.

63 **"Evidence suggests that writers":** Bruce McCall, "The Dog Wrote It," *The New York Times Book Review,* November 14, 1999, p. 43.

64 **But Goodwin never admitted:** See Jon Wiener, *Historians in Trouble* (New York: The New Press, 2005), pp. 182–95.

64 **"I felt vindicated":** See Bo Crader, "Lynne McTaggart on Doris Kearns Goodwin," weeklystandard.com, January 23, 2002.

64 **"Where would Dante send":** Sandra Beasley, "Nice Poem; I'll Take It," *The New York Times Book Review,* April 28, 2013, p. 31.

66 **"Oddly enough, most of us":** See "Novelists Speak Out in Defense of Colleague," *The New York Times,* December 7, 2006, C1.

67 **"Fiction," he wrote:** See Charles McGrath, "Plagiarism," p. 33. A 1920s *Punch* contained this verse written by its editor, Sir Owen Seaman—quoted in H. M. Paull, *Literary Ethics* (London: Thornton Butterworth, 1928), p. 126: "There's nothing new this time of day/ No bard should blush to be a debtor/To those who had the earlier say,/So long as he can do it better;/The form's the thing; to poets dead/And crowned in heaven we give the credit/Not half so much as what they said/As for the jolly way they said it."

67 **"I was sitting at home":** Malcolm Gladwell, "Something Borrowed: Should a Charge of Plagiarism Ruin Your Life?" *The New Yorker,* November 22, 2004.

68 **"immediate freshening":** The phrase is critic and poet Peter Schjeldahl's. Janet Malcolm deploys it in *Forty-One False Starts: Essays on Artists and Writers* (New York: Farrar, Straus and Giroux, 2014), pp. 9–11.

69 **It was used first in something like its modern sense:** See Richard Posner, *The Little Book of Plagiarism,* p. 50.

69 **"Writing is an act of thievery":** See *The Week,* June 1, 2013, p. 8.

69 **"Within this kind of work":** Alexander Stille, "The Body Under the Rug," *The New York Times,* February 10, 2013, p. 8.

70 **"It would be some fifty thousand words long":** See Michael Holroyd, introduction to *A Dog's Life* (London: Cape, 2014).

71 **Salman Rushdie did not deny:** See Zoë Heller, "The Salman Rushdie Case," *The New York Review of Books,* December 20, 2012, p. 8.

71 **"For the wolf of a writer":** Roger Rosenblatt, "The Writer in the Family," *The New York Times Book Review,* May 13, 2012, p. 43.

72 **"recognize a portion of an old diary":** See Thomas Mallon, *Stolen Words,* p. 126.

73 **"I have sinned against you":** *Letters of Thomas Mann, 1889–1955,* introduction by Richard Winston (Berkeley: University of California Press, 1990), p. 4.

73 **"As a younger man":** Peter Carey, *The Paris Review,* pp. 134, 144.

73 **"The novelist destroys the house of his life":** Milan Kundera in *Art of the Novel* (New York: Harper, 2003); used as the epigraph to Hilary Spurling, *Paul Scott: A Life of the Author of the Raj Quartet* (New York: Norton, 1991).

73 **"a dirty business":** See Adam Begley, *Updike* (New York: Harper, 2014), pp. 6–9.

74 **The Norwegian writer:** See "Completely Without Dignity: An Interview with Karl Ove Knausgård," *The Paris Review,* December 26, 2013.

4. THE TRICK OF IT

77 **"Remember that writing is translation":** E. B. White quoted in Michael Sims, "Some Book," *The New York Times Book Review,* April 22, 2012, p. 27.

77 **"And who are you?":** Laurence Sterne, *Tristram Shandy,* vii, 33.

79 **A difficulty with this approach:** See Diane Johnson, "At the Slumber Party," *The New York Review of Books,* November 8, 2012, p. 32.

80 **This is particularly true in *Anna Karenina*:** For a fuller discussion of the episode, see Janet Malcolm, "Dreams and Anna Karenina," *The New York Review of Books,* June 25, 2015, p.12.

80 **"How these papers have been placed":** Susan Rieger, *The Divorce Papers* (New York: Crown, 2014).

81 **"You adopted exactly the right method":** See *Editor to Author: The Letters of Maxwell E. Perkins,* p. 38, letter of November 20, 1924. *The Great Gatsby* was published the following September.

81 **"The story is told thirdhand":** Joan Didion, "The Art of Nonfiction No. 1," *The Paris Review,* no. 176, Spring 2006, p. 66.

83 **"A lying first-person narrator":** Peter Carey, *The Paris Review,* p. 131.

83 **In an essay of 1992:** Salman Rushdie, "'Errata': Or, Unreliable Narration in *Midnight's Children*," *Imaginary Homelands: Essays and Criticism, 1981–1991* (London: Granta, 1992), pp. 22–24.

84 **"You have to figure out":** *Conversations with Ann Beattie,* p. 83.

85 **"The book I have been doing":** Quoted by Elif Batuman, "Get a Real Degree," *London Review of Books,* September 23, 2010.

86 **"First person is always more":** Norman Mailer, "First Person Versus Third Person," *The Spooky Art: Thoughts on Writing* (New York: Random House, 2003), pp. 32–37.

88 **"The change to first person":** For Rose Tremain, the art of characterization is to arouse in the reader both recognition and surprise. It was the duty of a historical novelist to give a "different twitch" to what the reader knows, so that he thinks, "I thought I knew all about that period, but I didn't know that." She then added a lesson she had been taught years ago—that in all fiction one should have a hope/dread axis.

89 **In his preface to *The Ambassadors*:** Henry James, *The Art of the Novel* (New York: Scribner, 1937), p. 321.

91 **"I found myself increasingly drawn":** See Marc Chénetier, "An Interview with Steven Millhauser," *Transatlantica,* October 1, 2003, available at transatlantica.revues.org/562.

93 **This appears to be neutral third person:** See Michael Wood, "Report from the Interior," *London Review of Books,* January 9, 2014, p. 29.

93 **Not only in fiction:** See David Nokes, *Samuel Johnson: A Life* (London: Faber, 2012).

93 **William Faulkner's *The Sound and the Fury*:** See Frederick R. Karl, *William Faulkner: American Writer,* p. 533.

94 **Faulkner focused on the transformation:** See the Wikipedia entry on the novel—an excellent précis.

95 **In his review of the book, William Skidelsky observed:** See William Skidelsky, "*In a Strange Room* by Damon Galgut," *The Observer,* July 24, 2010.

95 **Letters have the advantage:** The material on Richardson is based on David Lodge, *The Art of Fiction,* p. 22.

96 **which even went through a phase:** See Elif Batuman, "Get a Real Degree."

97 **"One of Beckett's narrators reports":** Marc Chénetier, "An Interview with Steven Millhauser."

97 **One of their number:** Wendy Roberts, "The Art of Narrative Distance: The Sun Tzu Approach for Writers," manuscript in preparation.

98 **"In October 1805":** See *War and Peace,* trans. Richard Pevear and Larissa Volokhonsky (New York: Vintage, 2008), p. 112.

100 **Using this disembodied narrative voice:** The phrase is critic Wayne C. Booth's. See *The Rhetoric of Fiction* (Chicago: University of Chicago Press, 1961).

100 **In the end, he chose to sacrifice:** For these insights see estowell .edublogs.org/files/2011/09/The-Principles-of-Uncertainty-in-Crime -and-Punishment-1dwwd6z.doc.

100 **Francine Prose, who with Norman Mailer:** Francine Prose, *Reading Like a Writer,* p. 92.

101 **It is also likely that Raskolnikov:** See Joseph Frank, "The Making of *Crime and Punishment,*" in Robert M. Polhemus and Roger B. Henkle, *Critical Reconstructions: The Relationship of Fiction and Life* (Stanford, Calif.: Stanford University Press, 1994).

5. SAYS YOU

104 **"I took it out":** Di Trevis, in a talk at the 92nd Street Young Men's and Young Women's Hebrew Association, New York, January 2014.

104 **"If I picked up a book with no dialogue":** Nell Leyshon, "Dialogue," *The Author,* Winter 2013, p. 128.

105 **"The centrality of dialogue in *Pride and Prejudice*":** Azar Nafisi, *Reading Lolita in Tehran: A Memoir in Books* (New York: Random House, 2003), p. 268.

106 **"Too much of the action":** Sebastian Faulks, *On Fiction: A Story of the Novel in 28 Characters* (London: BBC Books, 2011), pp. 59–60.

106 **"Pierre sees that everyone, everyone is smiling":** Leo Tolstoy, *War and Peace,* trans. Richard Pevear and Larissa Volokhonsky (New York: Vintage, 2008), p. 212.

108 **"To read in these days":** Quoted in Charles Burkhart, ed., *The Art of Ivy Compton-Burnett* (London: Gollancz, 1972), p. 55. For this discussion of Compton-Burnett's use of dialogue cf. Jeanne Perry Sandra, *Disclosure and Ivy Compton-Burnett: A Guide to Reading Her Dialogue Novels* (Seattle: University of Washington Press, 1977); Frederick R. Karl, "The Intimate World of Ivy Compton-Burnett," in *A Reader's Guide to the Contemporary English Novel* (New York: Farrar, Straus and

Cudahy, 1962), pp. 201–19; and Walter Allen, *The Modern Novel* (New York: Dutton, 1964), p. 191.

109 **"She drops us—as if from a great height":** Francine Prose, introduction to Ivy Compton-Burnett, *A House and Its Head* (New York: New York Review Books, 2001).

110 **"lost more than it gained":** Edith Wharton, *The Writing of Fiction*, p. 54.

111 **"Put down the gun, Utterson!":** Stephen King, *On Writing* (New York: Scribner, 2010), p. 120.

111 **"Oh," growled Ralph:** Charles Dickens, *Nicholas Nickleby* (New York: Barnes and Noble), pp. 42–46.

112 **"The unconscious critical acumen":** Anthony Trollope, *An Autobiography*, chapter 12.

112 **"The question is a fascinating one":** Tim Parks, "Poor with Words," letter in *The London Review of Books*, July 28, 2011, p. 4.

113 **In 1968 Tom Stoppard wrote:** Tom Stoppard, *The Real Inspector Hound* (London: Samuel French, 1968), p. 15.

117 **This is not to say:** See Kingsley Amis, *The Paris Review,* no. 64, Winter 1975: "A novelist is a sort of mimic by definition." Amis himself was a wonderful mimic, and could produce a range of voices— not just on the page, but also in conversation.

117 **"A narrative style that faithfully imitated":** David Lodge, *The Art of Fiction,* p. 18.

117 **"There is a sense in which":** David Lodge, ibid., p. 172. He also mentions what he calls "the ultimate telephone novel"—*Vox* by Nicholson Baker.

117 **"I amend dialect stuff by talking":** See Andrew Levy, *Huck Finn's America* (New York: Simon and Schuster, 2015), p. 44.

118 **"I followed Hartley to her home":** John Crace, "The Sea, The Sea," *The Guardian,* January 21, 2010.

119 **"Asked, by one of our more distinguished":** Paul Scott, *On Writing and the Novel,* p. 49.

119 **"A single sentence will deploy":** James Wood, "Away Thinking About Things," *The New Yorker,* August 25, 2014, p. 68.

121 **"the brain has to process":** See Jonah Lehrer, "The Eureka Hunt," *The New Yorker,* July 28, 2008, pp. 40ff.

121 **"In her whole insignificant figure":** Thomas Mann, *Buddenbrooks,* trans. H. T. Lowe-Porter (Harmondsworth: Penguin, 1957), pp. 67, 159.

6. SECRET TRAPDOORS

125 **"Just don't forget irony":** See Joachim Fest, *Not I: Memoirs of a German Childhood,* trans. Martin Chalmers (New York: Other Press, 2014).

126 **"Irony may be defined":** Julian Barnes, *A History of the World in 10½ Chapters* (London: Vintage, 1990), p. 54.

126 **"Irony, in the sense of finding":** August Boehm, "Boehm on Bridge," *Bridge Bulletin,* December 2012, p. 47.

126 **"never quite without irony":** Kafka, *The Trial,* postscript to the first edition (1925) by Max Brod (New York: Knopf, 1957), p. 327.

127 **"hurts like irony":** Ali Smith, *Artful* (New York: Penguin, 2013).

127 **"was new to her and tasted oddly good"**: Meg Wolitzer, *The Interestings* (New York: Riverhead, 2013).

128 **"Sometimes, in spite of himself"**: Marcel Proust, *Remembrance of Things Past*, vol. 1, trans. C. K. Scott Moncrief (London: Chatto, 1966), p. 290.

131 **"never to articulate the idea"**: Søren Kierkegaard, *On the Concept of Irony with Continual Reference to Socrates*, trans. Lee M. Capel (Bloomington: Indiana University Press, 1975), p. 86.

131 **"the outer and the inner"**: Ibid., p. 50.

131 **"As one sees the trees"**: Ibid., p. 56.

"What's the right age to tell a child that she's ironic?"

132 **"A secret trapdoor had suddenly opened"**: Lila Azam Zanganeh, "His Father's Best Translator," *The New York Times Book Review*, July 22, 2012, p. 31.

132 **"In fiction two and two is always more than four"**: Flannery O'Connor, "Writing Short Stories," *Manners and Mysteries* (New York: Farrar, Straus and Giroux, 1970), pp. 99, 102.

133 **"I thought that we might see him"**: Hilary Mantel, *Wolf Hall* (New York: Holt, 2009), p. 186.

135 **"prefer the cold end"**: Roxana Robinson, "The Big Chill," *The New York Times Book Review,* January 7, 2001.

136 **"Your audience is your co-writer"**: David Carr, "HBO Bets on Two Thoroughbreds," *The New York Times,* January 29, 2012, p. AR1.

136 **When in 1946:** See "Animal Farm: What Orwell Really Meant," *The New York Review of Books,* July 11, 2013, p. 40.

137 **Kafka never completed many of his writings:** For this perception I am indebted to Alberto Manguel, *A History of Reading,* p. 92. Of all people, the physicist Robert Oppenheimer once remarked: "Precisely in philosophy you should know more than in poetry. It is the implicit missing that stimulates the argument."

137 **"A tale from which pieces"**: Rudyard Kipling, *Something of Myself: For My Friends Known and Unknown* (London: Penguin Classics, 1987), p. 156. Richard Holmes, in his introduction, calls this "implied" narrative.

138 **"You know what they do, Sybil?"**: J. D. Salinger, "A Perfect Day for Bananafish," *The New Yorker,* January 31, 1948.

139 **"that which writing suggests"**: Quoted in David C. Lindberg, *Theories of Vision from al-Kindi to Kepler* (Chicago: University of Chicago Press, 1996); cf. Alberto Manguel, *A History of Reading,* p. 39.

140 **For the part that shows there are seven-eighths more underwater:** See also John McPhee, "Omission: Choosing What to Leave Out," *The New Yorker,* September 14, 2015, pp. 42–49.

140 **"Art is not only the desire"**: See Penelope Niven, *Thornton Wilder: A Life* (New York: Harper, 2012).

140 **"They say that chess was born in bloodshed"**: Paolo Maurensig, *The Lüneburg Variation* (New York; Holt, 1998), p. 1.

141 **"ends as if the author"**: Spelling everything out may spoil the story's effect, but here goes: as I imagine it, Frisch and Meyer return to the old Nazi's home, and once again there is a chess match where a human life is at stake—only this time it is Frisch's. The board is the patchwork of cloth that years before was so laboriously stitched together so that Tabori could play chess inside the camp; it is his parting gift to Meyer. And Meyer wins the game by using the strategy he has been taught by his master—the Lüneburg Variation. As the two men make their way into the well-kept garden, it hardly matters

whether Frisch then takes his own life or allows Meyer to shoot him: the loser must pay.

7. GRABBING FICTION BY THE TALE

145 **For Aristotle, a plot had to have:** Aristotle, *Poetics*, 23.1459a.

147 **"They are far and away":** Christopher Booker, *The Seven Basic Plots: Why We Tell Stories* (London: Continuum, 2004), p. 2.

150 **These talks were later published:** See E. M. Forster, *Aspects of the Novel*.

150 **Story strips away all but the barest:** See Terry Eagleton, *How to Read Literature*, p. 115.

151 **"In my view, stories and novels":** Stephen King, *On Writing*, p. 159.

151 **"the good writer's last resort":** Ibid., p. 160.

151 **"sold like hotcakes":** Ibid., p. 164.

152 **"There is a huge difference":** Ibid., p. 167.

152 **"an elaborate puzzle":** Edith Wharton, *The Writing of Fiction*, p. 61.

152 **"the first essential":** Dorothy Sayers, "Aristotle on Detective Fiction," *Fiction: A Collection of Critical Essays*, ed. Robin W. Winks (Englewood Cliffs, N.J.: Prentice-Hall, 1980).

153 **In one of his books, Bloom commends Kermode:** Harold Bloom, *The Shadow of a Great Rock* (New Haven: Yale University Press, 2011), pp. 232–33.

153 **"A murder mystery needs a strong plot":** Joan Acocella, "Doubling Down," *The New Yorker*, October 8, 2012.

154 **"The A novelist":** Martin Amis, *The War Against Cliché*.

155 **"I cannot see what is meant":** Henry James, "The Art of Fiction," *Longman's Magazine*, 1884. It was written as a rebuttal to "Fiction as One of the Fine Arts," a lecture given by Sir Walter Besant, in which Besant argued that plot is more important than characterization.

156 **"the characters have been required":** E. M. Forster, *Aspects of the Novel*, pp. 126–27. How does one get the emotional and narrative arcs to mesh? Peter Dunne, in his book *Emotional Structure: Creating the Story*

Beneath the Plot, recommends that you write the headline of a scene on an index card and jot a few notes about the action, being careful to hit only the high points. Turn the card over and write a headline for the emotional content of this scene and jot a few notes about how the emotions change. Turning the card over in this way forces you to consider what your character would really feel in this situation, and connects the inner and outer conflict in a simple yet powerful way.

157 **"I sat down to another nine-day schedule"**: Ray Bradbury, *Fahrenheit 451* (New York: Del Rey, 2004), p. 111.

8. WAVES IN THE MIND

159 **"There are two kinds of written language"**: Ezra Pound, *ABC of Reading* (New York: New Directions, 1960), p. 20.

159 **"True wit"**: Alexander Pope, *An Essay on Criticism, Pt. II.*

"I think I've finally found my own voice."

160 **"Style is a very simple matter"**: *Congenial Spirits: The Selected Letters of Virginia Woolf,* ed. Joanne Trautmann Banks (New York: Harcourt, 1990), p. 204.

161 **"Rhythmic speech or writing"**: Henry Watson Fowler, *A Diction-*

ary of Modern English Usage (1926, reprinted by Oxford University Press, 2009).

161 **"the development of a symphony":** John W. Crawford, *The New York Times,* May 10, 1925.

162 **"About HB's [Brewster's] writing":** *Congenial Spirits: The Selected Letters of Virginia Woolf,* p. 282, letter dated March 23, 1931.

163 **"When a writer who is not a poet":** Mary Norris, *Between You & Me: Confessions of a Comma Queen* (New York: Norton, 2015), p. 108.

163 **"The harmony which is required":** Anthony Trollope, *An Autobiography,* ch. 12.

163 **"Good writing has a musical quality":** Willis S. Hylton, "Unbreakable," *The New York Times Magazine,* December 14, 2014, p. 43.

163 **"I . . . have consciously set myself":** *The Letters of Robert Frost, Volume 1: 1886–1920,* ed. Donald Sheehy, Mark Richardson, and Robert Faggen (Cambridge, Mass.: Belknap Press, 2014), letter to John Bartlett, July 4, 1913.

163 **"The ear does it":** Ibid., letter to John Bartlett, February 22, 1914.

164 **"with an intoxicating fervour":** *The Trial,* postscript to the first edition (1925) by Max Brod, p. 326.

164 **"hundreds of times out loud":** See Barbara B. Bannon, *Publishers Weekly,* May 25, 1970, pp. 21–22.

165 **"in the absence of friends":** Frederick Brown, *Flaubert* (New York: Little, Brown, 2006).

165 **James Wood takes up:** James Wood, *The New York Times Book Review,* April 16, 2006, p. 11.

166 **"In Goethe's time":** Milan Kundera, *The Joke* (New York: Harper Perennial, 1992), p. 321. Other writers of note have agreed. For Allen Tate, the celebrated American critic, "It has been through Flaubert that the novel has at last caught up with poetry." *Essays of Four Decades* (New York: Morrow, 1970), p. 140.

167 **"was the first to consecrate himself":** Jorge Luis Borges, "Flaubert and His Exemplary Destiny," *Selected Nonfictions* (New York: Viking, 1999), p. 90.

167 **"There are times when it means nothing":** E. M. Forster, *Aspects of the Novel,* pp. 210–15.

168 **Rhythm implies continuities:** See Frank Kermode, *The Sense of an Ending* (London: Oxford University Press, 1967), p. 118.

168 **"It may be that its musical qualities"**: Thomas Mann, *A Sketch of my Life*, p. 32.

168 **"easy rhythm in fiction"**: E. M. Forster, *Aspects of the Novel*, p. 215.

168 **"Many men died"**: See Kurt Vonnegut, *Letters*, ed. Dan Wakefield (New York: Delacourt, 2012), pp. 7–8, 49.

169 **The best book on the subject of rhythm:** F. L. Lucas, *Style*, 1955, ch. 10, "The Harmony of Prose," pp. 214–50; cf. Littlehampton Book Services, 1974.

171 **"The profanity was not good"**: Mark Twain, *A Connecticut Yankee in King Arthur's Court*, ch. 35. See Garry Wills, *Lincoln at Gettysburg: The Words That Remade America* (New York: Simon and Schuster, 1992), p. 161, where Wills discusses Lincoln's use of word order.

172 **"The raging rocks"**: *A Midsummer Night's Dream*, Act 1, Scene 2.

172 **"I'll lead you about a round"**: Ibid., Act 3, Scene 1.

173 **"As she moved beside him"**: See Peter Mendelsund, *What We See When We Read*, p. 308.

175 **"I daresay I fancied myself"**: Henry James, *The Turn of the Screw*, ch. 3, p. 15.

175 **"but [Ernest's] heart"**: Michael Holroyd, *A Book of Secrets* (New York: Farrar, Straus and Giroux, 2010), p. 21.

176 **"good prose is rhythmical"**: "The Rhythm of Prose," by Robert Ray Lorant, originally published in *The Century Magazine*, 1920.

177 **"They say that I should quit"**: Ross Thomas, *The Porkchoppers* (New York: Morrow, 1972), pp. 170–72.

178 **Later I came across:** See Melvyn Bragg, *The Book of Books: The Radical Impact of the King James Bible, 1611–2011* (London: Hodder, 2011), p. 125.

179 **"Style," he says:** Norman Mailer, *The Spooky Art*.

180 **"I'm often drawn by tone"**: John Lahr, "By the Book," *The New York Times Book Review*, September 21, 2014, p. 8.

180 **"and indeed when he writes badly"**: Paul Hendrickson, author of *Hemingway's Boat* (New York: Knopf, 2011), lecture at City University of New York, November 2, 2011. In a later review of an audiobooks edition of Hemingway's work, Hendrickson wrote that the author "changed the look and sound of American speech on the printed page." "An Audible Feast," *The New York Times Book Review*, May 19, 2013, p. 18.

9. "JUST LIKE ZORRO"

183 **"Sex is our most intense form of communication":** Edmund White, *The New York Times Book Review,* October 3, 2013, pp. 14–15.

183 **"All this fuss about sleeping together":** Evelyn Waugh, *Vile Bodies,* 1930.

184 **"Sex"—no clerical headmaster:** Iris Murdoch, *The Paris Review.*

184 **"Each language draws taboo lines":** George Steiner, "The Art of Criticism No. 2," *The Paris Review.*

184 **Nicholson Baker's sexually explicit novel:** See Sam Lipsyte, "Story of O," *The New York Times Book Review,* August 14, 2011, p. 10.

185 **Perhaps there is something in common:** See *Angélique* for other fruit metaphors: "as firm as apples" (p. 109), and "like a melon ripening under glass" (p. 131).

186 **"The difficult task of conveying":** Tom Fleming, "O Glorious Pubes!" *Literary Review,* December 2007/January 2008, p. 72.

188 **And the 2005 prizewinner:** Giles Coren, *Winkler* (London: Cape, 2005).

188 **"BEAT thung BEAT thung":** Tom Wolfe, *Back to Blood* (New York: Little, Brown, 2012). See a discussion of Wolfe's writing in Nathaniel Rich, "Things You Never Thought Possible," *The New York Review of Books,* November 22, 2012.

189 **"Most of what we have learned":** Celia Brayfield, *Bestseller* (London: Fourth Estate, 1996), p. 125.

190 **Attitudes were changing:** See Faramerz Dabhoiwala, *The Origins of Sex* (London: Allen Lane, 2012).

191 **"if it is the same blood":** Laurence Sterne, *A Sentimental Journey,* ed. Graham Petrie (London: Penguin, 1986), p. 75.

191 **Everything is double meaning:** See Elizabeth W. Harries, *The Cambridge Companion to Laurence Sterne,* ed. Thomas Keymer (Cambridge: Cambridge University Press, 2009).

192 **"You will certainly hurt yourself":** Jane Austen, *Mansfield Park* (Ware: Wordsworth Classics, 1993), p. 99.

192 **"Jane Austen's delicate genius":** Edith Wharton, *The Writing of Fiction,* p. 48.

192 **"I could scarcely see my master's face"**: Charlotte Brontë, *Jane Eyre* (New York: Norton, 1987), p. 225.

193 **"the closest the Victorian novel"**: David Trotter, quoted in Rebecca Mead, *My Life in Middlemarch*, p. 190.

194 **"As Mrs. Tulliver uttered"**: George Eliot, *The Mill on the Floss* (London: Collins, date unknown), p. 10. See also the withered, flaccid Casaubon "shrinking with the furniture" in *Middlemarch*, pp. 321–32, and Grandcourt's "lively, darting . . . lizard" in *Daniel Deronda*, p. 177.

194 **"a gingerly fashion"**: See F. W. Maitland, *The Life and Letters of Leslie Stephen* (London: Duckworth, 1906).

194 **"improper explicitness"**: Thomas Hardy, *The Life and Work of Thomas Hardy*, ed. Michael Millgate (Athens: University of Georgia Press, 1985), p. 215.

195 **"a distinct epoch in English fiction"**: D. F. Hannigan in the *Westminster Review*, December 1892, reprinted in Claire Tomalin, *Thomas Hardy* (New York: Penguin, 2007), p. 230.

196 **"Here is a whole world"**: George Orwell, "Inside the Whale" (London: Penguin, 1957), pp. 11–12.

196 **"the dirty handkerchief side of life"**: Ibid., p. 17.

197 **"the two white, glistening globes"**: Observations taken from the foreword of the unexpurgated edition of *Sons and Lovers* (Cambridge: Cambridge University Press, 1992).

198 **"With a queer obedience"**: Ibid., pp. 163–64.

199 **"It is very rare"**: Jacques Bonnet, *Phantoms of the Bookshelves*, pp. 29–30.

200 **"A sex scene"**: Elizabeth Benedict, *The Joy of Writing Sex: A Guide for Fiction Writers* (New York: Holt, 2002).

202 **"She was just eating a maraschino ice"**: See Lisa Scottoline, "English Class with Mr. Roth," *The New York Times*, May 4, 2014, p. 9.

202 **"My father used to say"**: See Ben Hoyle, "Sex? It's Impossible to Do It Well, Especially If There's Any Emotion, Amis Tells Readers," *The Times*, October 11, 2010, p. 4.

203 **"The Naughty Bits"**: See *The New York Times Book Review*, October 6, 2013, pp. 14–17.

204 **"herniating conscientiousness"**: See Allan Gurganus, in conver-

sation with Sir Ian Dunham, "Fear of Sex in Fiction: The New Shyness," *The New Yorker,* October 8, 2013.

204 **"Updike's literary reputation":** Adam Begley, *Updike,* p. 294.

205 **"a great writer of the erotic":** See Claudia Roth Pierpont, "The Book of Laughter," *The New Yorker,* October 7, 2013, p. 35.

205 **"My guess is that Updike avoids":** Adam Begley, *Updike,* pp. 200–1. The novels quoted are *Gertrude and Claudius* (New York: Knopf, 2000); *Villages* (New York: Knopf, 2005); and *Seek My Face* (New York: Knopf, 2002).

206 **"not about sex as such":** See George Hunt, *John Updike and the Three Great Secret Things: Sex, Religion, and Art* (Grand Rapids, Mich.: Eerdmans, 1980), pp. 117–20. This Jesuit priest-scholar has become Updike's principal apologist.

10. VISION AND RE-VISION (PART 1)

209 **"If it sounds like writing":** Elmore Leonard, *The New York Times,* July 16, 2001.

209 **"The wastepaper basket":** Isaac Bashevis Singer, *Isaac Bashevis Singer: Conversations,* ed. Grace Farrell (Jackson: University Press of Mississippi, 1992). However, Singer was hardly the first to give such advice. Robert Graves, in *Goodbye to All That,* has his Charterhouse headmaster deliver the same comment (p. 5).

209 **In my hands is a slim volume:** See *Two Chapters of Persuasion, Printed from Jane Austen's Autograph* (Oxford: Clarendon Press, 1926).

210 **The long explanation for his conduct:** See pp. 20–21 in Oxford University Press edition of *Persuasion,* pp. 430–32 in the Doubleday edition.

211 **"The last two chapters":** Claire Tomalin, *Jane Austen: A Life* (New York: Knopf, 1997), p. 258.

211 **"The scene becomes a ballet":** Carol Shields, *Jane Austen* (New York: Viking, 2001), p. 169.

212 **Arundhati Roy, winner of the Booker Prize:** Siddhartha Deb, "The Not-So-Reluctant Renegade," *The New York Times Magazine,* March 9, 2014, p. 37.

213 **"Lines were drawn":** See Mary F. Sandars, *Honoré de Balzac: His Life and Writings,* p. 123.

213 **John Cheever in just boxer shorts:** See Mason Currey, *Daily Rituals: How Great Minds Make Time, Find Inspiration, and Get to Work* (New York: Knopf, 2013), p. 110.

214 **"Once he had started work on a script":** See Graham McCann, *Spike & Co.* (London: Hodder, 2007).

214 **The revised version sounds:** For a fuller examination of how Henry James rewrote his novels, see James Wood, "Perfuming the Money Issue," p. 5.

215 **"A glass was broken":** Diana Athill, "Too Kind?" in "From the Pulpit," *Literary Review,* December 2004/January 2005, p. 1.

215 **"Writing a book is like building a coral reef":** See P. G. Wodehouse, *A Life in Letters,* ed. Sophie Ratcliffe (New York: Norton, 2013), letter to William Townend.

215 **"'They make Sugar sound so good'":** Norman Mailer, *The Spooky Art,* p. 41.

216 **"tore the manuscript to pieces":** See Herbert Leibowitz, *"Something Urgent I Have to Say to You": The Life and Works of William Carlos Williams* (New York: Farrar, Straus and Giroux, 2012). The story is told by Adam Kirsch in "The New World of William Carlos Williams," *The New York Review of Books,* February 23, 2012, p. 34.

217 **"There is a busybody on your staff":** Recalled by Sir Sydney Cockerell in a letter to *The Listener,* September 4, 1947.

218 **"There are corrections on every page":** *The Letters of Nancy Mitford and Evelyn Waugh,* ed. Charlotte Mosley (London: Hodder, 1996), pp. 217–18.

221 **According to Charles McGrath:** My account of Carver's editing is taken from two articles: Charles McGrath, "I, ~~Editor~~ Author," *The New York Times,* October 28, 2007, pp. 1, 5; and Motoko Rich, "The Real Carver: Expansive or Minimal?" *The New York Times,* October 17, 2007, pp. E1, E7.

223 **"by now rather tattered typescript":** This description, and the editorial history of Golding's novel, is taken from John Carey, *William Golding: The Man Who Wrote* Lord of the Flies (London: Faber, 2009), pp. 150–69.

11. VISION AND RE-VISION (PART 2)

227 **"I have rewritten several times"**: Vladimir Nabokov, *Speak, Memory.*

227 **"I'm all for the scissors"**: Truman Capote, *Conversations with Capote* (New York: New American Library, 1985).

230 **"sentimentality, weak narrative"**: Jonathan Franzen, "On Autobiographical Fiction," *Farther Away*, p. 124.

230 **"ultimately, literature is nothing but carpentry"**: Gabriel Garcia Márquez, *The Paris Review.*

232 **"When things are few"**: See Jonathan Coe, "Clutching at Railings," *London Review of Books*, October 24, 2013, p. 21.

232 **The writer and critic**: Geoff Dyer, "Next Time, Try 'Unflagging,'" *The New York Times Book Review*, February 19, 2012, p. 17.

232 **In English alone, a new word**: See lexicographer Jonathon Green, quoted in Andrew Taylor, "Grub Street," *The Author*, Spring 2015, p. 26.

232 **"Dance first. Think later"**: This is a famous line of Beckett's, yet he never wrote it—not in this form.

233 **"Punctuation should be consistent"**: Robert Graves and Alan Hodge, *The Reader over Your Shoulder* (London: Macmillan, 1943).

233 **The comma was a High Renaissance invention**: See Mary Norris, *Between You & Me*, p. 98. She nicely adds: "Commas, like nuns, often travel in pairs."

233 **"Students of literary economy"**: Martin Amis, *The War Against Cliché*, p. 326.

234 **"A clever man might successfully"**: See Francine Prose, *Reading Like a Writer*, pp. 68–69.

234 **Morrell scrupulously follows**: See David Morrell, "The Tactics of Structure," *Lessons from a Lifetime of Writing: A Novelist Looks at His Craft* (London: Writers Digest Books), 2003.

234 **"Talent is developed in privacy"**: Marilyn Monroe, interview with Richard Meryman, *Life*, August 17, 1962.

234 **"If writers agree on anything"**: Mark Slouka, "Don't Ask What I'm Writing," *The New York Times*, August 25, 2013.

235 **"Good Master Schoolmaster"**: David Markson, *This Is Not a Novel* (Berkeley, Calif.: Counterpoint, 2001), p. 113.

235 **"I would greatly prefer to think":** Elif Batuman, *The Possessed*
(New York: Farrar, Straus and Giroux, 2010), p. 19.

"Nothing much. Reading a book by some dead white female."

236 **"The truth is, there's nothing very utilitarian":** Nick Hornby,
Ten Years in the Tub (San Francisco: McSweeney's, 2014), pp. 69–70.

238 **"I wanted to write about a woman":** Richard Holmes, in an
email to the author, April 19, 2014.

238 **Begin afresh, afresh, afresh:** See Philip Larkin, "The Trees," *The
Complete Poems* (New York: Farrar, Straus and Giroux, 2012).

12. THE SENSE OF AN ENDING

241 **"The end of a novel":** Anthony Trollope, *Barchester Towers*, ch. 53.

241 **"The good ended happily":** Oscar Wilde, *The Importance of Being
Earnest*, Act II.

241 **The last chapter was known as:** See "Ending," available at ap.krakow.pl/nkja/literature/konwersatorium/ending.htm.

242 **"a brilliantly theatrical close":** See Christian Lorentzen, "God Wielded the Buzzer," *The London Review of Books,* October 11, 2012, p. 9.

242 **it took genius to "make an end":** See Edith Wharton, *The Writing of Fiction,* p. 38.

242 **"the will or the capacity":** Saul Bellow, *Letters,* ed. Benjamin Taylor (New York: Viking, 2010), letter to Richard Chase, 1959.

243 **"Irving the Explainer":** David Kahane writes: "Hell, in Euro-cinema, *every* character is Sam the Explainer. The cousin/*cousine* who explains at great length, over cigarettes and coffee, and entirely in the nude, why he/she's sleeping with his/her father/mother/ brother/sister/uncle/random stranger/the St. Bernard/the beach ball." "Explaining *In the Morning:* Meet Hollywood Sam," *National Review,* April 12, 2007.

243 **"We cannot, of course":** Frank Kermode, *The Sense of an Ending,* p. 23; see also pp. 51, 145, 175.

243 **"Something like a shudder":** Sally Beauman, "Encounters with George Eliot," *The New Yorker,* April 18, 1994, pp. 86–97.

244 **"Every limit is a beginning":** George Eliot, *Middlemarch,* vol. 2, pp. 492–500.

249 **"Had Dickens wanted Pip":** See Rupert Christiansen, "Charles Dickens' *Great Expectations,*" an excellent blog (exec.typepad.com /greatexpectations). The most detailed study of the case is "Putting an End to Great Expectations," an essay by Edgar Rosenberg, published in the Norton Critical Edition.

252 **All of Huck's moral crises:** The Sparknotes summary of Huck's situation at the end of the novel is quite cogent. See www.sparknotes .com/lit/huckfinn/section15.rhtml.

253 **"We want to believe in":** Francine Prose, "Bookends," *The New York Times Book Review,* February 9, 2014, p. 31.

Index

Credits and Permissions

p. 226: Cartoon by DeeRing2011, © Cartoonists Group

p. 240: *And They Lived Happily Ever After (Do They?)* (Dina Goldstein's Fallen Princess series), © Dina Goldstein

pp. 263-90: Cartoons © The Cartoon Bank, The New Yorker/Condé Nast

TEXT PERMISSIONS

Grateful acknowledgement is made to the following for permission to reprint previously published material:

The New York Times c/o Pars International Corp.: Excerpts from "The Naughty Bits" by Nicholson Baker, Sheila Heti, and Edmund White, originally published in *The New York Times*, October 6, 2013, copyright © 2013 by The New York Times. All rights reserved. Used by permission and protected by the copyright Laws of the United States. The printing, copying, redistribution or retransmission of this Content without express written permission is prohibited.

The New Yorker c/o The Cartoon Bank: Excerpt from "Away Thinking About Things" by James Wood, originally published in *The New Yorker*, August 25, 2014. Reprinted by permission of The New Yorker c/o The Cartoon Bank.

The Wylie Agency LLC: Excerpt from "A Tale of Two Novels" by Martin Amis, originally published in *The Observer*, copyright © 1980 by Martin Amis; excerpt from "New Novelist Is Called a Plagiarist" by Martin Amis, originally published in *The New York Times*, copyright © 1980 by Martin Amis; excerpt from "Martin Amis Fears Age Will Rob Him of His Literary Bite" by Martin Amis, originally published in *The Sunday Times*, copyright © 2009 by Martin Amis; "Amis: Sex Is Impossible for Writers and Embarrassing for Readers" by Martin Amis, originally published in *The Sunday Times*, copyright © 2010 by Martin Amis; excerpt from *The War Against Cliché* by Martin Amis (New York: Talk Miramax Books, 2001), copyright © 2001 by Martin Amis; excerpt from *The Spooky Art* by Norman Mailer (New York: Random House, an imprint and division of Pen-

ABOUT THE AUTHOR

RICHARD COHEN is the former publishing director of Hutchinson and of Hodder & Stoughton, and the founder of Richard Cohen Books. The author of *By the Sword*, an award-winning history of swordplay, and of *Chasing the Sun*, a wide-ranging narrative history of the star that gives us life, he was for two years programme director of the Cheltenham Festival of Literature and for seven years a visiting professor in creative writing at the University of Kingston-upon-Thames. He has written for *The New York Times* and most leading London newspapers, and is currently at work on a history of historians. He lives in New York City.

richardcohenauthor.com
Facebook.com/RichardCohenAuthor
@aboutrichard

ABOUT THE TYPE

This book was set in Baskerville, a typeface designed by John Baskerville (1706–75), an amateur printer and type-founder, and cut for him by John Handy in 1750. The type became popular again when the Lanston Monotype Corporation of London revived the classic roman face in 1923. The Mergenthaler Linotype Company in England and the United States cut a version of Baskerville in 1931, making it one of the most widely used typefaces today.